Christina Rossetti's Gothic

Also available from Bloomsbury

Coleridge and Kantian Ideas in England, 1796–1817, Monika Class

Coleridge, Romanticism and the Orient, Edited by David Vallins, Kaz Oishi, Seamus Perry

Elizabeth Barrett Browning and Shakespeare, Josie Billington

Emily Bronte and the Religious Imagination, Simon Marsden

Christina Rossetti's Gothic

Serena Trowbridge

B L O O M S B U R Y

LONDON • NEW DELHI • NEW YORK • SYDNEY

Bloomsbury Academic

An imprint of Bloomsbury Publishing Plc

50 Bedford Square   1385 Broadway
London   New York
WC1B 3DP   NY 10018
UK   USA

www.bloomsbury.com

First published 2013

British Library Cataloguing-in-Publication Data
A catalogue record for this book is available from the British Library.

ISBN: HB: 978-1-4411-1443-3
ePub: 978-1-4411-7044-6
ePDF: 978-1-4411-4223-8

Library of Congress Cataloging-in-Publication Data
A catalog record for this book is available from the Library of Congress.

Typeset by Newgen Imaging Systems Pvt Ltd, Chennai, India
Printed and bound in Great Britain

Contents

Preface

When I am dead, my dearest,
　　Sing no sad songs for me;
Plant thou no roses at my head,
　　nor shady cypress tree:
Be the green grass above me
　　With showers and dewdrops wet;
And if thou wilt, remember,
　　And if thou wilt, forget.

I shall not see the shadows,
　　I shall not feel the rain;
I shall not hear the nightingale
　　Sing on, as if in pain:
And dreaming through the twilight
　　That doth not rise nor set,
Haply I may remember,
　　And haply may forget.

One of Christina Rossetti's most famous poems, 'Song', is emblematic of her oeuvre: it is melancholy, it refers to death, it refers to the possibilities of an afterlife in heaven and it draws on natural imagery. In its sad sweetness, it has captured imaginations for decades. It is, after all, a poem of solace, a poem which offers hope of 'haply' remembering or perhaps forgetting: it does not, in Rossetti's poem, matter which. The world of nature, upon which Rossetti so often draws, seems at one with the dead in the first stanza, but oblivious in the second. The corpse, however, is left 'dreaming through the twilight' in a limbo state which seems peaceful, even desirable; the ghoulish aspects of death are suppressed in favour of an attitude of renunciation towards the world. The poem manifests the aesthetics of Gothic which are, as this book will discuss, apparent throughout her work, and which are specifically related to Rossetti's faith; the poem draws on a Gothic, graveyard atmosphere: full of 'sad songs', a 'cypress', 'shadows', 'pain' and 'twilight'. Though the poem appears to negate these items ('Sing no sad songs', 'I shall not see the shadows'), it is these sublimated images which fill the poem, creating a tension between the present and the absent, the living and the dead. It offers a gently aestheticized Gothic which, when dismantled, owes more to the renunciation of the world and the possibilities of a peaceful afterlife, than to the horror of early Gothic literature. Twilight, after all, is the time when Gothic heroines dream of a beautiful future, and, in its own way, that is what Rossetti's poetry offers.

Acknowledgements

This book grew out of my Ph.D. thesis, and my work owes a great deal to my supervisors, Fiona Robertson and Gavin Budge, who were endlessly helpful and knowledgeable. My colleagues at Birmingham City University have been supportive and encouraging throughout, for which I am grateful. Particular thanks must also go to my parents, for proof-reading and moral support, and to my husband whose interest in my work is both surprising and gratifying.

I was the fortunate beneficiary of a scholarship at Gladstone's Library, Hawarden, where much of my thesis was written, and some of this book revised.

Abbreviations

CS   Christina Rossetti, *Called to be Saints: The Minor Festivals Devotionally Studied*, ed. Maria Keaton (London: SPCK, 1881; repr. Bristol: Thoemmes Press, 2003)

FD   Christina Rossetti, *The Face of the Deep: A Devotional Commentary on the Apocalypse* (London: SPCK, 1892; Bristol: Thoemmes Press, 2003)

GR   John Ruskin, 'Grotesque Renaissance', in *The Stones of Venice*, X, pp. 135–95, in *The Works of John Ruskin: Library Edition*, 39 vols, ed. E. T. Cook and Alexander Wedderburn (London: George Allen, 1903–12) and on CD-ROM (Cambridge University Press for the Ruskin Foundation, 1996)

KGR   John Ruskin, *The King of the Golden River*, Cook and Wedderburn I, pp. 305–48

LS   Christina Rossetti, *Letter and Spirit: Notes on the Commandments* (London: SPCK, 1883; repr. Bristol: Thoemmes Press, 2003)

NG   John Ruskin, 'The Nature of Gothic', Cook and Wedderburn X, pp. 180–269 (p. 183)

TF   Rossetti, *Time Flies: A Reading Diary* (London: SPCK, 1885)

WMR   William Michael Rossetti, *The Poetical Works of Christina Georgina Rossetti, with Memoir and Notes* (London: Macmillan, 1904)

The many references to biblical sources throughout this book are taken from the Authorized Version of the Bible, and are noted by chapter and verse rather than by page. The references to Rossetti's poems are similarly noted by line number rather than by page, since there are several editions of Rossetti's poems currently in print. The edition referred to in this book is *Christina Rossetti: The Complete Poems*, edited by Rebecca W. Crump (2005).

Note on Referencing

The referencing follows the Modern Humanities Research Association (MHRA) style, with in-text citations for references throughout the book and a full bibliographic list at the end. The text follows the MHRA guidelines on spelling and usage, quotations and other stylistic issues.

Introduction

This book explores the possibility that the poetry and prose of Christina Rossetti manifest attributes of Gothic, developed through her adolescent exposure to Gothic fiction, and entwined with her Tractarian beliefs. It is well known that Christina Rossetti was, at various stages of her life, an avid reader of Gothic fiction, particularly that of Charles Maturin, Ann Radcliffe, Walter Scott and Edgar Allan Poe. Though both during her lifetime and in subsequent scholarly work on her poetry, she has been read primarily as a writer of religious poetry, this book will argue that Rossetti's work is preoccupied with the Gothic genre, which appears in her poetry in forms that may be barely recognizable as Gothic in some cases, but which represent its complex influence within her work. A reading of Rossetti's work in the light of Gothic both complements and augments, rather than superseding, readings of the religious aspects of her work. The question of the complex intertwining of Gothic and Christianity is raised by Rossetti's work, and I suggest that nineteenth-century Christianity is expressed in Gothic in ways which are easily overlooked. In the case of Rossetti's work, her label as a religious poet may cause aspects of her poetry which belong to a different tradition to be ignored. While her preoccupation with death can be explained by her faith (although her approach is not always consistent with her beliefs), other features of her work, such as the grotesque and the spectral, owe much to Gothic. Each of the chapters examines a specific aspect of this fractured Gothic, exploring and testing potential Gothic tropes in Rossetti's poetry and prose and working cumulatively, with each chapter building on the last.

Gothic, I argue, cannot be seen as a single coherent entity, but is used as a collective term for an assortment of tropes and styles. What is termed Gothic thus constitutes a genre which has been fractured since its inception, and these fractures have continued and deepened as the form developed, with further rupturing caused by its absorption into more mainstream Victorian literature, including novels such as *Wuthering Heights* and *Jane Eyre*, as well as elements of the works of Dickens, Browning and Tennyson. Such fracturing is akin to the 'disjunction' in Gothic defined by Elizabeth Napier, in which the genre owes a great deal to other structures and forms, such as the romance novel, causing ruptures from its origins. To read Rossetti's work as fractured Gothic permits a new reading of Rossetti, one which situates her in a different milieu, and which is significant for the study of Rossetti's work, but which also provides a different way of reading Gothic. This exploration of Rossetti's work as fractured Gothic, inherited from her early reading and reshaped by her cultural and religious position, will examine aspects of Rossetti's work which have been neglected, particularly in a sustained consideration of poetry as a vehicle for Gothic.[1] This introduction therefore aims to establish three essential issues: the critical context in which I am writing; the problematic nature of Gothic and its potential relation to Rossetti's work; and the important issue of Rossetti's Tractarian faith.

Rossetti's work, like that of her near-contemporaries, Elizabeth Barrett Browning and Emily Brontë, is frequently discussed in terms of gender, sexuality, the poetess tradition, or more specific issues such as anorexia, lesbianism or marriage.[2] These readings have provided the critical impetus for new work on Rossetti, and many are indispensable, but to read Rossetti's poetry as Gothic raises and examines issues that have been overlooked, as well as opening up works by Rossetti that remain largely neglected. The issue of gender, for example, is frequently pertinent to a study of nineteenth-century poetry, but to situate Rossetti's poems in the context of Victorian Gothic changes the emphasis. Her heroines do not always conform to Gothic stereotypes; she rewrites Maturin's heroines, for example, in a way which strengthens their characters and emphasizes religious faith. I examine this as a specific case-study of the influence of a traditional, though not conventional, Gothic novelist on the work of Rossetti. Though Rossetti read widely in the genre, it was only the novels of Maturin which prompted her to write dramatic monologues such as the early poems discussed here. It is interesting to note that the novels of Radcliffe, for example, framed in terms of the heroines' consciousness, are much more closed to interpretative readings than Maturin's novels. Little critical attention has been paid to the Maturin poems, in part because they are often classed as juvenilia, but in their voicing of Gothic heroines and some emerging themes, such as love, loss, and the threshold between heaven and earth, they are significant for her later work. In particular, Rossetti's poetic responses to Maturin provide an illustration of the theological significance of Gothic in her work, an exploration of which culminates in Chapter 5. The starting-point for this chapter is Diane D'Amico's essay (1981) which considers the Maturin poems, one of very few works to take them seriously. Particularly as an early example of Rossetti's engagement with heroines, something which is most often associated with the poetess tradition, these poems provide a useful barometer by which to gauge the extent of her poetic involvement with Gothic texts.

To look at the poems as fractured manifestations of already-fractured Gothic is to remove the tendency to read Rossetti's poems as largely biographical,[3] a trend begun by her brother William Michael Rossetti (1904) in his 'Memoir' of his sister and perpetuated by many critics since then.[4] Though it would not be impossible to read Gothic novels as biographical, this would be unusual and difficult, with their exotic settings and melodramatic plots; instead, they tend to be read as providing access to the subconscious. In my consideration of Gothic, I read it as an open text which moves away from the fallacies of authorial intention towards a reader-generated meaning. While Rossetti's personal faith is essential to her poetry, it is misleading to read her work as experiential or biographical; rather, her poems are experimental, exploring potential situations rather than recreating existing ones. This notion is further complicated, however, by Rossetti's avowed intention of writing to influence others for good, and the potential effects that this can create in the reader. Throughout these discussions it is evident that the Tractarian emphasis on reader-response is in tension with the similarly Tractarian concept of the exertion of positive influence through literature. My approach stops short of historicism, and instead aims to reconstruct a literary contextual history for Rossetti's work.

The critical context

Little work has been done on Rossettian Gothic, though many critics refer to 'Goblin Market' as Gothic. 'Goblin Market' is Rossetti's most widely read and anthologized poem, popularly seen as central to her oeuvre. The poem may be described as a Gothic poem, but rarely with any discussion of potentially Gothic attributes; it seems to owe its 'Gothic' label to Ellen Moers, who discussed it as an example of the 'Female Gothic'. Subsequently the descriptor is frequently used of the poem with little or no qualifying commentary, while web searches imply that the poem is an accepted part of the genre, which is fallacious. 'Goblin Market' has been discussed extensively by many critics who provide a range of interpretations, and in Chapter 4 I aim to supplement these readings by a sustained consideration of the poem as Gothic. The poem, with the sisters Laura and Lizzie, the goblins with their enchanted fruit, and motifs of redemption and salvation, lends itself to interpretations of Gothic, drawing on tropes such as the double, the fallen woman, monsters and vampires, and the potential influence of, and parallels with, fairy tales. Examining these aspects of 'Goblin Market' permits me to draw out new themes of Gothic in the poem, and to consider how the poem might be related to other texts which Rossetti read, including Milton's *Comus*, Spenser's *The Faerie Queene* and John Polidori's *The Vampyre*. Considering these sources offers a historical perspective on Rossettian Gothic which contextualizes her use of Gothic tropes.

In addition to her childhood reading of Gothic literature, there are compelling arguments for examining Rossetti's Gothic throughout her work.[5] However, it is not enough to suggest that Rossetti's work bears the imprint of her early Gothic reading; it is necessary also to determine exactly what is meant by the difficult and capacious term 'Gothic', which this introduction will endeavour to do. The Rossettian Gothic also owes a debt to Christianity and to biblical texts, on which Rossetti draws heavily throughout her oeuvre. Her Gothic imagination transforms familiar scriptures into alien and unsettling phrases, remaking them for her poetic purposes. For example, her poem 'Despised and Rejected', based on a text from Isaiah, is preoccupied with images of the blood of Christ, closing with the lines: 'I saw upon the grass | Each footprint marked in blood, and on my door | The mark of blood forever more' (ll. 56–8). Rossetti takes the dramatic and macabre images provided by the Bible and links them closely to the familiar world, and it is in this biblical usage, transformative rather than reproductive, that her Gothic roots lie.

It is not my intention to argue that the poetry of Rossetti is itself Gothic, or that it constitutes an addition to an already-defined body of Gothic literature, but rather that it reflects the wider cultural influence of Gothic and mirrors, echoes and transforms its identifiable modes and tropes.[6] Consequently, this is not a direct study of influence, but rather an exposition of how a genre can be reshaped and reformed to suit specific ends. In particular, this book will attempt to demonstrate that it is possible to read specifically Christian meanings into Rossetti's reworked Gothic. It seems more pertinent, therefore, to consider not what Gothic *is*, since there have been many helpful discussions of this, but rather to examine what it *does*: to what ends it is deployed, what effects are created and how it shapes the text. This book demonstrates that the Rossettian Gothic is closely linked to religious belief, and that many preoccupations of Gothic, such as thresholds, the sublime, the spectral and the grotesque, follow a distinct trajectory which moves the reader (and indeed the poet) towards heaven, this progress culminating in Rossetti's devotional prose.

A considerable proportion of the body of work on Rossetti is biographical, much of it drawing on William Michael Rossetti's somewhat patronizing notes on his sister's life and work in her posthumously published collected poems. The most significant biography is by Jan Marsh, which is detailed in its research and provides new material not available in previous works. Though Marsh draws some speculative conclusions (such as that Rossetti was abused by her father during his long illness), she seeks to contextualize Rossetti's poetry and to provide a biographical way into her work. This biographical approach is one which this book will avoid, but Marsh's discussions are frequently illuminating, and this, along with Antony H. Harrison's editions of Rossetti's letters, remains the standard work for information on her life.

After a period of neglect in the early twentieth century, Rossetti's work has been the focus of a considerable amount of recent criticism. A rediscovery of her work was initiated by feminist readings in the 1970s and 1980s, some of which relied on biographical information to 'reclaim' Rossetti as a feminist, for example, and in particular to recover a repressed sexuality for her.[7] This particular aspect of feminist readings led to the prevalence of 'Goblin Market' in criticism of her poems, since it lends itself to such interpretations, unlike the more mature work which is focused on the relationship between humanity and God. The work of feminist critics has often ignored the significance of religion, and there is little work which takes account of both Rossetti's self-conscious awareness of herself as a woman in a masculine literary world and as a human being in abject relation to God. Sharon Smulders, however, is concerned with the contrast between poet and saint that Rossetti embodies, and how these elements fit in with her views on women's place in society. Crucially, Smulders suggests that 'William felt her claim to poethood injured by her claim to sainthood' (1992, p. 569). Like other critics, Smulders seeks to reconcile apparently differing aspects of Rossetti's character, but in doing so suggests that Rossetti's Christian beliefs negated her womanhood, on the premise that all are equal in Christ.

More recently, there has been a revival of interest in her work as a religious poet, including criticism which considers the necessity of recovering her theological context in order to understand her work fully, especially her later poems, which still remain less generally known than her earlier work, while her devotional prose has received little attention. Jerome McGann, one of the earliest critics to consider seriously her status as a religious poet, argues that Rossetti's work was for a while seen as lacking serious intellectual qualities, due to a 'lapse of historical awareness' (1983, p. 131). Instead, he suggests that belief, or disbelief, should be suspended, and her work should instead be read in the light of contemporary theological debates, which will demonstrate her profound intellectual interaction with her religion. This interaction increased as she aged: although her personal theology appears to change little, as she grew older and her work matures there is an increased emphasis on faith. While some of her earlier poems, particularly those dealing with death, for example, seem to offer views which contradict Tractarian doctrine, this occurs less frequently over time.

Subsequent critical work has therefore engaged more fully with the religious dimension of Rossetti's poetry. Diane D'Amico considers the 'problem' of religion in Rossetti's poetry by persuasively arguing that in an attempt to reclaim her as a feminist icon, critics have not sufficiently addressed her genuine faith (1999, pp. 7–9). This is an aspect that has been considered by a number of other critics recently, including Constance Hassett, Dinah Roe and Antony H. Harrison.[8] Hassett examines the restraints and silences of Rossetti's poems which themselves speak volumes, and which form an integral part of the poetry. Patience is therefore also required of the reader of Rossetti's work, in order to hear the silences and attempt to uncover the reserve. Rossetti's aesthetics are examined minutely, with faith that they reward the reader's patience. Hassett endeavours to detach the poetry from accusations of dogmatism and excessive religious fervour, though it is perhaps surprising that the notion of reserve is not discussed within its Tractarian context. Roe, however, places Rossetti's work specifically in its Christian context, providing close readings of Rossetti's poems which contextualize them, emphasizing Rossetti's faith and demonstrating how Rossetti both draws upon and imaginatively reworks scripture. Roe's argument is that Rossetti's understanding of prosody and the nature of poetry demonstrates that her faith did not adversely affect her judgement. Moreover, Roe refers to Rossetti's 'gothic imagination', and relates her work to her reading of the Romantic poets (p. 69). In contrast, Lynda Palazzo (2002) specifically sets out to reconsider Rossetti's theology as feminist, rejecting the notion of the renunciatory women in Rossetti's writing and instead figuring them as both feminist (in a broader cultural sense rather than in the framework of modern liberal feminism) and as theologically coherent with Rossetti's faith. Moreover, she suggests that Rossetti used her imagination to liberate scripture from historical 'patriarchal oppression' (p. xi), though Palazzo's description of Rossetti's theology as increasingly 'radically feminist' seems at odds with what one can observe in Rossetti's work (p. 54).

Such works attempt to reconcile her gender with her religion, and begin to suggest that, far from suppressing her poetic talent, her beliefs gave her the opportunity both to express her views and to establish herself as a poet. Moreover, given Rossetti's absorption in her faith, an understanding of this context is vital to truly comprehend her poetics. Such contextualization can be productive to readers of Rossetti's poetry. Harrison, in particular, offers an interesting commentary on reading Rossetti in a range of contexts:

> We can properly understand Christina Rossetti's artistic values and procedures only when they are placed within the relevant contexts of their development and implementation. Such contextualization also enables enhanced perceptions of the 'meaning', relative canonical value, and reception history of her work. Reconstructing the aesthetic, social, and religious ideologies of Rossetti's immediate environment, out of which her poetics emerged, clarifies the interaction in her poetry among Pre-Raphaelite, Ruskinian, and aestheticist impulses. These impulses uniquely accommodated the High Anglican values with which she grew up and which increased in importance to her as she aged. (1988, p. 23)

This suggests the peculiar yet fitting blend of aesthetic values which her ideologies combined to create. Harrison's point that to reconstruct these is the only way to understand her work is, however, both a truism and almost impossible in any real sense. Harrison examines how it is possible for these ideologies to correlate, considering how her contemporaries perceived her as a Pre-Raphaelite poet despite her religious beliefs. With the important exception of devout religiosity, Harrison argues, these characteristics of Rossetti's poetry are still considered major components of Pre-Raphaelitism.

Alison Chapman's work on Rossetti's 'afterlife' (2000), however, emphasizes the dangers of reconstruction while simultaneously seeing its potential value. Chapman considers the critical recovery of Rossetti's work, and discusses the problematic nature of this recovery, and its tendency to produce a ventriloquized character rather than impossibly conjuring the original poet. Chapman's argument is mainly against New Historicist tendencies towards an 'unproblematic uncovering' in relating poetry to its context and biography. This argument is in part based on the notorious absence of Rossetti from the text, which has led critics to attempt to trace her life through abstruse clues.[9] New Historicist approaches, Chapman argues, merely serve to disguise the absence of Rossetti from her work, since they are predicated on the illusion of an authentic subject. Chapman goes on to doubt the validity of a feminist methodology which 'voices the silent', implying that ventriloquism, not interaction, is the result. However, she also comments that this recovered voice can rescue some poets from 'presumptive biography', citing Elizabeth Siddal as an example of this.[10] In its discussion of the haunted text and spectral writer, Chapman's work informs my chapter on spectrality in Rossetti.

In discussing Rossetti's work in the context of spectrality, an influential recent critical discourse in the field of Victorian studies, it is possible to consider what this approach might offer for a study of Rossetti's work.[11] Though writing itself is spectral, as this chapter discusses, for Rossetti this is particularly pertinent. A consideration of the spectral also permits a consideration of the ways in which Rossetti's work is itself haunted by earlier writers, including Gothic novelists, other poets and, particularly, Dante. Most significant here, however, are Rossetti's revenants, characters in her poems who come back from the dead, or who are haunted by dead lovers. The concept of crossing the barrier between life and death recurs in her work, and begins to dissolve this barrier, as ghosts return and the dead speak. This chapter raises a number of issues to which this book will itself return, raising and endeavouring to answer questions of the thresholds of earth and heaven in Rossetti's work which recur throughout. In investigating the role of the spectral in the Rossettian oeuvre, this chapter opens up Rossetti's work to the possibilities of Gothic.

Though there is little work on Rossetti and Gothic, studies of Gothic literature have offered a range of possible connections. The notion of Rossetti's work as pertaining to, and influenced by, Gothic, however, is one that is mostly unexplored, with a few notable exceptions. These exceptions include an essay by Diane D'Amico (1981), which considers seriously the impact of Rossetti's early readings of Maturin. D'Amico examines particular concerns in the work of Rossetti which can be traced back through her work to the early Maturin poems, and argues that these issues have an impact on Rossetti's mature work. D'Amico's work is discussed in more detail within this book, particularly the chapter on Maturin's poems, for which D'Amico's essay is crucial.

An essay by Jan Marsh uses as a starting-point Rossetti's 'self-haunted spider' which appears in *Time Flies* (in Liebregts and Tigges, 1996, pp. 21–30). Marsh explores a possible synergy between the work of Rossetti and the emerging discourses of aestheticism and decadence, particularly in terms of her 'morbidity' and her interest in the supernatural which is manifested in many of her poems (p. 24). Marsh's article was in part the instigator of my research, since it hints at Gothic possibilities in the work of Rossetti without fully exploring the potential of such a direction. Moreover, Marsh links Rossetti's poetry to perceived personality, which seems to foreclose any exploration of Rossetti's work and Gothic:

> [T]his dark side *is* Christina Rossetti, both in literary terms and in devotional terms: her final book was of course a long meditation on the Apocalypse, that most Gothic of biblical texts. As well as being the most powerful element in

her work, it is the mainspring, the fountain, the innermost self of her creative imagination, the source of her art. [. . .] She is truly a poet of horror and despair, death and putrefaction. (p. 29)

Though Marsh's article suggests some important avenues for Rossetti studies, such as Rossetti's depiction of evil, the Rossettian Gothic is complex, and is worked and reworked to provide a moral Gothic which is closer to the moral aesthetics of Ruskin than the death and decay of the early Gothic novelists.

This 'dark side' of Rossetti's work is also examined by Brad Sullivan (1996), who views Rossetti's secular and devotional poetry from an angle which is sympathetic to a reading of female Gothic. Critics have failed Rossetti, he suggests, by concentrating on her as a religious poet and thus simplifying her poetry and the concepts behind it. Instead, he suggests, the poetry subtly represents the secret potential of women, locked away and creating a tension that can only be resolved by death. Nature represents this potential, with threatening images such as birds and the sea engendering a sense of lurking danger, which suggests her 'profound uneasiness' with the 'natural order of things' (p. 234). Sullivan posits that this uneasiness is at odds with the Tractarian principle of God's ordered universe; however, I shall argue that it is in reflecting this postlapsarian world that Rossettian Gothic is at its most coherent, since the universe is ordered to God's plan rather than to mankind's, and was not intended to be fully intelligible to fallen humanity.

The use of 'Gothic' as a descriptor for Rossetti's poems appears frequently in a recent book, which discusses the 'clash between religion and romanticism' which features in Dante Gabriel and Christina Rossetti's expressions of desire (Waldman, 2008, p. 5). Taking a psychoanalytic approach, Suzanne Waldman devotes a chapter to 'The Superegoic Demon in Christina Rossetti's Gothic and Fantasy Writings', though she does not explicitly examine why Rossetti's work might be considered Gothic. The implication is that many of Rossetti's poems are Gothic in narrative content: 'Rossetti composed many explicitly gothic poems in which women are lured to isolated locales where all prospects of human delight are absent' (p. 39). Waldman's primary concern, however, is with the projection of the ego and its manifestations of desire and denial; Gothic provides the setting for this struggle, but no more than that. Gothic is described as a subgenre of Rossetti's work, which 'draws on gothic conventions that she likely came across in the Rossetti library' (p. 15). Waldman's close readings of Rossetti's poetry, while not explaining the label of Gothic used, nonetheless provide a valuable context in which to read Rossetti's work as Gothic.

Finally, an essay by Anna Jamison (2006) considers the poems in *Goblin Market and Other Poems* as transgressive, suggesting that their shock value is comparable to that of Baudelaire's *Fleurs du mal* (first published 1857). Concentrating on poems in which the speaker is dead, and female, Jamison places Rossetti's poems in the context of Victorian poetry to argue that Rossetti uses a poetics of stealth to provide a subtle break with the aestheticized dead woman of nineteenth-century poetry. Contrary to the expressive poetics with which the female poet was traditionally linked, Rossetti's poems are restrained and interior, in contrast to the objective and exterior corpses of women frequently appearing in men's poetry. While Rossetti ostensibly conforms to the Pre-Raphaelite exploitation of the female corpse, she reconstructs 'death as textual strategy' by providing a voice to the inviolate, emotionally detached woman (p. 271). The unsettling tone of Rossetti's poems is frequently overlooked even in modern criticism, and Jamison's essay helps to redress the balance.

The problem of Gothic

The first novel which describes itself as Gothic, Horace Walpole's *The Castle of Otranto: A Gothic Story* (1764), provides the original for many of the conventions now considered to be hallmarks of the genre, such as the castle, family, ghosts, a hero or heroine in a difficult situation, a preoccupation with history and hidden identities. Significantly, it also features the unexpected appearance of parts of a giant knight, whose 'fatal helmet' crushes the son of the house on his wedding day (Walpole, 1990, p. 23). The helmet appears periodically throughout the novel and serves as a reminder of its owner; this allusion to a 'whole' Alonso perpetuates the fallacious concept that there might have once been a 'whole' Gothic, complete and coherent. Next, a colossal foot is seen by servants, who suspect the creature is lying down but is too large to be seen in its entirety; an enormous sword is delivered to the castle; and later a hand is seen. The reader, like the inhabitants of the castle, only glimpses Alonso throughout most of the novel; the closest one gets to seeing him completely is in the marble statue of him in the church, and his portrait in the gallery of the castle. The giant is not seen in his entirety until the final denouement, but, instead, as apparently disembodied parts, engendering all the more fear for their grotesque dismemberment. This 'knight of the gigantic sabre' (p. 57), it transpires, represents the first great owner of the Castle, Alonso the Good, whose lineage has been usurped by its current occupier, Manfred. It is significant that where Alonso can be seen most fully, prior to his appearance at the climax of the plot, is rooted in religious history (the church) or in family history (as a portrait in the ancestral home). Moreover, the novel is scattered with broken images and things half-seen or heard, such as voices which speak in the dark, and dreams and revelations from saints, permitting the reader only glimpses of the narrative. Alonso's fragmented body has been read as a portent of the fracturing of the house of Otranto, and a semi-biographical representation of paternalistic relationships.[12] In such readings, it is possible to trace how this seminal novel encapsulates so many tropes and conventions, both physical and abstract, of what was to become Gothic tradition. In its representation of the giant knight, who threatens the established traditions of the castle, a partially obscured representation of Gothic itself can be traced. Critical readings of Gothic, themselves giant, sprawling and apparently dismembered, make it clear that it is not now, and perhaps never was, possible to view the form as a coherent and cohesive whole. Instead, aspects appear where least expected throughout the literature of subsequent periods, and these traces appear to be connected to the larger form of Gothic. Consequently, there is little critical agreement on what constitutes Gothic, other than the deployment of certain physical motifs and aspects of psychology, including isolation, despair, evil, loss and faith. As a result, studies of the genre tend to give broad overviews – an obscured glimpse of the giant – or else detailed studies of motifs or themes, such as castles and the ancestral house, the supernatural or the novels' heroines, providing a sight of a single aspect of Gothic.

There have been many critical attempts to define Gothic, many of which take into account its wide variety of forms and motifs. As critics have suggested, it is 'a form that escapes anything but the loosest definition' (McEvoy and Spooner, 2007, p. 29). Early studies of the genre tended to focus upon the physical features of Gothic, with some even providing a list of such items.[13] Such satirical discussions of the aesthetic tropes highlight the significant issue that in many ways the identifying features are often considered to be purely aesthetic, with plot, tone and literary merit being of less significance.[14] If, for example, as *The Age; A Poem* ironically suggests, a romance can be turned into a Gothic novel by the substitution of certain objects, and such substitutions were considered to be successful, then both genres are exposed as purely decorative, relying only on the external for their imaginative power over readers. Since, as historians of the reading public have argued, the majority of readers of Gothic novels were likely to have been women, this also has unpleasant connotations for the appetites and intellects of women readers, such as those satirized by Jane Austen in *Northanger Abbey* (1818).[15] However, the considerable critical interest in Gothic, particularly in the latter part of the twentieth century, suggests that it is both possible and worthwhile to read more closely into the texts that are considered to adhere to Gothic conventions, however these might be defined. Perhaps the most helpful definition of Gothic is John Ruskin's definition of Gothic architecture, which has parallels with Gothic in literary form. Though one might argue that it is more straightforward to define the outward forms of Gothic principles in architecture than in literature, Ruskin's comments make it clear that the outward signs point to the inward, and are shaped by them, and that it is a combination of elements which make up the form:

> Now observe: the chemist defines his mineral by two separate kinds of character; one external, its crystalline form, hardness, lustre, etc.; the other internal, the proportions, and nature of its constituent atoms. Exactly in the same manner, we shall find that Gothic architecture has external forms and internal elements. Its elements are certain mental tendencies of the builders, legibly expressed in it; as fancifulness, love of variety, love of richness, and such others. Its external forms are pointed arches, vaulted roofs, etc. And unless both the elements and the forms are there, we have no right to call the style Gothic. It is not enough that it have the Form, if it have not also the power and life. It is not enough that it has the Power, if it have not the form. (NG, p. 183)

Ruskin's abstruse argument is clearly applicable to literary Gothic, linking inner and outer forms. While modern literary criticism is less likely to take the writer's 'mental tendencies' into account, it is nonetheless possible to see the manifestations of the inward workings of Gothic in the aesthetics.[16] It is, as Ruskin says, the combination of the two which permits a work the title of 'Gothic'.

A sense of the difficulty encountered in attempting to define Gothic can be grasped from the excellent introduction to *The Gothic Revival*. Michael Charlesworth, in introducing an interdisciplinary 'cultural history of the Gothic revival' (2002, p. 5), considers the concept of 'living the Gothic' as a point where the architectural and the literary intersect. The desire to 'live' the Gothic was both inspired by literature, and inspired the writing of further Gothic literature; he considers the cases of Byron and Beckford, among others, but explains the difficulties and possibilities of living this fantasy:

> Once the Gothic [building] had been located, however, a multiplicity of events could devolve from it, depending in large part on the preconceptions, specific interests, and purposes in view, of the subject involved. To put it another way, the experience of living the Gothic depended on all sorts of factors, not least

the way in which the Gothic had been discursively constituted and ideologically framed in the life of the subject. (pp. 28–9)

It is perhaps unsurprising that the subjects of whom Charlesworth writes are male; the female Gothic 'subject' has historically been more of an object, less likely to choose to 'live the Gothic'.[17] Yet Charlesworth's point is significant: how one chooses to live out a fantasy is dependent on the subject's circumstance, be they fictional or otherwise. To read Gothic is to interpret it, as with any other text, but the monolith of Gothic turns out to be fractured and inchoate, often resistant to traditional methods of interpretation.

In 'The Nature of Gothic', Ruskin outlines the main tenets of Gothic architecture as he saw them, which he describes as 'characteristics or moral elements of Gothic' (NG, p. 184). These attributes are Savageness, Changefulness, Naturalism, Grotesqueness, Rigidity and Redundance. Significantly, he points out that 'every building of the Gothic period differs in some important respect from every other; and many include features which, if they occurred in other buildings, would not be considered Gothic at all' (NG, p. 181). The grotesque is one such characteristic: frequently but not always present in Gothic, whether considering literature, architecture or art. Ruskin's considerations of the morality of Gothic can be applied to literature as well as to other forms. It becomes clear that Ruskin viewed Gothic as splintered, just as he saw Venice itself, consisting of the various 'verities of Venice'. Ruskin recorded his views of Venice in a fragmented manner, noting down measurements, architectural details and personal impressions in order to piece them together in *The Stones of Venice*. 'Rossetti, Ruskin and the Moral Grotesque' sets a discussion of Rossetti's grotesques in the context of Ruskin's exposition of the grotesque as a fragment of Gothic in 'Grotesque Renaissance' and 'The Nature of Gothic'. The grotesque is an important and underexamined aspect of Gothic, yet Ruskin is unequivocal in his inclusion of it in 'The Nature of Gothic', and, in its reliance on disproportioned or misshapen elements, it is present in Gothic in various forms from Walpole onwards. While it is not at the centre of modern critical studies of Gothic, it provides an apposite approach to many of Rossetti's poems. This chapter provides a discussion of the grotesque and its potential effects and purposes, and relates them to Rossetti's poetry in order to construct an argument for a moral grotesque which corresponds to the sublime as well as the fearful, and relates to her understanding of the earthly and the sublime. This is also an area where a Gothic aesthetic is at work, filling the poems with grotesques which can also attempt to teach a moral and gesture towards heaven despite their physical unattractiveness. Close readings of Rossetti's poems which incorporate the grotesque, including 'Goblin Market', lead to the conclusion that the grotesque is an intrinsic aspect of the fallen world, human-focused and fallible.

This ruptured approach to Gothic is helpful in considering a mode of female Gothic, which necessarily regards the genre as a mode of fragments rather than a coherent whole corresponding to a monolithic patriarchal order. Readings of 'female Gothic', particularly after Ellen Moers's use of the term in *Literary Women*, have mined the conventions and aesthetics of Gothic, but it has proved difficult to produce a sustained and convincing association between the surfaces and depths of the genre. Many studies of Gothic, therefore, tend to provide motif-related studies, examining, for example, the use of the castle in the novels, relating them to the psyche and the boundaries of the self. For Rossetti, physical motifs such as these are used sparingly; her poetry tends to concentrate on the psychological rather than the physical. This is not to suggest that Rossetti is not concerned with surface appearance; rather, she either contrasts the surface appearance with the depths, or the hidden elements, or suggests a sympathy between appearance and character. To take the castle as an example, critics such as Anne Williams have argued that the building serves as a physical representation of the ancestral 'house' and pervading notions of patriarchy which are associated with this, combined with the concept that the castle also represents the body of the heroine, both in its limits and the limitations it thus places upon her, and in its depths to be explored, both psychological and physical. It has become a truism about Gothic for the domestic home to become a place of terrors and threats, where safety is no longer assured:

> [A] castle is a man-made thing, a cultural artifact linked with the name of a particular family. This structure has a private and a public aspect; its walls, towers, ramparts suggest external identity, the 'corridors of power', consciousness; whereas its dungeons, attics, secret rooms, and dark hidden passages connote the culturally female, the sexual, the maternal, the unconscious. It is a public identity enfolding (and organizing) the private, the law enclosing, controlling, dark 'female' otherness. (Williams, 1995, p. 44)

Though the notion of enclosure, whether within a building or by psychological barriers, features in many if not most of Rossetti's works, it is precisely this 'enfolding' which Rossetti's poems avoid. Rossetti's female protagonists, of whom there are many, from Laura and Lizzie of 'Goblin Market' to 'Cousin Kate', 'Sister Maude' and the speaker of 'The Convent Threshold', are rarely cloistered, at least at the moment of speaking. For example, the speaker of 'The Convent

Threshold' may be hesitating on the brink of a cloistered life, but the true barrier is to her love, since she says, 'There's blood between us, love, my love | There's father's blood, there's brother's blood | And blood's a bar I cannot pass' (ll. 1–3). This 'blood' itself points to Gothic, both in the impression of physical excess of gore, but also in its sense of the barrier of patriarchy and family. Yet these heroines' freedom to speak enacts their freedom to move away from the physical boundaries of the castle or domestic space, and instead demonstrates a concern with social structures and the boundaries of the self, particularly in the 'fallen women' poems. The traditional villain, meanwhile, is virtually absent in any coherent form. While David Punter suggests that 'The villain was always the most complex and interesting character in Gothic fiction', Rossetti's villains, if they can be termed such, are mostly characters whose villainy lies in weakness of character and moral turpitude rather than the pursuit of evil, such as the Prince in 'The Prince's Progress' (Punter, 1996, p. 9). Rossetti's focus is on heroines, or genderless narrators; even those men who have rejected her ballad-heroines are weak-willed rather than wicked. Men, it seems, are not a threat per se, but a diversion from the path of righteousness.

Such readings of the physical/psychological aspects of the castle and other motifs have now become commonplace in criticism of Gothic, and as such are open to a variety of interpretations. Norman Holland and Leona Sherman (1977) have argued that it is wise to treat all interpretations of physical motifs with caution; they propose that what Gothic offers depends on the mental and emotional state of the reader, among other things. How the reader 'matches' the inner and outer worlds of the Gothic novel varies widely, opening up a space of subjectivity which is by no means fixed.[18] While the castle provides a liminal space in which to project not the heroine's but the reader's fears and fantasies, the 'receptive function of the habitation' does not limit the reader (p. 282). This suggestion opens up the possibilities of the Gothic novel, to the point where reader-interpretation becomes its strongest characteristic:

> [P]sychoanalytic criticism would have assumed a one-to-one equation: the castle symbolizes the body. [. . .] Rather, each of us resymbolizes reality in our own terms. A gothic novel combines the heroine's fantasies about the castle with her fears that her body will be violated. The novel thus makes it possible for the literents to interpret body by means of castle and castle by means of body, but it does not force us to do so. (Holland and Sherman, 1977, pp. 281–2)

The notion of an enclosed or enclosing space, which may appear physically threatening, is significant in Rossetti's work in that it offers the heroine-reader the potential to escape and to cross boundaries or thresholds. In Rossetti's poems, however, these thresholds are more often metaphorical and interior than physical and exterior; Rossetti deploys the Gothic motif of the threshold without always requiring a physical barrier.

The castle, and indeed the Gothic text, thus forms a 'potential space', in which 'the individual experiences creative living', producing meaning through the act of creative reading (Winnicott, 1971, p. 103, cited in Holland and Sherman, 1977, p. 286). Though the text, in tone as much as in content, may be suggestive to the reader, it does not proscribe or coerce the reader's interpretations. This notion has particularly pertinent implications for Rossetti's work. Into this space, Rossetti wrote her poems, growing out of her own interpretations of a psychological and, most significantly, theological Gothic. If this reader is also a writer, as in the case of Rossetti, a doubled reading of Gothic is thus possible. Barthes states:

> Thus is revealed the total existence of writing: a text is made up of multiple writings, drawn from many cultures and entering into mutual relations of dialogue, parody, contestation, but there is one place where this multiplicity is focused and that place is the reader, not, as was hitherto said, the author. The reader is the space on which all the quotations which make up a writing are inscribed without any of them being lost; a text's unity lies not in its origin but in its destination. (1977, p. 148)

This concept of writing as a fractured form which finds meaning in the reader is particularly applicable to Gothic, itself a collection of ambiguous tropes of varied derivation, and appearing in forms which the reader must piece together. Thus '[t]he "text" itself embodies no more than the possibility of a certain kind of relationship between its words and its literents' (Holland and Sherman, 1977, p. 188). Napier goes so far as to suggest that Gothic is 'disruptive and subversive to read', being fractured to breaking-point into manuscripts which break off, or which cannot be read, letters and overheard words (p. 44). This, she suggests, causes the reader 'displeasure' which is an intrinsic part of the experience of reading Gothic:

> Part of the distinctive appearance of the Gothic may actually derive from the reader's unconscious displeasure [...] with its characteristic pattern of alternating static moralizing passages with scenes of often hectic action, it seems to demand an activity of consolidating on the part of its readership that its own design subverts. The result is a form that is fundamentally unstable, both in theory and in practice. (p. 44)

Critics tend to concentrate on the pleasure produced by Gothic literature, particularly in the way in which it permits subconscious fantasies to come into play, and in its 'escapist' reputation. Napier is suggesting the reverse; that, far from being a form in which the reader loses herself, and moreover a form which does not demand anything of the reader, it is in fact a genre which requires action on the part of the reader in order to make sense of the clues in the text, a theory which is clearly applicable to Rossetti's work. Similarly, other critics have suggested that since Gothic concentrates on the external, it leaves the reader to deduce the psychological aspects of the work.

Coral Ann Howells, for example, who concentrates on 'feeling', 'the whole non-rational side of experience – emotional, imaginative and sensational' which Gothic manifests distinctively, describes Gothic as a representation of 'the darker side of awareness' (1978, pp. 1, 5).[19] Howells emphasizes the 'sense of imprisonment' which creates the interiority of the Gothic novel, concerned as it is with boundaries and the self as well as literal prison walls (p. 6). The Gothic heroine 'is the prime example of this febrile temperament', irrational, oversensitive, intuitive and often sickly (p. 9). Rossetti's heroines, by this definition, are not Gothic at all; they may find themselves in circumstances appropriate to Gothic, such as trapped or abandoned by a lover, mourning a loved one or awaiting a ghastly fate, but they do so with stoicism, patience and Christian forbearance. While Howells links the heroine's 'persecution mania' to a 'dread of sex' (p. 13),[20] Rossetti's heroines include Maude Clare and Jessie Cameron, among others, who have borne an illegitimate child, been abandoned, and continued with their lives, shamed but strong. The moral consequences are clear in Rossetti's work, not shrouded in mystery and fear as Howells suggests; perhaps it is in the depiction of her heroines that Rossetti's pragmatic Victorianism is most apparent. Unlike Radcliffe, for example, who 'exploits almost continuously a double point of view: her heroine's and her own, that of participant and of the objective observer, or that of the feelings and that of the rational judgement', Rossetti does not appear to impose her own point of view upon a narrative, and eschews Radcliffean ambiguity for more forthright narrative (p. 59). Yet this is only completely true for Rossetti's ballads; in her more abstract poems, a careful reading is necessary, to extract a Christian message, and to reflect and to unpick the strands of Gothic contained within.

This close reading is appropriate for Rossetti's milieu in light of her beliefs, since she draws upon the Tractarian notion of reserve in both the content and aesthetics of her work. G. B. Tennyson, in his book *Victorian Devotional Poetry*, one of very few to consider Tractarian poetics, describes reserve as 'a sense of dignity and limit to expression in order that it not become mere effusion' (1981, p. 143). Rossetti's poems can be read repeatedly, opened up and unfolded in order to develop the spiritual mind of the reader. A significant aspect of Tractarian poetics is its highly developed theory of reader-response. Keble summarizes this, suggesting: 'It is to the awakening of some moral or religious feeling, not by direct instruction (that is the office of morality or theology) but by way of association, that we would refer all poetic pleasure' (Keble, *Occasional Papers and Reviews* (1877), p. 152, cited in Tennyson, p. 25). He goes on to suggest that authorial intention is irrelevant, since what signifies is the uplifting moral value which the reader may gain from the work. The use of reserve and typology requires the reader to have a certain amount of prior knowledge in order to read poetry as an active participant rather than a passive observer. Simply to read was not enough; the reader would be expected to interpret and reflect. This is particularly true of devotional poetry, such as Keble's *The Christian Year*, used by many Victorian readers, including Rossetti herself, as a meditative aid to devotions. A conscious ambiguity appears in many of her poems, placing the responsibility of interpretation onto the reader by leaving the message of the poem open.

This ambiguity is further complicated by Rossetti's mode of Gothic, in which she uses the aesthetics of the form sparingly while concentrating on the abstract to which the motifs are usually seen to point. For example, it is, of course, not possible to divorce the atmospheric settings and objects of Gothic from its potential meaning, but it has been established by a number of recent critics that the aesthetics of the genre may vary widely, according to their historical period and the oeuvre of the writer. Napier, for instance, argues that Gothic is itself so unstable a form that it cannot be defined in final terms, since, she implies, the conventions of Gothic are largely aesthetic and do not run deeper than the surface of a text. Significantly, Napier suggests that the abstract notions of psychology which are now critically associated with Gothic owe more to readings of these conventions than to the novels themselves, though it is clear that even criticism of the genre is now splintered or ambiguous.

The aesthetic tropes of Gothic, although they do in some instances occur in Rossetti's work, are of less significance.[21] Her poems operate in a more complex way, in which the aesthetics can be associated with the Pre-Raphaelite Brotherhood and her Tractarian faith as well as Gothic. Yet if one assumes that Gothic exteriors point to Gothic interiors, and that one signifies the other in a 'langue' of Gothic which is specific to its own needs, it should be possible to trace in the interiority of Rossetti's poetics some of the concerns of Gothic. Concepts such as fear and evil, which recur in the situations of Gothic heroines, can be related to Rossetti's devotional poetics in a Christian context. Although, in much of her work, fear is related to the fear of God, there is also a considerable exercise of fear within the world, of its seductiveness to the Christian focused on Heaven, and of the evil which exists, particularly within the society in which she was situated. Consequently, she writes of social ills such as the fallen woman and the double standard towards sexually incontinent men, and, particularly in her later devotional poems, examines herself inwardly for sin.

This self-examination which divides the internal from the external is a concern which Rossetti makes explicit in several of her poems, where the striking contrast between the inner and outer being is emphasized. Unlike the conventional Gothic tropes of heroines who are blameless and villains who are evil, however, Rossetti's poems demonstrate a complex understanding of the world more akin to Maturin than to Ann Radcliffe. It seems likely that this tendency to self-scrutiny derives at least in part from Tractarianism, with its emphasis on personal purity, frequent devotions and, in some instances, use of the confessional. There has been increasing recent critical interest in Rossetti's faith as a contextual tool for reading her poetry, although the recovery of Rossetti's status as a poet was initiated by feminist criticism.[22] This has also led to increased reading of her mature works, which are more devotional than many earlier poems, though her volumes of devotion and exegesis remain rarely discussed.

Tractarianism and Gothic

Tractarianism, the High Church movement which grew from *Tracts for the Times*, was undoubtedly the greatest single influence on Rossetti's work. Some of its followers later converted to Catholicism, but the majority maintained a High Church Anglicanism which concentrated on personal holiness, social responsibility and the aesthetics of worship, among other things. However, '[g]rasping Tractarian beliefs can be a slippery task due to internal disagreements regarding key doctrines like reserve, the Eucharist, confession, the Incarnation and analogy. The *Tracts for the Times*, however [. . .] grant us some idea of their collective philosophy' (Knight and Mason, 2006, p. 87). The Oxford Movement had a complex relationship with Catholicism, particularly in its later developments into Ritualism. The aesthetic of the movement, with ornate churches, candles and incense, confessionals and sisterhoods, seemed suspiciously Roman Catholic to many.[23]

It was a remarkably literary movement, and its adherents, including Newman, Keble, Pusey and Isaac Williams produced a great deal of poetry and prose which Rossetti read enthusiastically.[24] Moreover, in some ways the Oxford Movement provided a point of cultural intersection for the literature and architecture of the Gothic revival. The architectural significance of the Gothic revival also cannot be overestimated for its interest in the medieval, particularly in ecclesiology; for example, Isaac Williams's lengthy poem *The Cathedral: Or the Catholic and Apostolic Church in England* (1843) 'makes unmistakably clear the connection between a Gothic church and devotional feeling. While *The Baptistery* and *The Altar* are less intimately tied to Gothic, they too reinforce the growing Gothic inclinations of serious-minded churchmen' (Tennyson, 1981, p. 170). With its emphasis on sacraments and the ability of beauty to uplift the soul, the Tractarian church became increasingly Gothic in its aesthetics as well as its literature.[25] Alongside this poetry, the *Tracts for the Times* were published between 1833 and 1841, setting out the often controversial beliefs of the movement's principal adherents.

Keble's *Lectures on Poetry* provide invaluable insight into the literary aspects of the Oxford Movement, suggesting, for example:

> Let us test whether a writer overshoots the mark, whether his imagination runs riot without any reserve, whether he unworthily intermingles sacred with secular themes [. . .]. He cannot bring himself to confess all to all men, but like a harp lightly touched, he needs but very few notes to convey his real meaning to sympathetic hearts. (Keble, 2003, I, p. 73)

In Tract 80, 'On Reserve in Communicating Religious Knowledge', Isaac Williams writes of the Old Testament: 'We may notice the silence observed, respecting a future and eternal life in the books of Moses, as one of "the secret things which belonged unto God". Further on, Williams discusses the use of 'figurative expressions', suggesting:

> [W]e cannot but apply the remark of Bishop Butler, where he observes the vast difference between Holy Scripture, and any human composition in this respect, that in the latter our object is by words to convey most fitly our meaning to others; we cannot say this of God's written word. It may have objects quite of another kind, which its very obscurity serves, better than its distinct meaning would do.

Rossetti's writing tends to follow this biblical model, by use of veiled allusions, and especially typology. This latter was particularly significant in her work, since throughout her poetry the natural world, for example, serves as a metaphor for the workings of God, to which our eyes must be opened before we can understand. Furthermore, when the writer is 'unburdening himself' in poetry, 'Such exercise must always be done with the utmost circumspection and reserve, most often achieved through an indirect expression that includes allegory and other veiled modes of utterance' (Tennyson, 1981, p. 34). Indeed, a lack of reserve was seen as a potentially female failing, relating to an excess of emotion and a necessary spontaneity, as opposed to intellectual logic, in writing. This note of Tractarian reserve, however, is one in which Rossetti excelled, and, as Charlotte Yonge proposed in her book *Womankind*, she was 'writing as a Christian, with the glory of God in view' (1889, p. 228). Roe suggests that in her essay 'Dante, An English Classic' (1867), 'Rossetti connects the Tractarian doctrine of reserve and analogy to literary production. Just as the world is only a shadow of heaven, so a translation is a shadow of its original' (Roe, 2006, p. 66). Shadows and reflections of Heaven, for Rossetti, imbued the world with a spiritual hue which one ignored at the cost of one's salvation.

The fallen world is thus the natural home of Gothic, but in Rossetti's case this is a moral Gothic, which accepts fear, terror and the supernatural, as a part of the everyday life of a Christian. This book concludes with a chapter on Rossetti's prose works, examining the devotional and exegetical works which Rossetti wrote towards the end of her life, building upon the findings of the previous chapters and extending into new areas of Rossetti's work, which exposes both the presence and the complications of Gothic in her work. These lengthy texts remain a little-read part of Rossetti's work, but provide conclusions to some of the issues raised throughout her life, from the earliest Maturin poems onwards. *Letter and Spirit* and *The Face of the Deep* in particular offer some resolutions for Rossetti's fractured Gothic, especially the latter. An exegetical work on the book of Revelation, *The Face of the Deep* contrasts a beautiful and idealized heaven with a fallen and increasingly grotesque world, and this complex binary offers clarity to a Rossettian Gothic. Since the Fall, the world can only be figured as Gothic, filled with evil, decay, horror and fear; heaven seems all the more perfect by contrast, while humanity can cross between the two, through the grace of God. *The Face of the Deep* is concerned with the crossing of thresholds between heaven and earth, the dissolving of boundaries with which Gothic is concerned, and with resolving the division between humans and God.

The Christian faith, particularly Catholicism, and Gothic have a troubled and complex relationship;[26] in the nineteenth century this was particularly the case for Tractarianism due to its perceived theological and sacramental affinities with Catholicism. Closer investigation, however, suggests the theory that

Gothic is essentially a Christian-based mode of literature, which this book will support. Montague Summers (himself an Anglo-Catholic) writes that the main characteristics of Gothic are 'aspiration, yearning, desire, mystery, wonder', though he overlooks the darker side of Gothic, which I find is present in Rossetti (1968, p. 24). These traits are, of course, supplemented by other aesthetic and abstract characteristics to form a mode of Gothic, as this book will discuss, but these are notable qualities for their shared language of faith. These terms could certainly be used to describe most, if not all, of Rossetti's poetry, though this observation alone is not sufficient to prove the Gothic affinities of her work, but they provide a useful signpost to the direction which my hypothesis will take. Murphy, similarly, cites Eleanor Sickels's work on melancholy in poetry in his work on Shelleyan Gothic, to illustrate the relationship between faith and Gothic:

> [T]he elements which terror-romanticism took from the medieval revival were the very elements which it had in common with black religious melancholy. It took the backgrounds of dim cathedrals, midnight churchyards, ghastly charnel houses, and gloomy monastic ruins. It took the death theme, and embroidered it with all the terrors of physical corruption and spectral visitation. It took the theme of sin, and added domestic and exotic demonology, age-old tales of contracts with Satan, and the expiatory sufferings of the Wandering Jew. And out of the theme of sin, which is never far from the theme of death, it built its arch-types – the criminal monk, the tyrant, the strong dark hero inwardly consumed by remorse. (Murphy, 1975, p. 19, citing Sickels, 1932, pp. 159–60)

Though Sickels's account is a simplified version of the history of Gothic from the medieval to its revival, it serves to emphasize the essentially religious nature of Gothic, its preoccupation with the complex themes of good and evil, heaven and earth, life and death, dramatized to provide both moral teaching and a discursive framework. Sickels links the graveyard poets directly to earlier religious culture and continues their tropes into the Romantic poets and Gothic.[27]

Poetry and Gothic

This slippery term, Gothic, is rarely applied to poetry, and when it is, the claim is frequently unsustainable, or at least unexplained. Certainly there is virtually no critical material which considers the nature of poetry and Gothic.[28] It is interesting that such significant manifestations of Gothic have received little critical attention, since certain formal aspects of poetry might make it particularly fruitful for Gothic. This book explores the possibility that poetry is a form positioned to manifest elements of Gothic, since it is by nature fractured. In its subjective presentation of a wide range of subjects divorced from their surroundings, and in its ability to fragment further its content in stanzaic form and even fractured syntax, it bears a structural relation to Gothic. Moreover, in its reflective and psychologically complex subject matter, it frequently provides rich material for Gothic, and indeed it has been suggested that the genre itself draws much upon the work of the graveyard poets, such as Thomas Gray, Edward Young, Robert Blair and Thomas Parnell.[29] While these poets' work may have been an inspiration for Gothic largely in their grisly subject matter, the poems themselves bear further investigation as early examples of Gothic. Certainly poems such as Parnell's 'A Night-Piece on Death', reflecting on mortality by the light of a 'blue taper' (l. 1), and featuring revenants, corpses and graveyards, moving rapidly from melancholy to the sublime and back again, fit well into the genre of Gothic. Moreover, in its fragmentary effect of closed couplets, mixing interjections and vivid visual description, it gives an impression of trying to make sense of the world by focusing on the afterlife.[30] It is possible to trace a developmental arc from the work of the graveyard poets to Rossetti's, and indeed further, in the work of poets such as Sylvia Plath. It would be convenient to label Rossetti a late 'graveyard poet', but this classification is too neat and takes no account of the developments overlaid on the genre by the Gothic novel. Furthermore, for Rossetti it is not death itself, or the contemplation of it, which is her focus; it is death as a barrier to be crossed, a transitionary stage to enable the Christian to pass into heaven.

Yet there are clear parallels between Rossetti's poems and those of the graveyard poets. Though Gray's poetics in 'Elegy Written in a Country Churchyard' are very different from those usually employed by Rossetti, the defining premise of the poem, of the futility of human life and the inevitability of death which also characterizes 'On a Distant Prospect of Eton College', is reminiscent of the resignation and reflection of many of Rossetti's poems.[31] The graveyard poets, including Gray, Thomas Warton, Blair and Young, offer reflection on time, death and human life as a kind of *memento mori*, set in an appropriately melancholy setting, if not always a graveyard. These defining features of the genre are shared by much of Rossetti's poetry, though Rossetti sometimes permits her dead to speak; in 'From House to Home', for example, a ghost returns to its family to find it has been forgotten.[32] Moreover, Rossetti's dead, whether speaking or silenced, come out of the graveyard and into the home; for her, such reflection is not confined to the appropriate place, where the dead are buried, but instead can walk in the world as a constant reminder of imminent and inevitable death. Rossetti usually avoids the grisly and the decaying, but the ideas which characterize such poems are present. Poems such as 'Song (When I Am Dead My Dearest)' feature a potential, future graveyard in which the corpse 'may remember' or 'may forget' (ll. 15–16), for example, shifting the emphasis from the living to the already-dead, which has the dual effect of both reminding the living that their life is finite, and simultaneously providing hope that after death an earthly consciousness might remain.

Other poems which have been described as Gothic include those written by Gothic novelists, notably Matthew Lewis and Ann Radcliffe. Rossetti is likely to have read Lewis's *Tales of Wonder* (1801), which includes poems written or translated by him as well as some 'collected'. The first poem in the book, 'Bothwell's Bonny Jane' (pp. 1–10), provides an interesting study; the poem is a traditional ballad in its form, with a narrative which conforms to motifs of Gothic. It tells the story of Jane, who wishes to marry a 'village clown' rather than the rich man her father has chosen; the abbot offers to help her escape by boat, but is treacherous and seizes her for himself. In the ensuing struggle, he falls overboard, and the boatman turns out to be a fiend, with 'blood-shot eyeballs' and 'iron fangs', who takes them to the bottom of the ocean. The poem is reminiscent of Scott's 'The Daemon Lover', in which a woman is spirited away by a ghost, and of Bürger's 'Lenore', both of which are acknowledged sources for Rossetti's 'The Hour and the Ghost'. Such a poem as 'Bothwell's Bonny Jane' conforms to traditional concepts of Gothic in both its plot and its aesthetics; it is closer to the Gothic novel than to graveyard poetry in content. Yet it is a precedent, and moves the ballad form closer to Gothic; Rossetti's ballads seem to have developed by way of Lewis's and Scott's.

Such plot-driven poems owe their Gothic nature mostly to the content of their narrative form, while the poems of Ann Radcliffe (usually as a voice for the emotions of a heroine) utilize a quite different tone.[33] This sonnet, placed in *The Mysteries of Udolpho* at a point where Emily is remembering her recently deceased father, works as an artefact of Gothic even when taken out of context:

> Now the bat circles on the breeze of eve,
> That creeps, in shudd'ring sits, along the wave,
> And trembles 'mid the woods, and through the cave
> Whose lonely sighs the wanderer deceive;
> For oft, when melancholy charms his mind,
> He thinks the Spirit of the rock he hears,
> Nor listens, but with sweetly-thrilling fears,

To the low, mystic murmurs of the wind!
Now the bat circles, and the twilight dew
Falls silent round, and, o'er the mountain-cliff,
The gleaming wave and far-discover'd skiff,
Spreads the grey veil of soft, harmonious hue.
So falls o'er Grief the dew of pity's tear
Dimming her lonely visions of despair. (Radcliffe, 1980, p. 96)

The twilight and the imposing scenery combine here with the melancholy mind to provide a pensive tone. The aesthetics – the bat and the breeze, the woods, the cave, lonely sighs, the mountain-cliff and the tear, when juxtaposed with the emotional – the melancholy, 'sweetly-thrilling fears', the 'grey veil of soft, harmonious hue' and the 'lonely visions of despair', form a slow-moving and languorous sonnet which is appropriate to the reflective mood of the Gothic heroine. It offers none of the drama and grisly horror of the Lewis ballad, and in its use of natural imagery to evoke emotions, it recalls Rossetti's introspective poems, such as 'An October Garden' and 'On the Wing'. Radcliffe's poems tend, in fact, to operate in a similar manner to graveyard poems, recalling what is past and remembering the dead while using towering scenery to provide a reminder of the comparative frailty of humankind.

Since poetry is often without a plot, it becomes increasingly crucial to distinguish between Gothic that is a function of the plot, and Gothic which is inherent in the subject matter. Though it is not possible to separate trope from abstract in such a way, it becomes necessary to rely on the significance of 'tone', which is one way of identifying Gothic in literature. In poetry, then, it is possible for Gothic to emerge through a combination of factors, including tone and tropes, and is rarely reliant on plot. The more obvious aesthetics of Gothic appear in the poetry of Tennyson in the nineteenth century, for example, in his 'moated grange' and medieval preoccupations, but it is possible to trace elements of Gothic in a much wider range of works, such as the poetry of Thomas Hood, Mary Elizabeth Coleridge and others. Earlier poetry, written in or before the heyday of the Gothic novel, appears, like the novels themselves, to maintain more consistently the connection between the aesthetics (or 'recipes') of Gothic and its deeper preoccupations. For example, Gray's 'Elegy Written in a Country Churchyard', preoccupied with the transitoriness of life and reflections of death, and linked not only to Gothic but also to an earlier tradition in the *memento mori* vein, also contains 'moping owls', a picturesque churchyard, gravestones and enough moonlight to see by; it would make a perfect setting for Buffy the Vampire Slayer as well as for Ann Radcliffe's heroines. Yet no tryst takes place here. Gray appears to have perfected the inner psychological intensity of Gothic, in which inward reflection is manifested by the surroundings in which it takes place, a pathetic fallacy which is reflected in Gothic novels. Rossetti's poems frequently demonstrate this, particularly in poems such as 'Birchington Churchyard', written to commemorate her brother Dante Gabriel Rossetti, who was buried there. The inexorable movement of time is set against the unchanging landscape, and the grief is carefully restrained.[34] Rossetti's poetry manifests certain aspects of Gothic, appearing in her poetry throughout her life, and which is fractured, sometimes incoherent and contradictory, from her earliest poems to her mature prose works.

Rossettian Gothic is concerned with the passing of time and with the contrast and barriers between man and God, earth and heaven, good and evil. The besetting fears of this world are the result of the Fall, and Rossetti's poetry suggests a constant striving to reach beyond the bounds of this world to the next, leaving Gothic behind. Even when she depicts the beauties of this world, as in the poem 'De Profundis', the urge to leave behind the fallen world is strong:

> Oh why is heaven built so far,
> Oh why is earth set so remote?
> I cannot reach the nearest star
> That hangs afloat.
>
> I would not care to reach the moon,
> One round monotonous of change;
> Yet even she repeats her tune
> Beyond my range.
>
> I never watch the scatter'd fire
> Of stars, or sun's far-trailing train,
> But all my heart is one desire,
> And all in vain:
>
> For I am bound with fleshly bands,
> Joy, beauty, lie beyond my scope;
> I strain my heart, I stretch my hands,
> And catch at hope. (ll. 1–16)

Rossetti's speaker is not bound in the grave, or even reflecting in a graveyard, but she has bypassed the melancholy aspects of death and wishes to exceed only her 'fleshly bands' and reach up to heaven.

The Spectrality of Rossettian Gothic

The preoccupations of a Rossettian mode of Gothic – from the solemn Christian issues of life, death and immortality, to the graveyard aesthetics of Gothic, including spectres, corpses and revenants – point to the spectral as a productive starting-point for a consideration of her Gothic. Because of Rossetti's interest in the unknowable and supernatural, her poems frequently suggest a spectrality which has been little considered in criticism of Rossetti.

Yet there are a range of approaches to Rossetti's poems which are illuminated by an examination of the spectral. Many of her poems certainly lend themselves to this approach: some of her earlier poems, which critics commonly refer to as the 'ghost poems', and also several ballads, offer narratives of haunting. These spectral poems include 'At Home', 'After Death', 'The Hour and the Ghost', 'The Poor Ghost' and 'The Ghost's Petition'. These poems depict the return of ghosts to the site of their lives, troubling the living with their reappearance and demands. The spectres present themselves as reminders of a life the ghost-seers would rather forget, opening up the possibility of a psychological reading of a cycle of repression and return. The ghosts also embody a reminder of death, a memento mori for the haunted, who point out that 'tomorrow you shall know this too' ('The Poor Ghost', l. 8). Theologically, these poems are at odds with Rossetti's beliefs; she firmly rejected occultism and attempts to interact with the supernatural, such as séances, and her personal, Christian approach is represented by poems such as 'Song (We Buried Her among the Flowers)', which closes with the lines, 'And we shall see her wake, and rise | Fair, with the selfsame smile' (ll. 19–20). There are many poems throughout her oeuvre which make it clear that she believes in a reunification with the dead, but one that is specifically Christian and will take place in Heaven. Despite this, anticipating death with a Gothic shudder is a feature of many of her poems, from the spine-chilling line

'His death is full, and mine begun' ('A Peal of Bells', l. 30), to the description of the corruption of the grave in 'Death':

> The grave-worm revels now
> Upon the pure white brow,
> And on the eyes so dead and dim,
> And on each putrifying limb. (ll. 1–4)

Her poems manifest a Gothic interest in death as an aesthetic category, as an event and as a strategy for exploring the guilt-ridden psyche of the living. Though her ghost poems deploy the motifs of Gothic, they investigate the reaction to the revenant, and are more interested in the living than the dead. The poems rely on fear, both that of the ghost-seer and of the reader: fear of death and fear of the unknown, rather than on the Christian patience and hope of so many of her other poems. For this reason alone an investigation of how the spectral operates in Rossetti's work offers an intriguing challenge.

Spectrality as a mode of criticism

Both Julian Wolfreys[1] and Alison Chapman suggest that the idea of spectrality is apposite to the study of nineteenth-century writers.[2] Aspects of Victorian texts, notably the forms of uncertainty which appear both manifestly and covertly, point critics towards the spectral, and allow a response to the self-expressed uncertainties of poets. For example, in 'Dover Beach', Arnold formulates and displays many of the anxieties of the age, describing the period as 'a darkling plain | Swept with confused alarms of struggle and flight, | Where ignorant armies clash by night' (ll. 35–7). In this dark and fallen world, the spectres that haunt it are many, and the poetry of the period frequently seems to be seeking to represent them.[3]

The nature of Victorian poetry thus lends itself to considerations of the spectral, owing in part to the uncertainties of the historical period, in which many writers express a sense of being trapped between the world they knew and a modern world of which they know nothing. Arnold's concern for what he saw as the potential cultural disintegration of Britain is reflected in his exhortations to resist this disintegration and rely upon man's better nature. Culture in all its forms represented for Arnold the means to perfection in humanity. It is clear that he saw, and feared, a kind of twilight world opening up before him, in which the restricted cultural climate clouded the prospects of humanity forever, as though he saw in the nineteenth century a kind of second 'fall' of mankind. The realm of spectres is a convenient analogy for the darkness and disorder of which Arnold speaks, since it is both out of our control and beyond our comprehension.

The essence of the peculiarly nineteenth-century spectre, at least in literary terms, is an aspect of poetics which Bloom examines in *The Anxiety of Influence*. How poets influence, are influenced, and perhaps most significantly fear influence, provides a web of spectral relationships between living and dead poets. In his introduction, Bloom suggests:

> For every poet begins (however 'unconsciously') by rebelling more strongly against the consciousness of death's necessity than all other men and women do [. . .] from his start as a poet he quests for an impossible object, as his precursor quested before him. (1973, p. 10)

It seems, to the poet, that poetic precursors have overcome death, by leaving their poetry, and thus traces of themselves within it, to haunt later generations. The poet, or at least the strong poet, is destined to struggle with the ghosts of the past, only to become a ghost herself in time.[4]

Bloom goes on to discuss the anxiety of 'latecomers', and the fear of haunting that accompanies the nineteenth-century poet. His suggestion is that post-Keats, Wordsworth et al., the fear of becoming a 'copy' rather than an original increased, causing a distinctive belatedness in the Victorian poet which makes a haunting by predecessors inevitable. In fact, Bloom's discussion of influence relies heavily upon notions of haunting and other Gothic images; he describes the poet's development as both fear of unification with the 'other', that is, the precursor, and fear of separation from it. The 'family romance' of poetic influence culminates in a Gothic scene:

> The strong poet peers in the mirror of his fallen precursor and beholds neither the precursor nor himself but a Gnostic double, the dark otherness or antithesis that both he and the precursor longed to be, yet feared to become. (Bloom, 1973, p. 147)

The 'mirror' of poetry provides a space in which neither the reader nor the writer is quite herself, but instead is something in between, something not necessarily pleasant or welcome. Between reading and writing lies the ghost, Bloom implies, and it is both to be feared and welcomed.

The construct of spectrality as it is discussed in criticism today springs largely from the work of Derrida, notably *Specters of Marx*. Derrida's interest in Marx lies primarily in Marx's own 'spectropoetics' and how Marx's legacy is interpreted and misinterpreted in contemporary society. Just as Marx said in 1848 that '[a] spectre is haunting Europe – the spectre of communism', so the spectre of Derrida haunts modern literary criticism (Marx and Engels, 2009, p. 38). The multiple ghosts of Marx, which will not die, return because they must, Derrida states, because they have a mission to accomplish in society, in common with popular conceptions of ghostly visitants (see Derrida, 1994). The binaries Derrida presents – being/not being, living/dead, open up a space in between, which is either filled by an already-present spectre, or is an empty space which we fill with a constructed ghost of our own making. He suggests that we can only live between the two binaries, implying that life is dependent on death for its meaning, and that therefore death and its subsequent spectres are an intrinsic part of human life. The binaries thus become less clearly defined than we might expect. Derrida argues that this space and its spectres are quite unavoidable, and that where such a space occurs, a ghost will rise up to fill it. This space in which a ghost appears is defined by Wolfreys, applying Derrida's ideas to textual matters:

> The identification of spectrality appears in a gap between the limits of two ontological categories. The definition escapes any positivist or constructivist logic by emerging between, and yet not part of, two negations: neither, nor. A third term, the spectral, speaks of the limits of determination, while arriving beyond the terminal both in and of identification in either case (alive/dead) and not as an oppositional or dialectical term itself defined as part of some logical economy. (2002, p. x)

This is, in terms of categorization, a simpler definition than that of Derrida, since it reduces the nature of the spectral to a 'third term', similar to adding 'maybe' to the binaries of 'yes' and 'no'. As Derrida suggests, and as this chapter will argue, the spectral is more than a third option; it is inextricably linked to the living, and yet it is necessary for it to be dead. It can relate to both categories yet belongs to neither.

The spectral and the psychological

Schopenhauer suggests that 'we have a capacity for intuitively representing objects that fill space', confirming the idea that the psyche creates its own ghosts for specific reasons, often unknown to the ghost-seer.[5] This gap which we fill is, in Freudian terms, the space of repression. Schopenhauer goes on to suggest that ghosts come from the intellect, not the senses, since our perceptions of the world external to ourselves exist primarily cerebrally rather than physically: 'The notion of a spirit or spectre really consists in its presence becoming known to us in a way quite different from that in which we know the presence of a body' (p. 227). The implication is that we do not need the physical senses to see or understand the presence and potential message of the spectre. Since it is derived from the intellect, this is how we understand it, and it is no less real for that. Humans are programmed to believe in ghosts, he says, pointing out the affiliation between dreams and ghost-seeing. Discussions of this kind, relating to the imagination and its spectres, have a long history. Defoe, for example, suggests that:

> [W]e form as many Apparitions in our Fancies, as we see really with our Eyes, and a great many more; nay, our Imaginations sometimes are very diligent to embark the Eyes (and the Ears too) in the Delusion, and persuade us to believe we see Spectres and Appearances, and hear Noises and Voices, when indeed, neither the *Devil* or any other Spirit, good or bad, has troubled themselves about us. (2005, p. 43)

Defoe does not suggest that apparitions and spirits (which he clearly differentiates) do not exist, but is inclined to be sceptical about the proliferation of tales of them. In fact he is clear that he is not suggesting that 'there is no Intercourse or Communication between the World of Spirits, and the World we live in' (p. 44). As the editor of this volume, G. A. Starr, makes plain, Defoe's intention is to demonstrate how 'the "natural" and the "supernatural", the "visible world" and the "invisible world", are not separate and opposed but connected and permeable' (p. 1). Not unlike Rossetti, Defoe sees an understanding of the interlinked spiritual and physical worlds as an integral part of Christian belief.

Terry Castle (1995, p. 161) has argued that, post-Enlightenment, spectres were increasingly likely to be understood as a product of the mind rather than as separate entities. Certainly Schopenhauer provides a list of nine reasons for seeing ghosts, ranging from madness and fever to guilt and a premonition of coming death. Castle proposes that '[i]n the very act of denying the spirit world of our ancestors, we have been forced to relocate it in our theory of the imagination' (p. 143). This gives rise to theories of haunted consciousness, and has provided rich material for psychoanalysis, particularly in relation to repression within the subconscious. However, if ghosts are a product of the troubled mind, then a spectral visitation becomes something not to be avoided but to be cured.

In the psychological terms in which we understand Gothic today, the work of Freud has become indispensable. In his *An Outline of Psychoanalysis* (1940),

Freud examines the ghosts which haunt the mind, and throughout his work prescribes what can be understood as a kind of exorcism. The parallels here are distinct: a ghost is confronted, and a resolution proposed in order for it to cease its haunting. For ghosts in the mind, the confrontation and resolution take the form of psychoanalysis and therapy. His famous essay on 'The Uncanny' has provided an analysis which examines and is applicable to literature as well as to psychoanalysis which is frequently referred to in studies of Gothic literature. The uncanny in literature and life, Freud explains, is the effect of a disruption of the familiar, which acts upon the mind:

> The German word *unheimlich* is obviously the opposite of '*heimlich*', *heimisch*, meaning 'familiar', 'native', 'belonging to the home'; and we are tempted to conclude that what is 'uncanny' is frightening precisely because it is *not* known and familiar. Naturally not everything that is new and unfamiliar is frightening, however; the relation cannot be inverted. (1949, p. 370)

The return of the familiar, in the form of the ghost of a figure once known, provides an appropriate example of the familiar/unfamiliar, often appearing within a homely scene where a threat is least expected. The transformation, from familiar and alive, to unfamiliar and dead, when least expected, is sufficient to fill the viewer with horror. As Derrida suggests, however, the return of a spectre is always both a first time and a last time, a doubling and a separation. Since each instance of an event is unique, and since the ghost is recently dead and transformed into a spectre, it is a first time. Yet it is returning; therefore it is a recurrence, even despite death. This is explained in *Specters of Marx* as 'Repetition *and* first time, but also repetition *and* last time' (p. 10). This is one of the many paradoxes of the spectre, doubling its nature and arguably its impact by being the 'double', and yet different from the living person it represents. Both the transformation of the ghost (from corpse to spectre) and the viewer (from passive character into active spectator) disrupts identity and displaces the ego. The dead are changed substantially from their state when alive, yet remain entirely recognizable to the living. It is this disruption of identity which is a significant aspect of Rossetti's spectres. For example, the respectable young wife in 'The Hour and the Ghost' is proved by the appearance of the spectre of her dead lover to be 'fair and false', with a guilty aspect to her personality previously unsuspected by her husband. The appearance of a ghost not only demonstrates the disruption of the ghost's identity, but can, most importantly, significantly disrupt and alter the world into which it enters.

The most significant aspect of Freud's analysis, however, is that 'the uncanny is nothing else than a hidden, familiar thing that has undergone repression and then returned from it' (p. 399). Like Defoe's argument that the ghost is a product of the conscience, Freud's argument suggests that guilt, fear or anger, for example, when repressed, are transformed into a revenant. These emotions eventually emerge as ghosts of the mind. The 'ghost' can also be an example of a projection of the unconscious in the form of a doppelgänger, appearing in an apparently material form, thus haunting the mind of the ghost-seer yet seeming to occupy a physical space.[6]

Rossetti's poem 'A Peal of Bells' uses a doubled perspective to indicate approaching death, in which the speaker's fears are transferred to her friend. The first stanza is filled with sights, sounds and smells to block the senses and emphasize the vitality of the speaker, while the second stanza doubles death with life:

> My friend is passing to his bed,
> Fast asleep;
> There's plaited linen round his head,
> While foremost go his feet –
> His feet that cannot carry him.
> My feast's a show, my lights are dim;
> Be still, your music is not sweet, –
> There is no music more for him: (ll. 18–25)

Though this stanza speaks of a 'friend', the narrator is clearly sensing the approach of her own death. The closing lines of the poem, however, not only contrast life with death, but demonstrate the narrator's awareness of her mortality, with the death of her friend representing her own: 'My blood is chill, his blood is cold; | His death is full, and mine begun' (ll. 29–30). The implication of these lines is that death is beginning as soon as life starts, but moreover, that the frenetic life represented in the first stanza has faded, and the narrator, somewhere between death and life, is becoming a ghost in her lifetime, filling the neither/nor space suggested by Derrida.

Rossetti wrote several poems in which the speaker is a ghost, as though imagining reactions to her own death.[7] The surprisingly self-sacrificing notion expressed in the last few lines seems to imply a woman who has died of a broken heart:

> He did not love me living; but once dead
> He pitied me; and very sweet it is
> To know he is still warm tho' I am cold. (ll. 12–14)

George Landow (2002) argues that Rossetti's poems such as this one offer a rare example of an aestheticized dead woman as an object of beauty and pathos who has a voice. Like Edgar Allan Poe, who suggested that the death of a beautiful young woman was a sublime subject for poetry, Rossetti appears to aestheticize the dead in her monologues from beyond the grave, as Landow discusses. However, in voicing the woman, she subverts tradition by permitting her a voice at all, albeit one which sounds somewhat subservient, taking on the sexual implications of the passive, beautiful corpse, which are left unspoken by Poe.

Landow satirizes 'After Death' as seeming 'to embody the standard self-pitying adolescent fantasy expressed in the words, "they'll miss me when I'm gone (sob)"'. More complicated, however, is Rossetti's puppeteering of the ghost, for to assume that the dead girl still has thoughts and feelings is to deny what we understand of death – and, incidentally, to contradict the closing lines of 'Song (When I Am Dead My Dearest)':

> And dreaming through the twilight
> That doth not rise nor set,
> Haply I may remember,
> And haply may forget. (ll. 13–16)

The uncanny effect created by the introduction of a talkative corpse in a deathbed scene is not necessarily the element of surprise (since where could it be more obvious for a spectre to be?) but the construction of the poem which permits the dead narrator to communicate to us, the reader, while allowing the mourner no sign of her feelings. The lover is unaware that a second transformation has occurred – first from living to dead, and then from dead to spectral.

An uncanny disruption occurs in 'At Home', where a ghost returns to familiar surroundings. These poems of spectral narrative, in which the words are spoken by the ghost, provide a more complex relationship between reader and ghost, since here the phantom cannot be explained as a product of the ghost-seer's mind (particularly since in 'At Home' the living do not see the ghost, essentially placing the reader in the position of the ghost-seer). Instead, Rossetti has created this ghost to haunt her reader. The scene is both familiar and generic, of friends eating and drinking and talking of the future, in contrast with the dead who have no tomorrow. By making the scene both universal and specific, readers may identify not with the speaker, who is dead, but the oblivious living, unaware of the ghosts among them. The final verse, in which the spectre refrains from allowing her erstwhile friends to feel her presence, can only make the reader wonder what ghosts might revisit them:

> I passed from the familiar room,
> I who from love had passed away,
> Like the remembrance of a guest
> That tarrieth but a day. (ll. 29–32)

As Rossetti makes clear in other poems, a guilty conscience about forgotten loved ones can itself conjure ghosts. Those who feel no guilt are merely silently observed by spectres. The discomfort that such poems can generate is itself a form of haunting.

Rossetti wrote several poems about nightmares in which the dreams of the narrator are haunted, which is apposite since this encapsulates the interior drama of haunting that Freud has elucidated and which appears in the novels of Radcliffe. Rossetti's poem 'A Coast-Nightmare', for example, describes a nightmare world of ghosts, where the narrator's lover resides, yet, at the same time, haunts her: 'All night long I feel his presence hover | Thro' the darkness black as ink' (ll. 31–2). How the phantom inhabits the 'towers and towns from sea to sea' (l. 20) of 'ghostland' and yet also haunts his lover's nightmares can only be explained by his existence within her mind, detailed in this chilling poem of night terrors. Perhaps the silence the poem implies is one of its most frightening aspects, since this ghost neither speaks nor causes the narrator to speak. In this dream-sequence noted for its subtle eroticism, there is no interchange between the woman and the spectre. Nonetheless, he tells her secrets of death, consistent with Rossetti's poetic preoccupation with secrets that cannot be told. The final stanza is most descriptive of this haunting:

> Without a word he tells me
> The wordless secrets of death's deep:
> If I sleep, he like a trump compels me
> To stalk forth in my sleep:
> If I wake, he rides me like a nightmare;
> I feel my hair stand up, my body creep:
> Without light I see a blasting sight there,
> See a secret I must keep. (ll. 33–40)

Since death is commonly referred to as sleep, this is the rhyme to be expected at the end of the second line; instead, Rossetti subverts our expectations and instead transforms sleep into something which involves no rest or even numbing of senses. The physical effects of haunting upon the senses are detailed, yet there is no explanation for the haunting itself, except the cryptic first line, 'I have a love in ghostland.' The interiority of the ghost to the narrator is in no way acknowledged, making this poem, with its Gothic landscapes and 'indistinguished hazy ghosts' (l. 17) one of her most inexplicable and terrifying. It is possible, however, to read it with the idea that the narrator may be verging on insanity, perhaps driven mad by a haunted consciousness, or conscience.

Spectrality and writing

In fact, the spectre is a part of the poet, according to Bloom, inextricable, and existing both in and because of the poet. Since the word 'spectre' derives from the Latin *specare*, to look at, it is on the gaze of the viewer that the emphasis lies – the essence of the spectre is derived from the spectator rather than the apparition.[8] This suggests that the poet or ghost-seer is entirely complicit in her own haunting. Derrida hints at this, but few critics have developed this crucial suggestion:

> What seems almost impossible is to speak always *of the* specter, to speak *to the* specter, to speak with it, therefore especially *to make or let* a spirit *speak* [. . .] Finally, the last one to whom a specter can appear, address itself, or pay attention is a spectator as such. (Derrida, 1994, p. 11)

Derrida is here highlighting the supposed difficulty of interaction with the spectre, while making central the role of the spectator. To engage with the spectre causes the spectator to be no longer a viewer but a participant, just as Bloom refers to critics as 'necromancers', attempting to bring the dead to life in their reading of texts.

Derrida asks questions about responsibility and justice to the dead in *Specters of Marx*. The acknowledgement of the ghostly presence/absence, or spectral space, needs to occur in order for 'justice' to be possible.[9] This raises questions for literary criticism, since Derrida claims that justice relies upon 'the principle of some responsibility beyond all living present', a responsibility which is due by the living to the dead, though the examples he cites here are the wronged dead, victims of oppression or injustice (p. xix). This poses crucial problems: that of the responsibility of living critics to dead writers, and also, and perhaps separately, to their works. What debt of responsibility do critics owe to now-spectral authors? This is particularly pertinent for feminist critics who may consider that they owe a debt to 'oppressed' or excluded women writers.[10] This sense of responsibility appears to manifest itself in the recent critical desire to reclaim and revoice silenced poets such as Rossetti, problematic as this is, and to suggest the spectral nature of writers themselves.

One such argument has been proposed by Chapman, who has offered the most sustained discussion of the spectrality of Rossetti as a writer, while acknowledging the difficulties this presents:

> What does it mean to recover Victorian women's poetry? Is it really an unproblematic uncovering of lost, forgotten or silenced works, or is this somehow always a re-covering? How do we let the poetry speak once its imposed silence within the literary canon has been exposed? (p. 2)

To revoice the silent, Chapman posits, is all too often to submit to the inherent difficulties of New Historicism – that is, to use the spectre as a puppet by inflecting the words of the poet with the cultural networks of the critic. Bloom similarly considers that past poets are revivified through their poetic inheritors:

> The mighty dead return, but they return in our colours, and speaking in our voices, at least in part, at least in moments, moments that testify to our persistence, and not to their own. (1973, p. 141)

This revoicing is, for many 'mythologised' writers, a common position, and one of which critics are increasingly wary (Chapman, 2000, p. 3). However, recently there have been several examinations of the notion of spectrality in relation to various mythologized authors, including Shakespeare, Blake and Plath.[11] Garber, for example, describes the relationship between '"Shakespeare" and western culture' as analogous to 'the transferential relationship Freud describes as existing between the analyst and the patient' (p. xiv). This relates to Bloom's argument about the patterns of influence traceable through generations of poets, where influence may occur, but must also be overcome in order for the poet to succeed in becoming a poet in her own right. While the process of reading is vital to the poet, it is also necessary then to exorcize the demons of previous poets in order to write oneself.

Not only writers, but writing itself, are spectral, according to Wolfreys, who discusses the 'virtual network of spectro-technical relations' (p. 1), and highlights Derrida's theory that ghosts are never something purely of the past but relate immediately to the double present in which they appear – the present of the character who sees them, and the present of the reader of the text (see Derrida, 1989, pp. 60–74). Ghosts are commonly associated with history: either the past

in a historical sense or part of an individual's past. That they might be entirely
of the present is perhaps an uncommon idea, but one which is logical. When a
ghost appears, it is the present for the character who sees it; it is also *a* present
for the reader who reads of it. Equally, the ghost always has some bearing on the
present and usually appears for a reason which can be explained by the present,
such as wishing to take the spectator to the grave with them. This may be in
retribution for past wrongs, but has nonetheless an immediacy to it which places
it in the present. Furthermore, all stories are ghost stories, and every narrative
is haunted, since:

> to tell a story is always to invoke ghosts, to open a space through which something
> other returns, although never as a presence or to the present. Ghosts return via
> narratives, and come back, again and again, across centuries, every time a tale is
> unfolded. (Wolfreys, 2002, p. 3)

This concept also insists on the immediate nature of ghosts, in that they return
and revisit every time a narrative is read or reread. The text itself is a liminal
space in which the oppositional binaries we might take for granted (alive/dead)
are blurred, and the text itself acts as a space in which the ghost can manifest
itself.

The acts of writing and reading, Chapman suggests, are spectral acts which
allow the living to connect with the dead. This concept is particularly appropriate
for examining the work of Rossetti, for the connection between the living and
the dead is something she explores in a variety of ways in her poems. Chapman
also considers Rossetti's absence from her own work, suggesting that as the critic
becomes closer to her work, Rossetti herself seems to draw away, making any
kind of historicist reconstruction of character and context increasingly difficult.

Certainly Rossetti plays with the notion of her own absence and presence in
many of her poems, such as 'Winter: My Secret', where a secret, which may or
may not exist, is constructed to appear to be the key to the writer's personality,
as she deliberately masks herself from 'every one who taps' (l. 13).[12] The speaker
uses the reader's curiosity, drawing out the suspense in a teasing manner, only to
admit finally that there may be no secret at all. One might expect that the poem
serves as a warning to critics attempting to personalize Rossetti's poetry, since
one realizes in reading this poem that there is quite possibly nothing under the
layers – the poet has absented herself deliberately, becoming an invisible ghost
in her own poem. Of course, this playfulness is a manifestation of Rossetti's
'resistance to inscribing the personal', since for Rossetti it is the poem and not
the person which must remain paramount (Chapman, 2000, p. 15). Virginia

Woolf hints at Rossetti's desire for her name and work, but not her person, to be known. In her essay 'I Am Christina Rossetti', Woolf describes an event at a tea party:

> [S]uddenly there uprose from a chair and paced forward into the centre of the room a little woman dressed in black, who announced solemnly, 'I am Christina Rossetti!' and having so said, returned to her chair.
>
> With those words the glass is broken. Yes [she seems to say], I am a poet [. . .] Here you are rambling among unimportant trifles, rattling my writing-table drawers, making fun of the Mummies and Maria and my love affairs when all I care for you to know is here. Behold this green volume. It is a copy of my collected works. It costs four shillings and sixpence. Read that. And so she returns to her chair. (1986, II, p. 240)

Woolf uses contrasting past and present tenses here, in which Rossetti's actions are situated in the past (she 'uprose' and 'paced forward') and yet the effect of her words is very much of the present ('she seems to say', and then 'returns to her chair'). By the juxtaposing of past and present, opening up the neither/nor of spectrality, Woolf conjures Rossetti as a spectre herself, situated in a liminal space which leaves the reader with a feeling of uncertainty as to both the time and the purpose of Woolf's anecdote. In fact, this serves to emphasize the historical position of Rossetti herself, who was dead by the time this was written, and the living nature of her poetry, still accessible and available to readers.

Rossetti, like all writers, thus appears necessarily spectral: neither alive nor dead, neither completely absent nor actually present. In reading her work we revivify her poetry, yet acknowledge her historicity and thus her death. As Chapman submits, once an author has died, she is nothing more than a signature, though, according to Derrida's 'Signature Event Context', '[b]y definition, a written signature implies the actual or empirical non-presence of the signer. But, it will be said, it also marks and retains his having-been present' (Derrida, 1982, p. 314). The signature thus stands in for the existence of the poet who appended her name to her work while alive, as a kind of proof. However, it doubles as a monument of death or absence too, since it must serve in place of the poet herself. The signature or name itself therefore becomes a spectral representative. Rossetti's manifest consciousness in her dealings with publishers, for example, of the use of her name suggests that she was aware of the indelibility of the signature of the author to mark both an authorial presence and absence, and the significance of it to her literary career.[13]

Tim Armstrong, writing about haunting in Hardy's work, points out that Hardy 'repeatedly describes the dead as wronged, misreported or unreported by the texts of history' (2000, p. 90), and further concludes that:

> What saves the dead from history, then, is carried within the phrase 'mute thought' and its cognates: in the recollection of ghosts; in the evocation of the muttering and vanishing of the souls of the slain; in close attention to the curious calls of the dead. (p. 102)

Many nineteenth-century writers did indeed pay 'close attention' to the spectres of the past in their poetry, and as a consequence the spectral figure appears repeatedly, manifesting itself for a purpose. Rossetti's interest is in the spectres of her characters' personal histories, and her phantoms are frequently manifestations of guilt. She develops this issue sometimes through reworked ballads, in which a spectre is demanding a form of justice and acknowledgement of responsibility from those who loved them in life yet have forgotten them in death.

To address the question of the critic's responsibility to an author's works, it might seem that to locate work culturally and historically within the poet's milieu allows an authentication of the work, but this is almost impossible, since, as Chapman points out, valid authentication can never take place because it is always too much coloured by the present to allow any genuine historical reconstruction of the text. Furthermore, it is the interaction of writer and reader which prevents the poet from remaining dead in the usual sense. To illustrate the unexpected communication between the binaries, Garber quotes Keats's 'This Living Hand', 'with its *trompe-l'oeil* gesture across the boundaries of life and death, writing and reading' (1987, p. xv):

> This living hand, now warm and capable
> Of earnest grasping, would, if it were cold
> And in the icy silence of the tomb,
> So haunt thy days and chill thy dreaming nights
> That thou wouldst wish thine own heart dry of blood
> So in my veins red life might stream again,
> And thou be conscience-calm'd – see here it is –
> I hold it towards you. (ll. 1–8)

This quotation indicates the crossing of the boundary of life and death which can be traversed by the dead author as a text is read. Of course the reverse is also true, that as we read we may cross the threshold towards the tomb in interpreting the work of a poet. Where the critic's responsibility lies is difficult to define, and an answer to this question of critical responsibility is not easily provided, if it is possible to provide one at all. Certainly in the case of Rossetti there are particular problems with acknowledging a writer who deliberately absented herself from her work. Though many of Rossetti's poems are in the first person, one cannot assume she is speaking personally. Rossetti constructed her own absence to side-step the issue of her readers considering her own voice to be speaking through her poems. This allows her readers to develop their own spiritual selves, partly perhaps by placing themselves in the space of the speaker. Since many of her poems are devotional, speaking in personal tones of a need for salvation and a longing for God, the reader finds herself apparently speaking these words, not unlike prayers. Rossetti thus forces her reader to align themselves unconsciously with the poem, rather than the poet, using her absence and ambiguity to require a personal response. For example, 'A Better Resurrection' is unspecific about the cause of grief, dealing instead with its effects and potential alleviation of suffering. The echoes of biblical phrases, which would have been familiar to her readers, give clues to the source of comfort even before the line 'O Jesus, quicken me' (l. 8). This use of familiar, biblical phraseology is indicative of the aesthetics of Tractarian poetics, and a form of justice towards Rossetti's work lies in the acknowledgement of her beliefs. For Rossetti, spectrality is further complicated by her religious views. Rossetti was herself 'haunted' by Tractarianism, by Gothic literature, by other women poets, and by her Italian heritage, to name but a few.[14] The haunting of Rossetti's texts by Dante provides a further spectral aspect to her work; the Bible and the works of Dante are crucial to understanding her poems fully. The significance of the many Dantean references is partly that they strengthen the argument for Gothic in much of her work, relating to the Christian understanding which is so important for Rossetti, as well as depicting the suffering of the damned. Alison Milbank attributes the Rossetti siblings' interest in Gothic to their familiarity with the work of Dante, suggesting that they lived literally under a shadow of Dante through their father's obsession, and also speculates that their interest in 'tales of spectres and doppelgängers' was formed by their early association with the *Divine Comedy* (1998, p. 124). These shadows still haunt her work when we read it today, but of course our readings are also haunted by our own cultural positions.[15]

Rossetti's spectres

In 'The Hour and the Ghost', an argument takes place between a bride, bridegroom and the ghost of the bride's former lover, which plays on the notion suggested by DeLaMotte: 'Two fears dominate this Gothic world: the fear of terrible separateness, and the fear of unity with some terrible Other' (1990, p. 22). As the ghost tries to take the bride away to 'our home' (l. 12), she clings to the bridegroom, who dismisses the ghost as 'dreams and terrors' (l. 49). In fact readers find themselves in a state of confused reality, as we can hear the ghost 'speak' in the poem, so we cannot doubt his existence, but the bridegroom clearly hears nothing. Rossetti only gives us the speaker's point of view, which the reader therefore must believe, while doubting its literal truth. The reason for the haunting becomes apparent as soon as the ghost speaks:

> Come with me, fair and false,
> To our home, come home.
> It is my voice that calls:
> Once thou wast not afraid (ll. 11–14)

This haunting, and her own eventual death, are the result of her betrayal of her former lover, and her punishment is to see her bridegroom betray her: 'To see one much more fair | Fill up the vacant chair' (ll. 57–8). Rossetti hints, however, that the conversation is in the mind of the bride, torn between guilt for her dead lover and love for the living. This suggestion is supported by Castle's proposition that literature on ghost-seeing began, in the early eighteenth century, to concentrate on the ghost being in the mind rather than a physical reality, and thus 'thought itself was a spectral process' (p. 164). Castle's discussion suggests that whereas before the Enlightenment it was considered both possible and even likely to see an external manifestation of one who had died, a gradual transition began which forced the spectre into the realms of the mind, considering it a projection of the ghost-seer's unconscious rather than of the spirit world. The guilt of the bride in 'The Hour and the Ghost' is tantamount to an explanation that the ghost has been conjured by her conscience, as the final lines of the poem emphasize:

> Forget not as I forgot:
> But keep thy heart for me,
> Keep thy faith true and bright; (ll. 43–5)

The ghost and bridegroom seem unaware of each other, and the bride's resolve to stay with the living fades as she says 'He draws me from thy heart, | And I cannot withhold' (ll. 22–3). She does not attempt to deny the ghost's claim on her, but admits her guilt. There is certainly more than a suggestion that the ghost is reasonable in exacting his punishment, and the bridegroom seems a sorry figure for his belief that he can protect her from a ghost which, as the reader may surmise, is internal to his bride. Crump states in her notes that Rossetti may have been influenced by the ballad 'The Daemon Lover', which tells a similar tale.[16] Typically, Rossetti has chosen a moment in the poem – just before the bride is taken away, when her fate is clear – and dramatized it, with her own emphases. In Scott's version, the bride is married already, with 'two babes also', and, though she goes with the demon lover, she soon 'espied his cloven foot', and he takes her to 'the mountain of hell' (ll. 47, 59). Rossetti's version, telling of the bride's sadness to leave her husband, and her fear of the unknown, is more chilling in its depiction of emotion and fear, and yet one senses that the bride brought it upon herself.[17]

Castle posits that, paradoxically, the act of seeing a ghost is an attempt to deny the possibility of death, since the ghost appears to have transcended death to return to the living. For a ghost to return, death cannot be final, and can seem to negate the possibility of one's own death, and also indicate a possibility of the spectral return of loved ones. However, the ghost is often, as it is here, a portent of death, an indication of approaching death which can be misread as a sign of life. The ghost as a production of guilt serves as a warning: the writer, now spectral, similarly demands acknowledgement. An examination of Rossetti's spectral poetics is supported by her faith, manifested in her poetry, although the theology of her poems is often at odds with the faith she expressed privately. She is interested in connections with the supernatural, in its broadest sense, and how it impacts on the lives of the living. In *The Face of the Deep* she states:

> Eyes that have been supernaturalized recognize [. . .] how darkness reveals more luminaries than does the day: to the eye pertains a single sun; to the night innumerable, incalculable, by man's perceptions inexhaustible stars. (p. 116)

The 'supernaturalization' of which she writes is that which comes through Christianity, which is inextricable from her use of language.[18] For Rossetti, there is a fine line between the aspects of the supernatural that are of God, and therefore acceptable, and those which relate to the occult and darker aspects which should not be meddled with.[19] As she wrote in *Time Flies*, it is only Christ 'Who seest the unseen' and 'Who knowest the unknown' (p. 106). Moreover, as Schopenhauer points out, the Protestant church cannot admit the existence of ghosts external to the mind, since after death souls are believed to go straight to heaven or hell, and 'cannot come out to us from either' (p. 293).

Catholicism, on the other hand, with its belief in Purgatory, has fewer theological difficulties with belief in ghosts, but Rossetti, as a Tractarian whose mind was set firmly against conversion to Rome, is likely to have considered ghosts as a product of the mind rather than of the spirit realm. Catholicism sustains the belief not only that souls are held in Purgatory, but also that they can be affected by the living while there. In Tract 79, *On Purgatory*, Newman cites the Creed of Pope Pius IV: 'Constanter teneo Purgatorium esse, animasque ibi detentas fidelium suffragiis juvari'.[20] Newman adds that proof of the existence of Purgatory 'would seem to lie in the popular stories of apparitions witnessing to it', and deconstructs it as a theological possibility.

Rossetti's references to the supernatural align her more with Christian mysticism than with the occult or spiritualist dabblings of the period. In setting Gothic in the context of Romanticism, Montague Summers argues that the mysticism of the Romantic age impacted on the Gothic novel of that period, suggesting that: 'Romanticism is, in effect, a supernaturalism, and the highest form of Romanticism, in its purest and best endeavour, raised upwards to the sublime, is Mysticism' (p. 18). Rossetti's attitude towards the supernatural is perhaps best described by the closing lines of *The Gothic Quest*, in which Summers states that 'everything in the last analysis depends upon the supernatural, since as S. Augustine tells us, God is the only Reality' (p. 412). Summers himself, as a high Anglican, perhaps demonstrates the cultural position of Rossetti with regard to Gothic.

Occult aspects of the supernatural were fashionable with many of her contemporaries, however, who maintained an interest in spiritualism, mediumship and mesmerism. Her brother, D. G. Rossetti, held séances after the premature death of his wife, Elizabeth Siddal, and, suffering from guilt for his neglect of her during her life, endeavoured on many occasions to contact her after her death. Their brother W. M. Rossetti took to attending professional séances, but Christina Rossetti declined to be involved on these occasions, remaining hostile to spiritualism in general. As Marsh suggests: 'With her poetic liking for voices beyond the grave, Christina might also have been intrigued by spiritualism's claims. Instead, she remained staunchly distrustful' (1994, p. 342). The rise of spiritualism in the nineteenth century was rapid, and many public figures attended séances in an attempt to communicate with the dead, which Rossetti must have been aware of through her acquaintances. She is explicit about her own feelings on this, however:

PLEASE GOD. I will have nothing to do with spiritualism, whether it is an imposture or a black art; or with mesmerism, lest I clog my free will; or with hypnotism, lest wilful self-surrender become my road to evil choice, imagination, conduct, voluntary or involuntary. Neither will I subscribe to any theory which would pursue knowledge by cruel or foul methods; or do evil that good may come. Neither will I either in jest or in earnest tamper with fortune-telling or any other fashion of prying into the future. (*FD*, p. 271)

To search for the supernatural, the other, she states emphatically, is wrong, though it is eyes attuned to the 'supernaturalized' which also help one to see the work of God. Indeed what is notable about the supernatural in her poems is that it is always the dead reaching out for the living, the other reaching towards the self rather than the other way around.

As an enthusiastic and informed reader of the Gothic novels of Ann Radcliffe, Rossetti was likely to have been aware of Radcliffe's essay, *On the Supernatural in Poetry*, since it was published as a preface to Radcliffe's only novel to include a genuine ghost, *Gaston de Blondeville*, published posthumously in 1826. In her essay Radcliffe emphasizes that the truly supernatural character is that of the writer, rather than the text: 'I am speaking of the only real witch – the witch of the poet; and all our notions and feelings connected with terror accord with his' (1826, p. 149). Radcliffe goes on to suggest that an explanation of the spectral is beyond human comprehension, saying 'If I cannot explain this, take it as a mystery of the human mind' (p. 152). This accords with Freud's notion that it is the repressed which resurfaces as something uncanny, related to the mind and to personal perception, and certainly Rossetti's spectres too seem to have psychological as well as aesthetic purposes.

Though the spectres in Radcliffe's novels tend to have rational explanations, the mystery which surrounds them remains, and in her essay she makes clear that not only is the supernatural a mystery, and should be accepted as such, but it is a mystery which relates to the mind; that is, it is the projections of the minds of readers that are significant, rather than the potential workings of the spectral world itself. The existence of spirits in this world and the next is irrelevant here; Radcliffe's essay hints at the ideas outlined by Defoe, that the spirit world is within the mind of the spirit-seer, and reflects their psychology.

This is the approach taken by Rossetti, where the focus of a poem is not on the ghost itself, but on the interrelation between the dead and the living, which sheds light on the mind of the living character, turning her ghost poems into a drama of emotional or interior life. As DeLaMotte explains in her discussion of Radcliffe's novels:

Radcliffe comes close to presenting the idea, if not stating it directly, that the imagination, though it cannot create real things, can provide valid insights through the delusions it produces. [. . .] In Radcliffe, the aura of mystery lingers long after the mystery itself is finally explained. (pp. 46–7)

The mystery, therefore, is not that of the supernatural, but that of the mind, and this interiorization of plot and narrative is indicative of the literary mode of Gothic. Despite this, Radcliffe goes on to discuss the conceivability of taking ghosts such as Banquo and Hamlet's father as literal truths:

> 'You would believe the immortality of the soul,' said W –, with solemnity, 'even without the aid of revelation; yet our confined faculties cannot comprehend how the soul may exist after separation from the body. I do not absolutely know that spirits are permitted to become visible to us on earth; yet that they may be permitted to appear for very rare and important purposes, such as could scarcely have been accomplished without an equal suspension, or a momentary change, of the laws prescribed to what we call *Nature* – that is, without one more exercise of the same Creative Power of which we must acknowledge so many millions of existing instances, and by which alone we ourselves at this moment breathe, think, or disquisite at all, cannot be impossible, and, I think, is probable. (p. 152)

The implication, with which Rossetti's poems suggest she would agree, is that the possibility of haunting must remain, due in part to faith in the immortality of the soul which readers would be expected to already maintain; and yet that is what they remain – possibilities, not to be fulfilled except by the witch-poet.

Castle, in refuting the claims of previous critics that Radcliffe's work is not Gothic enough because her ghosts are explained away, discusses the space created by critics looking at Gothic literature, particularly Radcliffe's *The Mysteries of Udolpho*. She argues that critics separate the 'Gothic core' of the novel from the domestic, familiar scenes which take up a considerable amount of the book (p. 121). The division of the world into homely and uncanny (in itself a troublesome proposition), and the division of the book into Gothic and domestic, is common in criticism of Gothic, and echoes the too-comfortable binaries of living and dead: 'Seldom at issue in any of these accounts, however, is the two-world distinction itself (with its normal/abnormal, rational/irrational, ordinary/extraordinary oppositions)' (p. 122). Rossetti, however, draws on domestic vignettes interrupted by ghosts. Her poem 'After Death' exemplifies this with its familiar (to contemporary readers) scene of a body laid out, with 'rushes, rosemary and may' (l. 2), the first two bearing the meaning of docility and remembrance. While this scene would have been recognizable, it rapidly becomes apparent that the speaker is the body on the bed, speaking from beyond the grave to an unspecified audience. The unsettling aspect of this is all the more effective for taking place in an apparently familiar setting.

Castle posits that this distinction is not present in Radcliffe's work due to her unifying use of spectral language, and that it is therefore in the domestic scenes where memories of the dead take over Radcliffe's characters. The result of this is that 'the supernatural is not so much explained [. . .] as it is displaced' into the 'everyday' (Castle, 1995, p. 124). That there is something neither living nor dead, not one thing or the other, is intrinsically difficult to verbalize, requiring resistance to commonly used critical terms such as 'vital', 'incorporate' or 'embodiment'. As Wolfreys points out, however, the spectral is about the 'limits', testing the boundaries, and yet while it is neither living nor dead, it is not not living, and not not dead – since a ghost is something that was once alive, and was also once dead. It defies a clear understanding, in terms of what it is and of its purpose, and by evading definition and appearing in a space apparently constructed for it, the spectre can serve a purpose which, while mysterious, could not be fulfilled by anything more concrete or deterministic. To enter this spectral space, a threshold must be crossed: from life to death, since the space exists between these binaries. DeLaMotte discusses the use of these thresholds in Radcliffe's work, considering the moment when a heroine enters a castle, for example, or a forbidden room, to be the moment when the domestic, 'real' world is left behind and a Gothic world inhabited by death and fear is entered. The threshold is also associated with knowledge, however, since death and knowledge are closely linked in theology.[21] As Rossetti herself says in *Time Flies*, 'The hardest step is at the threshold' (p. 4). This concept of a threshold, the crossing of which alters a situation completely and irrevocably, provides a helpful focus for a Rossettian Gothic.

In 'The Daemon Lover' and 'The Hour and the Ghost', the sea appears as a threshold which the bride has been condemned to cross, while in Dante's *Inferno* the air becomes the sea, the purgatorial representation for souls who, literally, cannot rest.[22] While in some instances crossing a threshold can be seen as transgression, where the supernatural is concerned it is death that is the threshold – literally, in the case of 'From House to Home', for example, or metaphorically, with the sea as a threshold in 'The Hour and the Ghost' and 'A Ballad of Boding'. The threshold of the house in 'The Ghost's Petition' serves as a metaphorical threshold between this world and the next. In 'The Hour and the Ghost', it is interesting to note that in several cases the words spoken by the Bride run over more than one line:

He bids my spirit depart
With him into the cold: –
[. . .]

Thro' the lone cold winter night
Perhaps I may come to thee. (ll. 24–5, 46–7)

Enjambments are used sparingly by Rossetti throughout her poetry, with most lines of her verse complete in themselves. The effect here is of a threshold being crossed by the reluctant Bride as her ghostly lover tears her away from her husband.

The repeated trope of the enclosed space in Gothic novels such as Radcliffe's, where castles, convents and caves provide barriers to the heroine's ambitions, is that the heroine is trapped inside waiting to be freed. Rossetti frequently reverses this, instead allowing her heroine the freedom of the world, and the lover who comes to take them away presents a threat rather than a release. This demonstrates her complicated position, that the world is both something to be left behind, and is not 'home', but equally that death is unknown and other, not necessarily to be welcomed. The threat is the loss of freedom, in which the lover comes to take his bride to the afterlife, implying a kind of imprisonment in the spirit world. Yet this poem suggests a terrifying space, with the sea and mountains appearing as a Gothic landscape. Far from the 'blissful renewal of domestic life' which many expected of heaven, fear of the other supersedes fear of death itself in this poem (Castle, 1995, p. 131). For all the morbidity of some of Rossetti's poems, however, a fear of death is rarely present (although she does not embrace mortality like Emily Dickinson, for example), and as her work matures, it becomes apparent, particularly in her prose works, that to cross the threshold between life and death is to find true freedom. While for some heroines crossing the threshold may lead to freedom, for Rossetti's it often leads to knowledge, and not, perhaps, always the knowledge they desire, which is particularly pertinent in the case of 'Shut Out', which can be read as representing Eve's expulsion from Eden. DeLaMotte says: 'Much of the complexity of knowledge as a Gothic theme derives from the fact that the word *knowledge* itself has meaning in two contexts' – factual knowledge and sexual knowledge, and while the first may be positive, the second, in many of Rossetti's poems where the haunting is by a lover, becomes a source of terror (1990, p. 49).

In 'The Poor Ghost', one of the protagonists is a spectre who, having crossed the threshold to death very recently, has returned due to the grief of her lover. Surprisingly, the ghost-seer shows little astonishment at her appearance, despite her 'face as white as snowdrops' (l. 3) and 'voice as hollow as the hollow sea' (l. 4), but instead asks the reason for her return. The spectre offers him knowledge of death and what comes after: 'You know the old, whilst I know the new: | But tomorrow you shall know this too' (ll. 7–8). However, his fear is of leaving the familiar: despite his grief, he is clearly more at home in the world than the 'poor ghost' had realized. She therefore asks the question Rossetti's spectres often ask: 'Am I so changed in a day and a night | That mine own only love shrinks from me with fright [. . .]?' (ll. 13–14). Her lover admits his love was more finite than either had anticipated – 'I loved you for life, but life has an end' (l. 18). The change wrought by death is a change which cannot survive love, he suggests. He loves her still, perhaps, provided she remains dead as expected. This unromantic response is met with sarcasm: 'Life is gone, the love too is gone, | It was a reed I leant upon' (ll. 25–6). It is only in the closing lines that the woeful spectre indicates that she returned because of his grief, which woke her from her supposedly eternal slumbers. In the context of rigid and extravagant nineteenth-century mourning rituals, this is an idea which might have either frightened or appealed to Rossetti's readers, particularly given the rapidly developing interest in spiritualism. Alex Owen claims that spiritualism was based on the dominant theory of woman's 'sphere', being the domestic and the spiritual, confined largely to the private world of the home, as opposed to the masculine sphere of the public and intellectual life. Owen describes one female medium, who had suffered illness in childhood, as therefore 'forced to turn in upon herself and to dwell upon the themes of Christian resignation and suffering', and that she was comforted by considering 'life and its sorrows as a necessary preparation for the future world' (Owen, 2004, p. 78). Yet Rossetti's narrative of revenance comes with a warning attached: that the dead might wish to take the living away with them. The spectre of love which exceeds death appears frequently in Rossetti's narrative poems, often with a veiled threat or intention of vengeance.

A slightly different approach can be found in 'The Ghost's Petition', where a woman waits for her husband, whose uncanny arrival is signalled by the blue flame burning in the fire. This spectre comes to gently chide his wife for her sadness, since 'there's no sleeping while you sit weeping.' The wife replies:

Oh but Robin, I'm fain to come,
If your present days are so pleasant;
For my days are so wearisome. (ll. 70–2)

This is perhaps indicative of the poor social standing of widows as much as her grief. In this instance, the living wish to accompany the dead to the grave, which may be lip-service, given the slightly shrewish note in the last lines, suggesting she sees herself as much as an abandoned wife as a widow:

> Yet I'll dry my tears for your sake:
> Why should I tease you, who cannot please you
> Any more with the pains I take? (ll. 73–5)

Once again, the grieving living find closure in the reappearance of a ghostly beloved. By contrast, 'From House to Home' provides a very different consideration of the life that follows death. Here, there are no recriminations, simply a hard-won acceptance that life is a preparation for death. D'Amico points out that 'in reading Rossetti's poems that urge the reader to renounce the world or to beware the temptations of the world, one must keep in mind her belief in a reward of individual immortality and spiritual joy' (1999, p. 64). The narrator, separated from the man she loves, finds that the world is a pale reflection of heaven where he awaits her. The ghost here is not from the afterlife, but is the world itself, with its illusions and fleeting joys, leading the speaker to conclude:

> Therefore, O friend, I would not if I might
> Rebuild my house of lies, wherein I joyed
> One time to dwell: my soul shall walk in white,
> Cast down but not destroyed. (ll. 201–4)

The transitory nature of the joys of this world are reflected in many of her poems, such as 'Beauty Is Vain', which concludes with the moralizing note, 'Time will win the race he runs with her | And hide her away in a shroud' (ll. 15–16). More permanent are the joys of heaven, and increasingly as the poet matures she concentrates on this aspect of the supernatural world. Notably, 'The World', a sonnet not of love but of fear, describes the world as a femme fatale, who seduces only to destroy. The nightmarish quality of the reality that the speaker faces when, in the night, she realizes the truth, is remarkable for its qualities of reasoned argument in the face of terror:

> But thro' the night, a beast she grins at me,
> A very monster void of love and prayer.
> By day she stands a lie: by night she stands
> In all the naked horror of the truth
> With pushing horns and clawed and clutching hands. (ll. 7–11)

Like 'A Coast-Nightmare', the visual imagery here is reminiscent of Fuseli's *The Nightmare* (1781), with which Rossetti may have been familiar through her brother's interest in his work. Comparable to the goblins in 'Goblin Market', 'The World' personified here is attempting an invasion of mind here figured as an invasion of the body. By recreating the supernatural in physical, human terms, Rossetti produces a warning for her readers, using a Gothic motif of fear of monsters in the dark to instruct and influence. The deceiving and destructive supernatural control of the world itself contrasts starkly in her work with the release of the soul to heaven after death, where reality is subject to God, and therefore more permanent. This is exemplified in 'A Portrait', where the reader is permitted a glimpse of the thoughts of a corpse surrounded by mourners, this time a devout and pious woman: 'Heaven opens; I leave these and go away; | The Bridegroom calls, – shall the Bride seek to stay?' (ll. 20–1). The boundaries of this world melt away, exposing its temporality, and indicating the deeper and permanent joys of heaven.

Wolfreys suggests that Gothic expanded beyond its boundaries in the nineteenth century, haunting texts and reforming itself: 'The gothic became other than itself, the meaning of the term changing, metamorphosing beyond narrow definition, promising the destabilization of whatever it came to haunt' (Robbins and Wolfreys, 2000, p. xiv). The implication that Gothic had 'spread far and wide' fits the concept that all texts are haunted, and that society is haunted: Gothic has become more than an eighteenth-century literary mode, but instead a pervading cultural atmosphere. It was no longer confined to the novel; though it had always exceeded its boundaries in some respects, including as it did excerpts of letters, poems, quotations and other fragments. In the light of this, Rossetti's poems provide a useful example of Gothic haunting. They are in themselves haunted by the unfulfilled promise of Gothic, never reaching fruition in the Gothic genre, but instead providing the reader with tantalizing Gothic fragments. Just as DeLaMotte and Wolfreys have argued that the nature of Gothic itself has always been fractured, relying on a splintered narrative often divided up with poems, letters, quotations and multiple narration, so Rossetti's poems present quasi-vignettes of Gothic, with poems which indicate a much larger narrative than they are able to explain. Poems frequently figure as fragments in Gothic novels, notably those of Ann Radcliffe, where they are used as a quotation to direct the reader at the beginning of a chapter, or to provide an outlet for the voice of a character. It is in this last that Rossetti's poems display the traces of Gothic, since she picks a moment in the imagined lives of her characters to dramatize, be it through her version of ballads, which comprise her 'ghost poems', or through the dramatic monologues she wrote for Maturin's heroines. The majority of Rossetti's poems which include ghosts are fragments of narrative – the thoughts of the speaker, or a ballad with a story only hinted at. The poems themselves present only a fraction of a tale: the reader is left to guess at the rest of the story, the context and preceding events. These aspects of larger imaginary tales work well perhaps because they often seem familiar, with Rossetti drawing on sources including ballads, novels, the Bible and the work of Dante. Most striking, however, are the poems which draw on the works of Maturin, which provide an especially intense and direct Gothic intertextuality.

Early Influences: Rossetti and the Gothic of Maturin

Some of Rossetti's early monologic poems demonstrate a direct response to her reading of Gothic novels, particularly eight poems based on the novels of Charles Robert Maturin: 'Eva' (1847), 'Immalee' (1847), 'Isidora' (1847), 'Zara (Now the Pain Beginneth)' (1847), 'Lady Montrevor' (1848), 'Zara (The Pale Sad Face of Her I Wronged)' (1848), 'Zara (I Dreamed That Loving Me)' (1855) and 'Look on This Picture and on This' (1856). Although Rossetti's reading of Gothic included a range of authors, she appears to have been most engaged by the novels of Maturin. These poems portray Maturin's Gothic heroines at a moment of crisis, both in the structure of the novel and in their lives, giving them a voice at a crucial moment. Divorced from their context, the poems can prove difficult to appreciate, but studied alongside Maturin's novels they provide a case-study of Rossetti's interaction with a particular Gothic author. These poems have been overlooked, possibly on the grounds that they were written in youth and do not easily fit in with the rest of her oeuvre. Marsh, for example, comments that 'Such works clearly supplied a need', presumably emotionally for the young poet, but does not consider them any further (1994, p. 45).

It is undeniable that the structure and language, as well as emotional content, of the first six Maturin poems are not as developed as her mature work. Moreover, in his edition of Rossetti's poems published in 1904, W. M. Rossetti designates these (and other) poems as juvenilia, and, as with so many of his decisions about his sister's poetry, the label has stuck. Juvenilia tends to present a critical problem, in that it is often easy to trace simplified connections between early writings and later works, and to draw biographical as well as literary assumptions that can be facile. It is therefore important to consider the early poems as works in their own right rather than as manifestations of teenage angst, for example. However, when Rossetti produced the first poem, 'Eva', in 1847, she was 16 – considerably older than the Brontës, for example, when their childhood writing began.[1] Critics consider the early writings of the Brontë siblings to be important not only in demonstrating and honing their developing literary talents but also in the complex plots of their later work. The Brontës' biographer, Juliet Barker, discusses Charlotte Brontë's early interest in the supernatural manifested in her Angrian writings (see Barker, 1995), while other critics go further. Sally Shuttleworth, for example, takes the early work of Charlotte Brontë very seriously, considering its interrogation of gender boundaries in a political and social context, and pointing out the value of these works: 'We find here the same sense of embattled selfhood, shying away from interpretative penetration, the same concerns with the instabilities of psychological and gender identity, which fuel the later work' (1996, p. 101). For Brontë, her 'juvenilia', in terms of the saga of Angria, was produced well into her twenties, yet Rossetti was not much younger when she began writing poems influenced by Maturin. It has been overlooked that the last two Maturin poems ('Zara – I Dreamed That Loving Me' and 'Look on This Picture and on This') were written in 1855 and 1856, just a year before the critically acclaimed 'A Better Resurrection' (1857), for example.

The Gothic novel, with its complex psychological heritage and subterranean explorations, may seem a surprising choice for a religious adolescent girl, but *Melmoth the Wanderer* became one of Rossetti's favourite novels from childhood onwards. Rossetti's early reading of Gothic novels is now common knowledge, yet her brother, W. M. Rossetti, reduced her choice of literature to a footnote in his 'Memoir', in her posthumous collected poems.[2] Here, in relation to the poem 'Lady Montrevor', which is based on Maturin's novel *The Wild Irish Boy*, W. M. Rossetti comments: 'Christina, as well as her brothers, was in early youth very fond of Maturin's novels, and more than one of her poems relate to these' (WMR, p. 477). D'Amico, in her essay 'Christina Rossetti: The Maturin Poems', suggests that since biographical references to Rossetti's interest in Maturin are merely cursory, we might erroneously 'expect this connection to be a minor one, perhaps involving only Rossetti's youthful fancies' (p. 117). Though Rossetti read other authors such as Ann Radcliffe with similar avidity, only *Melmoth the Wanderer*, *The Wild Irish Boy* and *Women* inspired her to write poems based on their heroines.

D'Amico's essay stands almost alone in its central argument that Rossetti's interest in Maturin's novels was more than an adolescent phase.[3] She argues that Rossetti's interest in his work forms three major strands, which are borne out in her later work. The first of these, she suggests, is 'a convent motif in which a woman is torn between her lover and her religious vows' (p. 118). This is an image which Maturin frequently employed, notably in *The Albingenses* (1824) and *Fatal Revenge* (1807) (neither of which inspired Rossetti to write, and there is no evidence that she read them, though it seems probable that she did). Rossetti wrote a number of poems which examined convent life, including 'The Convent Threshold', one of her most famous poems. Here, the world of the convent is seen as harsh and wearisome, as the novice cries:

> How long shall stretch these nights and days?
> Surely, clean Angels cry, she prays;
> She laves her soul with tedious tears:
> How long must stretch these years and years? (ll. 57–60)

The world beyond the convent, despite its temptations, is illusory, however, and the novice pleads with her lover to repent so that she might see him again in heaven, with a longing reminiscent of the close of her poem based on Immalee. Similarly, 'An Immurata Sister', though speaking with hope of the life to come, is an essentially melancholy poem which despairs of 'yearnings without gain' (l. 10). The convent itself features little in Rossetti's so-called convent poems, certainly not in the gloomy and forbidding style of convents in Gothic literature, since Rossetti focuses on the nuns themselves. Instead, it is the notion of enclosure, compulsory or otherwise, combined with a focus on God, which sets the tone of these poems, not necessarily in a positive way: Rossetti's view of convents was not enthusiastic.

In many of Rossetti's convent poems, however, the convent itself appears mainly as a device to provide a barrier between the repentant woman and her lover, a concept also present in Radcliffe's works which use the convent motif, such as *The Italian*, in which Ellena is cloistered in a convent by Schedoni. While D'Amico comments on the motif in Rossetti's poems, she does not explore it further. In fact, the convent, although it features in Maturin's fiction, is more easily traced to other concerns in Rossetti's life. The development of Anglican sisterhoods was supported by Reverend William Dodsworth of Christ Church, Albany Street, which Rossetti, with her mother and sister, attended. Dinah Mulock Craik also wrote vociferously in support of them, as a useful vocation for the single woman, though she emphasized that 'family life is the first and most blessed life' (Rossetti and Craik, 1995, p. 54). Newman and Pusey encouraged the development of Anglican sisterhoods, both in order that women might provide much-needed care within their communities, for example, working with the sick and with 'fallen women', and in order to provide a devotional alternative to spinsterhood. The first Anglican sisterhood, the Park Village sisterhood, was therefore created in 1845, associated with Christ Church. Later, in 1859, Rossetti began volunteering at the St Mary Magdalene Penitentiary in Highgate, and eventually became an associate sister, while her elder sister Maria entered a sisterhood in 1873, sensing a vocation that Christina Rossetti considered herself to lack. It seems probable that despite her religious devotion, Rossetti's depictions of the convent life in her poetry stem from her own nature, which she believed could not thrive under such conditions.[4] Lynda Palazzo even suggests that sisterhoods exploited women, by rendering them barren on all levels (p. 6). In fact, Rossetti's poems frequently tend to concentrate on love both earthly and spiritual, with its tensions and synergies, rather than on the cloistered life. The convent represents barriers to fulfilment or happiness, both earthly and spiritual.

The second strand of Maturin's influence on Rossetti's work, D'Amico posits, is the novels' 'concern [. . .] not simply with the secular aspects of such a love dilemma but with the religious as well' (p. 118). This is certainly a major issue in Rossetti's poetry, which, despite her concern about her poems being read as 'love personals', early critics tended to see as biographical, relating to her two broken engagements.[5] There is no doubt that the conflict between earthly and spiritual love was an issue which appealed to Rossetti, and which she developed in her poems based on Maturin's novels, particularly 'Isidora' and those drawn from *Women*. She expanded upon this motif in later poems, such as the sonnet sequence 'Monna Innominata'. While D'Amico suggests this might appear unlikely, this chapter will argue that it was precisely the conflicted nature of these heroines and their circumstances which drew Rossetti to Maturin's work and inspired her poetic representations.[6]

The final strand D'Amico explores is 'the theme of the strong soul in conflict' (p. 120). It is indisputable that Rossetti was drawn to the depictions of the 'active, heroic woman' (p. 120) in Maturin's fiction. Indeed the heroines of her poems were strong-willed and passionate, such as Maude Clare and Maggie, and the narrative thread of these poems is predicated on this. However, it is the aspect of the struggles the heroine faces which seem to have particularly attracted Rossetti. It is difficult to conceive of Rossetti producing a poem based on Matilda in Matthew Lewis's *The Monk* (1796), for example, since Matilda appears barely to struggle with her immorality, having little interiority in Lewis's narrative, and instead embraces her blasphemy. Rather, it is probable that the drama of the conflicts faced by Immalee/Isidora, Zaira, Eva and Lady Montrevor presented possibilities to Rossetti. These aspects continued to interest her for the rest of her writing life. To separate these three strands of Maturin's influence is difficult and perhaps unnecessary, since they point towards one overriding concept: the tension between earthly and spiritual love is resolved only by the renunciation of the former.

Though D'Amico rightly suggests that the Maturin poems are deserving of further study, and that they provide an element of influence on her later work, there has been little critical discussion of their significant impact upon her later poems. The assumption that there is an underlying division between the young and instinctive Rossetti and the reserved, mature poet is one that has driven much of the criticism of her work, yet the Maturin poems provide scope to revisit her earlier poems in the context of her more famous later work. The motifs and issues which she began with her earliest poems are in many cases maintained until her last. This chapter considers Rossetti's Maturin poems in the order of Maturin's novels, in order to provide a sense of continuity in both the novels and the poems. In fact this chronology also for the most part reflects the chronology of the poems, suggesting the development of Rossetti's work alongside her reading of Maturin's novels.

The Wild Irish Boy

Maturin's first major novel, *The Wild Irish Boy* (1808) was written following the success of *The Wild Irish Girl* (1806) by Sydney Owenson, later Lady Morgan. Since the later novel had little in common with its predecessor save the title, however, *The Wild Irish Boy* was not well received, though this may in part have been due to its complex and sometimes confusing structure. The novel is Gothic in its interiority of characters, who are beset by temptations and nightmares, while the text itself is fragmentary, but on the whole the book is less Gothic than Maturin's other works. E. F. Bleiler, in his introduction to the 1977 reprint of the novel, suggests that it is:

> best classified as a conglomerate novel [. . .] In this subform several genres could be combined to create a novel of potentially wide appeal. Gothic terror and exoticism, fairly realistic society material, intellectual speculation, satire and sentiment all might be worked into a single framework.[7]

The novel, which begins in an epistolary form and moves on to a somewhat disjointed narrative with multiple narrators, tells the story of a 'wild Irish boy', Ormsby Bethel, and his ill-fated love for the beautiful Lady Montrevor.

With its action moving between high society in London and Dublin, the novel was censured for its low morals and sordidness, though it is perhaps clearer to the modern reader, with the benefit of hindsight, that Maturin's somewhat heavy-handed portrayals of a corrupt society were intended as parody, with their exaggerated, almost grotesque scenes. The scene is set with the letters of Elmaide, a young girl who cherishes an unrequited love for Bethel. Expressing her misery in overblown, romantic terms, she tells her correspondent that she is 'obliged to listen to all that *can be said* with conviction and despair' (I, p. 20). In fact, throughout the novel it is what *cannot* be said which is paramount. Bleiler comments that 'The greatest strength of *The Wild Irish Boy*, as might have been expected, lies in its power of language, an area where Maturin excels' (I, p. ix). While Maturin's use of language is commendable, Bleiler comments only on the power of words. What Maturin exercises, and Rossetti's poetry consistently demonstrates, is an understanding of the power of what is beyond words.

In *The Wild Irish Boy*, it is initially intense emotion, or love, that is beyond words, though as the novel reaches its climax it seems to be truth itself that cannot be spoken; indeed Ormsby Bethel refers to the 'dark language' (III, p. 290) spoken in society, which aims to beguile and deceive. Maturin reinforces this on a number of occasions; for example:

> I know not how to speak at this moment; I wish I could borrow the common language of description, and tell as I would of any woman of fashion. (I, pp. 242–3)

> I can speak of her at no time, for every time I saw her she was different; it is difficult to speak of her mode of beauty, it is more difficult to speak of her age. (I, p. 246)

Language becomes both a medium of communication and a barrier to it. Like Elmaide, Bethel finds that love leaves him speechless, and that language appears too base or corrupt an instrument with which to express his feelings. This is a common enough rhetorical device, to declare words to be insufficient yet to use many of them; in this novel the failure of words is supplemented with those who have words for every occasion, such as Lady Montrevor, who, on being congratulated for her wit, replies:

> 'Tinsel, mere tinsel,' said she, almost with a sigh; 'but it does as well for common use. The value of wit, as jewellers say of plates, depends more on the fashion than the weight; and this light currency saves credit, and gains time, two great points in preventing a bankruptcy of – conversation.' (I, p. 258)

Her own consciousness of the levity with which words may be spoken and heard is to her credit, and attracts Bethel to her still further. With this speech she becomes a more than two-dimensional character, attractive to the reader, aware of her flaws despite her physical appeal.

It has been suggested that Maturin was influenced by Mme de Staël's *Corinne* (1807) in the creation of his characters of Lady Montrevor, and also Zaira in *Women*. If, as Taylor Monroe (1980) posits, Maturin read *Corinne*, this seems a not implausible argument, as the characters do seem to have at least their fatal magnetism in common, but furthermore a tragic aspect unites them. One particular trait the three characters share is their ability to communicate, or 'speak', through a variety of media including their appearance and demeanour, dance, music, painting and poetry as well as spoken language. The result of these abilities is that, as Lord Nelvil states in *Corinne*, beside such women, other women appear to speak only in 'insipid conventional phrases used to express neither their feelings nor their opinions truthfully' (de Staël, 1998, p. 166). The Gothic heroines which Rossetti depicts are aware of their ability to communicate, yet also conscious of the failures and problems of communication, and particularly language, which seems inadequate.

Corinne, Lady Montrevor and Zaira experience the failure of language under the pressure of intense emotion. Rossetti similarly emphasizes the value of silence in 'Monna Innominata', which gives a voice to the usually voiceless woman, she who loves passionately and cannot speak of it. The final sonnet of this series closes:

> The longing of a heart pent up forlorn,
> A silent heart whose silence loves and longs;
> The silence of a heart which sang its songs
> While youth and beauty made a summer morn,
> Silence of love that cannot sing again. (Sonnet 14, ll. 10–14)

In 'Monna Innominata' Rossetti makes the distinction between those who are dumb through convention, as women who love should be, and those who are silent because silence is more telling than words.[8] In this last sonnet, the latter is the case; the heart can no longer speak but the love remains. In another poem, 'Echo', she writes of the 'speaking silence of a dream' (l. 2), and it is in the 'speaking silence' that she excels; what is not said is as important as what can be put into words, and frequently more so.

Mr Corbett, the preacher in *The Wild Irish Boy*, perhaps provides the most sincere example of how language may be used. He too is talking of love, but in his portrayal of divine love he appears gifted with an eloquence lacking from those who wish only to talk of earthly love:

> Though his positions were strong and important, they were clothed in a language, whose peculiar and providential felicity is, that it is the universal language, the first language that religion talks to the ear of infancy, the language that genius reverences, and ignorance understands, the language of the poet and of the saint, the language of divinity and of the heart, the language of the Scriptures. (I, p. 209)

Mr Corbett's use of language is full of sincerity and spirituality, redolent of the poetic spiritual truths later voiced by the Tractarians. While it was accepted by the Tractarians that there was much that was divine that could not be either understood or expressed by human tongues, the eloquence afforded by the language of Scripture is a concept which clearly chimed with Rossetti. Her interest in language, as a poet, is to be expected, but her discussions of language in her later work, particularly defending the role of Eve in the Fall, give an insight into how deeply she considered the matter, and to what uses debates around language might be put.

The instability of language is both refuted and reinforced in Rossetti's work: she demonstrates, particularly in her later work, that the Bible is not immune to the vagaries of interpretation, which can have considerable theological significances. Her poems have a tendency to utilize ambiguity, in the sense which Empson gives it: 'any verbal nuance, however slight, which gives room for alternative reactions to the same piece of language' (1965, p. 1). Furthermore, Rossetti exploits such verbal ambiguities in her own interpretations of Scripture; for example, in *Letter and Spirit: Notes on the Commandments* (1883), Rossetti considers the Fall, and her conclusion suggests that language may be at the root of it (*LS*, pp. 17–18).

Several of her poems maintain this engagement with the slipperiness of language. In 'The World', a poem which begins softly with emphasis on the sibilants, and the juxtaposed seductive and loathsome images, Rossetti presents the temptations of the world as a Gothic monster, not unlike the fiends both mental and physical that afflict the characters of *The Wild Irish Boy*. In 'The Three Enemies', however, the speaker conducts a conversation with those who would tempt humans from righteousness (the Flesh, the World and the Devil). Here, the tempters speak fondly – 'Sweet, thou art pale' (l. 1), 'Sweet, thou art young' (l. 17) and are firmly answered, 'More pale to see | Christ hung upon the cruel tree' (ll. 2–3) and 'So was He young | Who for my sake in silence hung' (ll. 18–19). The speaker uses language rich in biblical allusions, and with echoes of the catechism, drawing on reserves of language which appear convincing in the context of the poem because of their familiarity and association with scripture. The poem appears like a catechism, with answers readily forthcoming to each temptation, yet the use of catechismic language may cause the reader to wonder if the answers are more learned responses than considered beliefs. However, the answers in the last section of the poem suggest that 'Knowledge' (l. 41) is 'helpless dust' (l. 42), yet 'Thy Word' (l. 48) can conquer all; Rossetti prioritizes the language of the scriptures over everything else, even knowledge, and thus the use of this language can be seen as strengthening her argument.

Rossetti is demonstrating here the use to which language may be put: to verbalize one's beliefs and to strengthen one's resolve, and, moreover, to pass this on to others. Language may be used for deception, but it can also be used to repel temptation.

In the penultimate line of her poem based on *The Wild Irish Boy*, 'Lady Montrevor' (1848), Rossetti picks up the thread of Maturin's preoccupation with the uses and misuses of language. Despite her fame as a wit, it is silence that Lady Montrevor wishes for, and her 'tongue shall not complain' (l. 13), as evidence of her stoicism and remorse for her misspent life. Though suffering, Lady Montrevor is not a character to be pitied, and her pride insists that she remain strong. In depicting her thus, Rossetti resists the broken-hearted woman as a figure of ignominy and replaces her with a stronger, more appealing character. She develops this concept throughout her Maturin poems as well as her ballads, as abandoned women speak out and demand to be heard. Here, Rossetti manipulates words and their power to create a monologue spoken by a beautiful and tragic heroine.[9] The society belle, Lady Montrevor, is speaking here presumably towards the end of the novel, when the extent of her misery and duplicitous life has been revealed to the reader:

> I do not look for love that is a dream:
> I only seek for courage to be still;
> To bear my grief with an unbending will,
> And when I am a-weary not to seem.
> Let the round world roll on; let the sun beam;
> Let the wind blow, and let the rivers fill
> The everlasting sea; and on the hill
> The palms almost touch heaven, as children deem.
> And though young Spring and Summer pass away,

And Autumn and cold Winter come again;
And though my soul, being tired of its pain,
Pass from the ancient earth; and though my clay
Return to dust; my tongue shall not complain:
No man shall mock me after this my day. (ll. 1–14)

The character's lexical range, emphasizing the natural world, may appear an odd choice for a society woman such as Lady Montrevor, yet at the moment of crisis when her accustomed world has failed her, it seems appropriate. The passing of time and beauty, echoed in the passing of the seasons, is a trope to which Rossetti returns, while the words of patience and stoic courage express sentiments which Rossetti's poems voice throughout her life, in poems such as 'A Better Resurrection', 'Where Neither Rust Nor Moth Doth Corrupt' and the sonnet sequence 'Later Life'. More particularly, however, Rossetti's 1854 poem 'A Study. (A Soul.)', unpublished until Crump's edition of her work, describes a woman who stands 'Like Cleopatra when she turned at bay | And felt her strength above the Roman sway', and '. . . stands there patient, nerved with inner might' (ll. 2–3, 12). Though the woman described is unnamed, it is possible that she may have her origin in Lady Montrevor, who, when describing her fall from fortune, and her resolve to face it with resilience, states:

We were fallen! fallen! fallen! Yet I was determined to fall like myself. I had been the Cleopatra of the revels for many loose and worthless years, I was now to be the Cleopatra whose departure was to throw dignity upon a clouded life. (III, p. 78)

It is not merely the reference to Cleopatra that is striking, but the notion of a woman braced to face an unpleasant life, or indeed death, in the case of Cleopatra. The strength and resolution of a woman such as Lady Montrevor, intelligent and intrinsically noble despite her immoral behaviour, clearly attracted Rossetti's attention throughout her reading of Maturin's novels.

Lady Montrevor has no Christian comfort such as the speakers of poems such as 'Where neither rust nor moth doth corrupt', and I suggest that in fact the sonnet is written within a framework of resignation, which no longer looks for comfort. Crump suggests that lines 6–7 refer to Ecclesiastes 1.7: 'All the rivers run into the sea; yet the sea is not full; unto the place from whence the rivers come, thither they return again' (Rossetti, 2005, p. 1108). Further, Crump refers the reader to 'A Testimony', which contains the lines, 'The rivers do not fill the sea, | But turn back to their secret source' (ll. 10–11). Here, the reference is quite unmistakeable. 'A Testimony' is a poem which owes much to Ecclesiastes; it considers the passing of time and the frailty of worldly possessions, which are apposite symbols for the tale of the doomed Lady Montrevor.

However, another poem which also draws heavily on Ecclesiastes 1.2–11 seems to provide a more useful context for 'Lady Montrevor'. 'One Certainty' opens with the words of Ecclesiastes 1.2, 'Vanity of vanities, saith the Preacher, vanity of vanities; all is vanity', a favourite theme of Rossetti's throughout her life. Vanity is at the centre of Lady Montrevor's corruption. In the first two volumes of the novel she is portrayed as a vain, heartless woman who survives on the excessive admiration of others; in the third volume, where she tells her own story, she admits that her need for admiration, and her own vanity, has been her undoing. The joylessness of 'Lady Montrevor' is reflected in the resignation of 'One Certainty':

> So little joy hath he, so little cheer,
> Till all things end in the long dust of death.
> Tomorrow is the same as yesterday,
> Tomorrow also even as one of them.
> And there is nothing new under the sun:
> Until the ancient race of time be run (ll. 7–12)

Like 'Lady Montrevor', this poem also emphasizes the passing of time, the enemy of beauty, as Rossetti suggests in many of her poems, such as 'Beauty Is Vain', which warns, 'Time will win the race he runs with her | And hide her away in a shroud' (ll. 15–16). 'One Certainty', though not suffering the same stigma of juvenilia as the Maturin poems, was written only a year later than 'Lady Montrevor', and follows the same Petrarchan sonnet form as the earlier poem. The similarities in tone and content are striking; it is only the narrator who changes.

Ecclesiastes inspired or is a point of reference in many of Rossetti's poems, though 'Lady Montrevor' appears to be the first. Over thirty poems include references to it, of which fourteen refer to 1.2, and six refer to 1.7.[10] Its resonance for Rossetti was evidently deep and personal, due perhaps to the philosophy of her stoical nature, but in the context of Lady Montrevor's character it is particularly appropriate. Even much later poems, such as 'A Vain Shadow', which appeared in *Verses* (1898), strike a similar note to Lady Montrevor's resigned renunciation of the world, commenting on the temporal and vain world and closing with reference to the fluctuations of the sea.

Women

This novel, published in 1818, inspired Rossetti to produce five poems, which I will examine in the order in which Rossetti wrote them. Once again these are monologues which reveal the inner turmoil of a character from the novels. By rewriting characters from novels, Rossetti is also creating her own space in the poetess tradition. D'Amico asserts that Rossetti is writing in this tradition at this stage, particularly in drawing on already existing narratives of women's lives, as did others, including Augusta Webster, Felicia Hemans and L. E. L., focusing on the lives of ill-fated women, though in the case of these poetesses, the characters were more frequently based on autobiography than fiction (1999, pp. 18–20). Rossetti's poems tend to feature lone heroines, particularly those who have suffered, perhaps through their own misdeeds, and she celebrates transgressive womanhood in the Maturin poems as much as she celebrates the pious and self-sacrificing. Her ballads are also prime examples of this, focusing on 'fallen women' who are redeemed through their own strength of mind, rejecting pity from the reader.

This novel also is remarkable for its interiority of characters, and focuses on the family, as well as the results of excessive faith. It tells the tragic story of Charles De Courcy, who falls in love with a young, extremely religious girl, Eva, who is portrayed as a victim of her family's zealous Evangelicalism. They eventually become engaged, despite her scruples about his lukewarm religious beliefs and her desire to focus solely on heaven. While being smitten with her youth and purity, De Courcy is fatally attracted to a well-known singer and society beauty, Zaira (though Rossetti always spells it 'Zara').[11] After some agonizing vacillations, De Courcy leaves Eva, and London, to travel abroad with the fascinating Zaira. However, his guilty thoughts are with Eva, and his fascination with Zaira wanes, until he returns to England, only to find Eva on her deathbed. After Eva's death, it transpires that Zaira was Eva's mother, who had been forced to give up her child in order to provide a better life for her. De Courcy also dies, hoping that Eva had forgiven him. Zaira must then live with her conscience, and it is this struggle that provides Rossetti with material for two of her 'Zara' poems.

Rossetti's poem 'Eva' (1847) appears to take place near the end of Eva's life, when, abandoned by Charles De Courcy, she falls ill and prepares for death, blaming herself for becoming too attached to him. Once again, earthly and spiritual love contend for primacy in this poem. There are no direct biblical allusions here, which is surprising given both Rossetti's and Eva's tendency towards this, though one line appears to derive from the *Book of Common Prayer*: 'It is good and meet and right.' Like so many of Rossetti's poems, and indeed much of Maturin's prose, the poem uses phraseology and syntax which sounds weighted with scriptural authority; for example:

> Lord, Thou knowest, I have said,
> All is good that comes from Thee;
> Unto Thee I bow my head.
> I have not repented me. (ll. 8–11)

The poem is strictly rhymed, representing not the overflowing of emotion from a dying woman that one might expect, but rather the tones of love and desire reined in by the scrupulous exercise of willpower and conscientious Christian belief typical of both Eva and Rossetti. The structure of the poem is particularly significant in its emphasis on certain aspects of Eva's concerns, concentrated in the mono-rhymed tercets which close each stanza, throwing the emphasis of each line onto the words in the middle; for example, the nouns 'sorrow', 'trial' and 'faith' in the first, and adjectives 'bitter', 'stubborn' and 'haughty' in the second:

> That the sorrow shall not last,
> And the trial shall be past,
> And my faith shall anchor fast.
> [. . .]
> Still, oh! still 'tis bitter ill;
> Still I have a stubborn will,
> And my heart is haughty still. (ll. 5–7, 12–14)

The catalectic trochaic metre provides a regularity of rhythm not typical of Rossetti's verse, though one trips slightly over the word 'Heaven' in the final two stanzas where it needs to be pronounced as one syllable, indicating a move towards death as heartbeat and strength fail. Eva speaks of her penitence, and her feeling that her punishment is deserved, since despite her remorse she continues to love De Courcy. In addressing herself as she does, she appears to be admonishing an unseen listener (or indeed the reader), which contains echoes of her deathbed scene in the novel, in which she abjures the children of the family to 'Love God, and him *only!*' (III, p. 381) and asks them to learn from her plight.

Of course, the alternative to Eva's fate of dying of an illness brought on by the desertion of Charles, might have been for her to have rejected him and continue to focus on God. Many of Rossetti's poems reflect this alternative, and present it as no more appealing. 'Memory' tells of a choice made, though the choice is not specified, and the poem tempts critics towards biographical readings:

> None know the choice I made; I make it still.
> None know the choice I made and broke my heart
> [. . .]
> I broke it at a blow, I laid it cold,
> Crushed in my deep heart where it used to live.
> My heart dies inch by inch; the time grows old,
> Grows old in which I grieve. (ll. 13–14, 17–20)

Eva, like the speaker of this poem, had a choice to make between earthly and spiritual love, and despite her innocence and initial reluctance, was persuaded by De Courcy to commit herself to him. The suffering and endurance of the speaker in 'Memory' seem barely preferable to Eva's fate of an early grave, and certainly Rossetti's poems contain many early deaths, some less lamented than others. However, Rossetti appears preoccupied with the idea of lovers parting, to be reunited after death, particularly with the self-sacrifice and endurance that this entails. Eva prays for this reunion at the close of Rossetti's poem; 'Memory' closes with conviction of reunification after death, and other poems such as 'One Day', 'Twilight Night' and 'Isidora' close on a similar note, with several poems using the word 'Paradise' to emphasize the bliss of the lovers' reunion.[12] This is a trope which emerges earliest in her work through her Maturin poems, however, and is a feature of all the Maturin poems except 'Lady Montrevor', who wishes only for forgetfulness, and 'Zara (I Dreamed That Loving Me)'.

   This concept of reunification in heaven is a complex one theologically. In cultural terms, Victorian writers, especially novelists, feature 'death-bed scenes [. . .] of "going to join" parents, or brothers or sisters who have died early, [which] presupposes the continuity of distinctive individuality and personal relationships' (Hick, 1976, p. 204). This assumption is clearly also made by Rossetti, not only in her Maturin poems but also in other works. Moreover, in 'Saints and Angels', published in 1875, Rossetti presents a biblical description of Paradise in which 'The road to death is life, the gate of life is death' (l. 33). Like other poems including the later 'Zara' poems, death as the gateway to heaven is something to be relished rather than feared. This poem also offers hope for reunions in heaven: 'The loves that meet in Paradise shall cast out fear, | And Paradise hath room for you and me and all' (ll. 39–40). As D'Amico suggests, '[f]or all these women, heaven is much more Pre-Raphaelite than Christian', akin to D. G. Rossetti's 'Blessed Damozel' (1999, p. 127). This is a poem in which the life to come is longed for not as a respite from daily toil or grief, though this is a common conceit in her work, but for the state of bliss it offers.

Her belief in the individuality of souls in heaven may come from her readings of Dante, especially the *Paradiso*. Not only does Rossetti's poetry reflect the concrete reality of Dante's heaven, which 'worked within current cosmology and astronomy in order not to contravene any cosmological truth set in his time', but Dante's assertion of being guided through the afterlife by Beatrice affords a similar hope for reunion to Rossetti's poetry (Burton Russell, 1997, p. 166). Dante also sees and speaks with some of the apostles, whom he evidently recognizes, as well as many other figures whose tales he tells. It is interesting to note that, like Rossetti, Dante is also concerned with what cannot be expressed verbally, commenting that he 'saw things which to tell | Lack power and skill' (Dante, 1887, 'Paradiso', ll. 4–5). The restraints of language which Rossetti learned early in her career as a poet may have stemmed from her absorption in the work of Dante as much as from her reading of Maturin.

Contrary to this belief are the words of Mark 12.25, which state unequivocally: 'For when they shall rise from the dead, they neither marry, nor are given in marriage: but are as the angels which are in heaven.' This passage 'abrogates not only the essential human faculty of sexual love and relationship and the need for procreation but even the very survival of human ties' (Simon, 1958, p. 217). Simon goes on to suggest that the wider family provided by the communion of saints in heaven is perhaps compensation for this. The implication is that there will be no recognition of individuality in heaven; rather, the earthly body will be discarded, which is also a concept which many of Rossetti's poems endorse, since she writes with a dualistic theological approach in many instances, in which it is the soul which travels on while the frail body decays.

A particularly explicit example of Rossetti's dualism can be found in 'Two Thoughts of Death', two sonnets which contrast the view that the body is dead with the continued life of the soul. The first sonnet opens, 'Her heart that loved me once is rottenness | Now and corruption; and her life is dead' (ll. 1–2). Rossetti's emphasis is on the 'life', or body, that is dead, in earthly terms. The second sonnet, however, considers the memory of the beloved, reflected in natural images which regenerate and live on. This sonnet concludes:

Then my heart answered me: Thou fool to say
That she is dead whose night is turned to day,
And whose day shall no more turn back to night. (ll. 12–14)

Just as Tractarian typology points all natural life on earth towards heaven, similarly nature is used here to remind the reader of eternal life, and provide hope for the bereaved – a concept, incidentally, not only promulgated by Tractarianism but also explained by Beatrice in lines 77–81 of Dante's *Paradiso*. Rossetti's poems, unsurprisingly, insist on the continuation of life after death; it is the exact nature of the continued life that is changeable.[13]

Rossetti's approach to death in her poems is flexible, which serves to indicate her inclination to use 'poetic licence' when it suited her, as well as a salutary warning that Rossetti's beliefs may not always be directly reflected in her poetry. For example, in 'Amor Mundi', there is a reference to 'a thin dead body which waits the eternal term' (l. 16), which relates to the belief that the body and soul may be reunited only at the Last Judgement. However, Rossetti's poems of heaven usually imply an immediate entrance to heaven as well as recognition of family and friends. Furthermore, her description of heaven in 'Paradise', for example, draws on Scripture to produce a sensory description of heaven that consistently relates to human understanding and senses. All the human faculties are overwhelmed with the beauty of heaven in this poem, and the implication is clear: that we are transformed yet retain human, or earthly, qualities of perception which seem to translate our understanding of individuality. Though Rossetti is not entirely consistent in her approach, and admits that after death one 'haply may remember, and haply may forget' ('Song (When I Am Dead My Dearest)', l. 16), this may be because she is prepared to use a certain amount of poetic licence to dramatize situations. Death may be a longed-for release or a keenly anticipated prize, but it is present in many of her poems as a destination no less real than earth.

This desire for death as a release from the pain of life is a feature of the poem 'Zara (Now the Pain Beginneth)'. Like 'Eva', it is written at a moment of crisis, with the first line indicating her awareness of the anguish that lies ahead of her. Despite this, the tone is restrained and rhythmic; the dignified heroine does not seem to stoop to untrammelled despair. 'The word' which is 'spoken' in line 1 is unspecified, but the effect is that the time for speaking is past, now replaced with the 'tolling of the churchyard chime' (l. 2). At the point in the novel at which this monologue is set, De Courcy has grown weary of Zaira and, overcome with remorse, returned to Eva. Since Eva's death is not yet imminent, the 'churchyard chime' may be for Zaira herself, representing not her death but her misery, which entombs her in a living death. The knowledge that her love is 'a crime' (l. 4) comes from her guilt that De Courcy left Eva to be with her; as yet she is ignorant that Eva is in fact her daughter.

The second stanza opens in a manner familiar from Rossetti's later poems of resignation and endurance: 'But the fear is over; yea, what now shall pain me? | Arm thee in thy sorrow, O most Desolate!' (ll. 5–6). Many of Rossetti's poems, such as 'And Now Why Tarriest Thou?', 'They Desire a Better Country' and 'Despised and Rejected' contain this sense of weariness with life and pleas for strength to continue if death cannot end the struggle. These later poems take an entirely devotional approach to this, but the concept of life as a struggle that must be borne is one which Rossetti explores repeatedly in her work. However, the stanza concludes in a more passionate tone, emphasizing the speaker's excessive emotions: 'Weariness and weakness, these shall now sustain me, – | Pride and bitter grieving, burning love and hate' (ll. 7–8). The emphasis in this poem is on changing moods, as the exuberant and uninhibited Zaira attempts to come to terms with her abandonment, and, like Corinne, displays great capacity for suffering. Despite the interlaced rhymes of each quatrain, in each there is a shift in emotion between the first two and last two lines: for example, the third stanza opens with a tone of relief that the fear of De Courcy's desertion is over, though realized, yet concludes with expressions of grief which border on insanity, though this is again belied by the regular rhythm of the metre. The purpose of the metre is realized as the poem progresses to become almost a curse; the last six stanzas suggest the chanting of imprecations, as part of Zaira's despairing reaction. Reading the poem with knowledge of the plot, and knowing that Zaira's heart will be again broken by Eva's death when she discovers her parentage, Zaira's extreme words contain an element of hubris:

> He shall leave thee also, he who now hath left me,
> With a weary spirit and an aching heart;
> Thou shalt be bereaved by him who hath bereft me;
> Thou hast sucked the honey, – feel the stinging's smart. (ll. 17–20)

In his Notes to Rossetti's poems, W. M. Rossetti comments that this was originally to be illustrated: 'The device to "Zara" is a foxglove plant, with insects sucking its poison-honey' (WMR, p. 467). This adds an interesting dimension to the poem, since the words portray Eva as a form of parasite, living off the honey of a plant; but the image of the foxglove, known to be poisonous, suggests rather that the source of evil is De Courcy himself, and logically the poem proceeds to ask why vengeance has not been forthcoming upon him: 'Hath the Heaven no thunder wherewith to denounce him? | Hath the Heaven no lightning wherewith to chastise?' (ll. 29–30). The irony here is that Zaira is still unaware of the relationship, yet her madness when the situation is revealed is not dissimilar to King Lear's ravings on the heath, invoking the natural elements in her call for vengeance. Zaira will suffer the punishment of remorse verging on madness after realizing her rival's true identity.

In the following stanza, however, she seems to repent, asking instead that she be struck – 'O ye thunders deafen, O ye lightning blind me, | Winds and storms from heaven, strike me but spare him' (ll. 35–6). As she softens towards him, Rossetti introduces a sacrificial stance, which is common in her poems. Finally, she reaches forgiveness, and prepares herself for the punishment for both their sins: 'May thy cup of sorrow be poured out for me; | Though the dregs be bitter yet they shall not grieve me' (ll. 38–9). Though Zaira's religious beliefs have been called into question by De Courcy, particularly given her career as an actress and the contrast with Eva's devotion, Rossetti's appropriation of Christian imagery here seems apposite. The lines echo Psalm 75.8:

> For in the hand of the Lord there is a cup, and the wine is red; it is full of mixture; and he poureth out the same: but the dregs thereof, all the wicked of the earth shall wring them out, and drink them.

Zaira offers herself as a sacrifice for the man she loves, wishing she alone could take the blame and punishment. Indeed the closing stanzas of the poem imply that only forgiveness and a form of martyrdom can wipe the slate clean for Zaira. Clearly for Rossetti this self-sacrifice is a sign of pure love, and it is an idea to which she returns in 'Isidora' and in 'Zara (The Pale Sad Face of Her I Wronged)'. The concept of sacrifice more generally runs throughout her poetry: many refer to Christ's sacrifice on the cross, but it is also a preoccupation of 'Goblin Market', in which one sister is prepared to sacrifice herself for the other.

The notion of rivalry is also strong in this poem. The critic Dolores Rosenblum considers this element of Rossetti's poetry, and posits that 'the fantasies of sexual rivalry, betrayal, renunciation, and apotheosis which underly [*sic*] *Women* must have matched closely with Rossetti's own youthful fantasies' (1986, p. 154). This is difficult to substantiate; instead, it seems more likely to have been the spiritual aspect of renouncing earthly love which attracted Rossetti. Rosenblum goes on to argue, however, that the interest in rivalry sparked by *Women* is re-enacted in many 'sister' poems, such as 'Noble Sisters' and 'Sister Maude', in which sisters are rivals for earthly love. The rivals become doubles, she argues, which is particularly apposite for Eva and Zaira, who are presented in the novel as two sides of one coin, so physically and intellectually opposite that between them they seem to present one whole individual:

> By dividing 'sisters' in narrative poems and by opposing the self who desires to the self who renounces in the lyric poems, Rossetti articulates her version of Romantic-Victorian divided consciousness: not the split between hero and villain, or between reason and emotion, but between the sister who is chosen

and the sister who is spurned, and between the self who romantically asserts and the self who stoically denies. [. . .] The spurned sister, though outwardly invalidated, endures as the authentic consciousness, while the rival becomes the 'other', reduced to her function as usurper. (Rosenblum, 1986, p. 146)

That Eva and Zaira turn out to be mother and daughter is another way of linking them; the obscured family connection is a familiar emblem in the Gothic novel. In the novel it is striking that De Courcy should be attracted to such diverse women, yet as the novel reaches its climax, Eva becomes stronger, though spurned and dying, while Zaira becomes weaker as her dependency on De Courcy grows. In her poems, Rossetti appears to emphasize this strength; 'Eva' is not a poem of weakness, despite its self-abnegation, while the 'Zara' poems with their increasing misery maintain the women's individual characteristics while bringing their emotional and spiritual attributes closer together.

Dante Gabriel Rossetti's poem 'Jenny' uses a comparable trope of doubling characters who ostensibly have no more in common than their gender. His often-used theme of sacred and profane love is barely comparable to his sister's concern with the struggle between earthly and spiritual love, not least because for her the two were closely related, and linked to her faith, but primarily due to Christina Rossetti's relative purity of tone in dealing with such subjects, compared with her brother's publicly criticized 'fleshly school of poetry'. D. G. Rossetti's well-known twinning of the prostitute Jenny and the narrator's 'cousin Nell' appears to contrast the two women, so different, and sharing only their femininity:

> Of the same lump (as it is said)
> For honour and dishonour made,
> Two sister vessels. Here is one.
>
> It makes a goblin of the sun.
>
> So pure – so fall'n! How dare to think
> Of the first common kindred link? (ll. 182–7)

However, his words seem to place Nell little higher than the prostitute, since he emphasizes that she is 'fond of fun, | And fond of dress, and change, and praise, | So mere a woman in her ways' (ll. 185–7) which is not so far removed from 'Lazy languid laughing Jenny, | Fond of a kiss and fond of a guinea' (ll. 1–2). Women, the poem suggests, may be 'fallen' through a variety of situations, not only sexual. Though complicit in Jenny's fall, the speaker clearly regrets the contrasting situations which make 'poor Jenny' an outcast while Nell, secure in 'another's pride in her' (l. 198), remains respectable. The double standard reflects the doubled women, and both Rossettis reflect on the nature of fallenness in such poems.

The rivalry of 'Zara (Now the Pain Beginneth)' contrasts with Rossetti's next poem, 'Zara (The Pale Sad Face of Her I Wronged)' (1848), where Zaira's remorse for De Courcy's desertion of Eva is growing, though her sadness for herself remains as her anger towards the unfaithful lover grows.[14] Though she does not as yet realize the true relationship between herself and her rival, Zaira is conscious of an almost supernatural connection between them, which Rossetti heightens in the opening lines of the poem. Eva's face seems to haunt Zaira, and her customary demure silence is replaced with a nightmarish vision:

> The pale sad face of her I wronged
> Upbraids and follows me for ever:
> The silent mouth grows many-tongued
> To chide me; (ll. 1–4)

The poem utilizes a scheme of near-rhymes, such as paradise/eyes, erred/ word, which serve to emphasize the disintegrating confidence of Zaira as she is overtaken by conflicting violent emotions. However, towards the end of the poem the rhymes become more confident with an increased number of perfect rhymes, as Zaira forms a plan and becomes calmer as she decides her own fate. For a woman such as Zaira, Rossetti seems to imply, being mistress of her destiny is vital; though alone, deserted and heartbroken, if she can maintain control over her life she will not be defeated by events.

Once again the problems and possibilities of language are a central issue of the monologue, particularly in its contrast with silence, which Eva represents despite the 'many-tongued' vision. In the third stanza Zaira asks if it is 'thought, or deed, or word' (l. 16) which caused De Courcy to desert her; perhaps it was her words, in contrast to Eva's submissive silence, which wearied him. Indeed Zaira continues in the eighth stanza to see silence as a sign of strength rather than weakness:

> Therefore because she did not speak,
> Being strong to die and make no sign;
> Because her courage waxed not weak,
> Strengthened with love as with new wine. (ll. 43–6)

This strength through silence, comparable to the silent woman of 'Monna Innominata', will win her De Courcy's love again, Zaira suggests, and despite her own misery she seems to desire for Eva that he 'may bring her health' (l. 49), yet with a presentiment she knows that 'it is too late' (l. 54). Zaira's words in Rossetti's poem suggest that she feels the contrast between her speaking and Eva's silence keenly as a crucial difference between them, which has caused the situation. However, in stanza 10 she challenges De Courcy himself to speak:

> Thou doubly false to her and me,
> Boast of her death and my despair.
> Boast if thou canst: on land and sea,
> I will be with thee everywhere. (ll. 55–8)

Rossetti, by writing monologues for Eva and Zaira, has thus far effectively silenced De Courcy himself, though her final poem based on *Women* allows De Courcy to speak. By challenging him in this poem, however, Zaira is silencing him by invoking his own guilt, especially since the stanza closes saying: 'My soul, let loose by mine own deed, | Shall make thee fear who would'st not heed' (ll. 59–60). The implication is clearly that her 'own deed' will be death at her own hand, and that should he speak of the women he has hurt, she will haunt him. By now, Zaira's stance seems to have shifted to a moral anger, which encompasses both herself and Eva. Since he was 'doubly false', the women-doubles shall reap a double vengeance.

As in the previous poem, Zaira moves on to call curses down on his head, and, having invoked Greek mythologies, including Endymion, Narcissus and Echo, her language suggests the Furies, or perhaps Euripides' Medea, in her desire for vengeance which supersedes reason, life and death:

> Come, thou glad hour of vengeance, come,
> When I may dog him evermore,
> May track him to his distant home. (ll. 61–3)

In fact, her situation has sad echoes of Medea, who murdered her children as revenge upon her faithless husband; Zaira's child too will die, and the remorse will drive her to madness. Rossetti's later poems have none of this anger and vengeance, yet Zaira appears akin to a pagan deity calling vengeance upon her enemies. Her own death will allow her to become an instrument of vengeance, although she is aware that it is she who will suffer most: 'Till he shall long for death; yet shrink | From the cold cup that I shall drink' (ll. 71–2). She returns to the trope of the earlier Rossetti monologue, recalling Psalm 75.8 once more. This time the theme is more fully developed, however, as she reaches a conclusion at which she hesitated in the previous poem. The 'cold cup' will provide her a numbness, and she expresses a desire that she might be buried 'dug deep', because 'Such quietness I would not break, | Not for my cherished vengeance' sake' (ll. 83–4). She demands the cup of bitterness and death, then, desiring 'nothingness' above all, perhaps still haunted by the face of Eva and sensing that if she, Zaira, were to die, Eva might continue living by De Courcy's side. Embracing this notion, she metaphorically toasts this future forgetfulness: 'On the grave brink I turn and think | Of thee, before I stoop to drink' (ll. 89–90). Death has become the solution to Zaira's life, and with this decision she generates a sense of calm, reflected in the verse rhythms, which lead to a serene closing stanza. Once again the poem closes with the suggestion that the lovers will be reunited in heaven, with no mention of what may happen to Eva after death. Since it is Eva who dies in Maturin's novel, rather than Zaira, however, it is Eva who eventually takes on the martyr role which Zaira seems to crave, and who presumably will be reunited in heaven with De Courcy.

In 1855, after a gap of some years, Rossetti wrote another sonnet based on *Women*, 'Zara (I Dreamed That Loving Me)'. Once again the idea of heaven, this time in the form of eternity, is significant. The monologue opens: 'I dreamed that loving me he would love on | Thro' life and death into eternity' (ll. 1–2). This poem returns the reader to the point where Zaira has been abandoned by her lover but is not yet aware of the true identity of Eva. It is only the title which indicates it is another 'Zara' monologue, since it is otherwise a conventional sonnet of lost love and ensuing pain. The sonnet follows an especially tight and formal scheme against which the passionate misery of the words seems to strain. In the line 'I dreamt that love would be and be and be' (l. 3), for instance, the repeated words provide a sense of dreary informality in a carefully rhymed and scanned line. Zaira is haunted by her dreams of happiness, and asks 'what drug will lull the pain?' (l. 9). It is probable that when Rossetti wrote this poem she placed it chronologically before the two earlier 'Zara' poems, since here Zaira mourns her loss and is stultified by the pain. The 'drug' she seeks here, the earlier poems suggest, lies in the 'bitter cup' she will drink, representing both the metaphorical cup of the Psalms which will allow her to exonerate both herself and De Courcy, and a physical cup of poison, with which she will end her life.

The bitterness and desire for revenge Zaira manifests in Rossetti's earlier poems are still incipient here; instead, her anger seems directed inwardly, to herself and her memory, that cannot let her reach oblivion:

Oh lying memory, when shall I forget?
For why should I remember him in vain

Who hath forgotten and rejoiceth still?
Oh bitter memory, while my heart is set
On love that gnaws and gnaws and cannot kill. (ll. 10–14)

Zaira's strength, in her battle with herself and reproach to her own memory, is demonstrated here as in the other Zaira poems. It is, of course, the aspects of relationships which cannot be forgotten that affect Zaira. In the 1857 poem 'Memory', a similar situation arises, in which the speaker both retains her memories and is pained by them. Elsewhere Rossetti mourns what cannot be remembered. In 'Monna Innominata', the speaker tries to remember 'that first day, | First hour, first moment of your meeting me' (Sonnet 2, l. 2) but it has gone from her memory; 'So unrecorded did it slip away' (Sonnet 2, l. 5). 'Monna Innominata', Rossetti's monument to women who love yet are usually silenced (Beatrice in Dante's *Vita Nuova*, Petrarch's Laura) may itself have its roots in the monologues of Maturin's female characters, whose power and genius as well as ill-fated love and eventual resignation appear in the later sonnet sequence.

The final *Women* poem, 'Look on This Picture and on This', takes its title from *Hamlet*, 4.3, 54–5, where Hamlet addresses Gertrude, saying, 'Look here, upon this picture, and on this, | The counterfeit presentment of two brothers'. The Queen's response to this is '[S]peak no more: | Thou turn'st mine eyes into my very soul, | And there I see such black and grained spots'. Rossetti's poem is a monologue, this time spoken by De Courcy, addressing himself rather than a third person, despite his invocation of Eva's name, and the Queen's fearful answer to the speech seems a possible response for De Courcy to make to his own speech, reluctant to turn his gaze inwards and face the painful truths of his behaviour. *Hamlet*, like *Women*, also manifests an anxiety for the inadequacy of language. Crump's notes to 'Look on This Picture and on This' suggest that the line 'You my saint lead up to heaven she lures down to sin' might echo the King's words in 3.3: 'My words fly up, my thoughts remain below: | Words without thoughts never to heaven go' (Rossetti, 2005, p. 1134). Eva's careful words and silences are ostensibly more heaven-bound than Zaira's ready wit, certainly in the early stages of this poem, so this is perhaps a suggestive context. Rosenblum states that not only are Zaira and Eva 'as incomparable as Claudius and the elder Hamlet', but that the context 'indicates violation of the incest taboos comparable to the violation that occurs in *Hamlet*' (1986, p. 155). Since Zaira is Eva's mother, De Courcy's position as the lover of them both, while not incestuous, is verging on taboo, and the experienced Zaira and pure Eva might well be compared in a similar manner to Claudius and Hamlet's father. There is also a similar concern for duality, or apparent duality, in characters. In 3.1, Hamlet tells Ophelia, 'I have heard of your paintings too, well enough; God hath given you one face, and you make yourselves another.' This division which Hamlet believed he saw resolves itself into madness in the case of Ophelia; while, if we are to take Zaira and Eva as one being divided and manifested as individuals, it seems logical that after Eva's death, Zaira's grief also results in her madness.

Lona Mosk Packer suggests that the poem may not be inspired by *Women* at all, but is simply a poem of complex, dual love, in which 'love is portrayed as a turbulent maelstrom of emotions in which sexual hostility, jealousy, self-pity, and self-contempt each strives for dominance' (1963, p. 101). Packer constructed a theory about Rossetti's life which involved a potential affair with William Bell Scott, and thus construed many of her poems as relating to this situation. It seems highly improbable that Rossetti would have used the name Eva and created a poem so bound to the plot of *Women* without intending it to represent the voice of De Courcy, and certainly her brother seemed convinced that the poem originated in *Women*, commenting that otherwise 'I should have been embarrassed to guess what directed my sister's pen to so singular a subject and treatment' (WMR, p. 480). That the characters of Maturin's novel might provide a screen for Rossetti to write a more personal poem is unintentionally suggested by her brother's comments, despite Rossetti's fears of her poems being thus construed. Such a possibility cannot be ruled out, but remains purely speculative.

Though this poem is her last directly inspired by Maturin, it also in many ways seems her weakest, though it is powerful in its description of the frantic state of the speaker. Written in rhyming triplets, with uneven rhythm and line lengths, it originally had 46 stanzas; W. M. Rossetti reduced it to 23, 'omitting those passages which appear to me to be either in themselves inferior, or adapted rather for spinning out the theme than intensifying it' (WMR, p. 382). The MS version shows W. M. Rossetti's deletions, which in many cases alter the sense of the poem and its interaction with the novel, especially in the light of the earlier *Women* poems. His first and only textual alteration is to move a word in the first line to improve its scansion; it seems likely that the irregular rhythm caused him to abandon any further attempts to regularize the poem.[15]

'Look on This Picture, and on This' is intense in its repeated rhymes, including internal rhymes, and the monologue has an unnervingly conversational tone, with the speaker interrupting himself, pausing, contradicting himself and demonstrating his divided loyalties despite his supposed commitment to Eva. The monologue appears to take place after De Courcy has begun to realize the dangerous attraction he feels for Zaira, when he is struggling against it, since at this point he is able to say 'Have I wronged you? nay not I nor she in deed or will.' Under the pressure of the situation his sanity seems to be crumbling, for he wildly addresses Eva and seems to confuse her with Zaira. This is the only poem by Rossetti which gives voice to a specifically masculine viewpoint, but in its internal debate it reflects the concerns of the Eva and Zaira monologues. The poem as a whole is underpunctuated, which may have been Rossetti's attempt to adopt a more conventionally masculine tone than usual, by removing some pauses in an endeavour to produce a more forthright, unhesitating voice and leaving the poem relatively uncluttered. The poem seems to rush ahead of the reader, with thoughts tumbling out of the speaker.

The poem begins with an emphasis on 'looking' – that he 'hates' himself when he looks at Eva, presumably for betraying her in her innocence, and then in the second stanza describing the charms of Zaira's appearance which he cannot resist, cruelly calling on Eva as a witness to her rival's beauty. Throughout the poem, Eva is portrayed as 'silent', 'dumb', and even, in one of the deleted verses, as speaking in Zaira's voice: 'Tho' your lips speak it's her voice I flush to hear so plain' (l. 26). The progressive confusion Rossetti creates in the poem is considerably altered by her brother's deletions, since the stanzas removed are mostly those which appear to project Zaira's characteristics onto Eva. Though at first De Courcy is mild towards her, first calling her his 'saint' while Zaira has 'a devil' dancing in her eyes, and asking rhetorically, 'How should I choose a peacock and leave and grieve a dove?' (l. 8), he also admits that he cannot ignore her, because of 'her eyes, her witching manner' (l. 12). Zaira is indeed presented as a seductive witch, a Lorelei or Melusine who tempts him against his will. While De Courcy tells the silent Eva 'You are winning', he also adds, 'You constrain me', and appears spellbound by Zaira (ll. 13–14).

His confusion increases as he admits in stanzas 8 and 9 of the uncut version that despite being in Eva's presence his heart and mind are filled with Zaira, while stanza 12 beatifies Eva, placing himself and Zaira on a level with each other – sinners cast out of heaven, but together and blessed with love:

One short pang and you would rise a light in heaven
While we grovelled in the darkness mean and unforgiven
Tho' our cup of love brimmed sevenfold crowns of love were seven. (ll. 34–6)

By stanza 15 De Courcy imagines Eva dead, 'at peace and dumb' (l. 45), though that is also how he has envisioned her in life. The deleted stanza 16, however, switches to referring to her in the third person, stating that 'the old love has driven the new away' (l. 46). It is this changing of both sentiment and mode of address which indicates the fluctuating emotion the speaker is experiencing, and also draws in the reader by forcing considerable concentration.

By sanctifying Eva, De Courcy is attempting to vindicate himself. Not only would she 'thank me for the freedom of that day' (l. 47), but he imagines her death by describing her as 'tiring for the Bridegroom till the morning star shall rise, | Then to shine a glory in the nuptials of the skies' (ll. 52–3). In elevating Eva's goodness to such an extent, he suggests she is too good for him – too precious for earthly life at all and thus not in need of a husband. Eva appears like a virgin saint who has a higher calling than marriage. In a burst of self-abnegation he wishes himself dead, yet then shifts the emphasis:

> I would that one of us were dead, were gone no more to meet,
> Or she and I were dead together stretched here at your feet,
> That she and I were strained together in one windingsheet. (ll. 58–60)

The sexual overtones of the last line are unmistakeable, and imply a desire to hurt Eva emotionally. The reason for this becomes apparent in the next few stanzas, with references to 'your keener scorn' (l. 62) and particularly the deleted twenty-second stanza:

> A pitiless fiend is in your eyes to tempt me and to taunt:
> If you were dead I verily believe that you would haunt
> The home you loved, the man you loved, you said you loved – avaunt. (ll. 64–6)

The strained rhyme aside, this stanza demonstrates most clearly the confusion that is growing in De Courcy's mind. Eva's character shows no hint of a 'pitiless fiend', since she is mild and demure throughout the novel. It is clear that Zaira and Eva are beginning to merge, though in fact even Zaira is neither as manipulative nor as intentionally tempting as this poem suggests. Read with the novel in mind, the poem provides an insight into the mind of the speaker as Rossetti saw it, and in her embellishments she brings a dimension of the temptress to Zaira that is not fully developed in the novel, where, while Zaira is a worldly woman, she is also often well intentioned and reluctant to cause pain.

By verse 24, which W. M. Rossetti did not delete, Eva has become an angel again, this time with wings and a halo. The next four stanzas, which are crucial to Rossetti's version, were deleted, but portray the fear that motivates De Courcy and causes him to become sadistic. In emphasizing the death of his love for Eva, he discloses his irreligiosity, saying 'The door will not unclose to you tho' long you wait and knock'. The image is evocative of Jesus standing at the door, for example, in Holman Hunt's painting *The Light of the World* (1851–3), and suggests that Eva's religion has put up a barrier between them which he stubbornly refuses to tear down. Insisting that he has not wronged her, he instead blames her for his failure to continue to love her, and tells her 'You it is alone that mingle the venomous cup' (l. 77). Zaira, in her guilt and misery, has in Rossetti's previous poems used the same imagery repeatedly, yet here De Courcy appears to apportion blame to Eva. Verse 30 is cruel in its desire to apportion blame:

> Sit you still and wring the cup drop after loathsome drop:
> You have let loose a torrent it is not you can stop;
> You have sowed a noisome fieldful, now reap the stinging crop. (ll. 88–90)

Clearly in De Courcy's mind, Eva has somehow transmuted into Zaira, and he is scourging her with his anger and misery at the situation that the three of them have created. The confusion between the two women in this monologue emphasizes the dual natures of the women, who between them seem to form one whole. As their characteristics become hopelessly confused, the reader too is uncertain whom the reader is addressing, and the women appear finally to merge into one being.

Towards the end of the poem, W. M. Rossetti's deletions become less severe, as De Courcy's sympathies swing back to Eva, telling her 'I love you yet' (l. 111), and asking for forgiveness. Her angelic status is confirmed as she enters heaven while he and Zaira are condemned to 'a searching fire and strict balances to weigh' (ll. 125). Optimistically, the final stanza seems to reunite the three of them, in a portentous omen of the relationship between the two women as yet unknown in the novel:

> Be open-armed to us in love – type of another Love –
> As she forgave us ones below will she forgive above,
> Enthroned to all eternity our sister-friend and dove? – (ll. 132–5)

The poem closes hesitantly, with a dash which suggests that there must be more to come, as if De Courcy himself is uncertain about the ending of the narrative. In fact this last stanza was also deleted, leaving instead a note of self-recrimination and pessimism. The reunion in the afterlife which Zaira and Eva imagine is far more complex here, suggesting that Rossetti was aware of the debate surrounding the problems of individuality in heaven, outlined in Luke 20, yet the conclusion is not in line with Rossetti's other imagined heavens, some of which envisage a blissful forgetting of the earthly life.[16] While this passage raises more theological questions than it answers, I would suggest that Rossetti depicted the reunion in the afterlife in many of her poems as a device which serves to emphasize the importance of earthly love as well as spiritual.

Despite the passionate and somewhat frenzied tone of the poem as a whole, Rossetti manifests some sympathy towards the situation by demonstrating the suffering and confusion which all three characters experience. Her brother's deletions remove the pity and love for Zaira, thus allowing De Courcy to seem both less deranged by love and less culpable. Moreover, the excisions emphasize Eva's saintly nature, thus causing Zaira to seem more to blame for the situation. W. M. Rossetti's 'embarrassment' at the subject matter that he mentions in the notes is perhaps responsible for his swingeing excisions, which produce a more restrained poem.

Melmoth the Wanderer

Maturin's most widely read novel, *Melmoth the Wanderer* (1820) is also his most Gothic novel, of a man who has given up his soul in return for eternal life, a concept that must have both shocked and fascinated the devout Rossetti. W. M. Rossetti describes the novel's plot in his Notes:

> Melmoth is a personage who has made a compact with the Devil, thereby securing an enormous length of life (say at least a century and a half), and the power of flitting at will from land to land. At the end of the term, Melmoth's soul is to be forfeited, unless he can meanwhile induce some one else to take the compact off his hands. Melmoth makes numerous efforts in this direction, but all abortive. One of his intended victims is a beautiful girl named Immalee, a child of Nature in an Indian island – a second Miranda. She becomes deeply enamoured of Melmoth, but resists his tamperings with her soul. She is finally identified as the daughter of a Spanish Grandee, and is then baptized as Isidora. At one point of the story she espouses Melmoth, and bears him a child. Christina's poem ['Isidora'] is her deathbed scene. (WMR, pp. 466–7)

The novel functions on the traditional anti-Catholic basis of Gothic, its Calvinist author producing bitter diatribes against the superstition, corruption and blasphemy that he sees as inherent in Protestant Christianity.[17]

Rossetti's sonnet 'Immalee' is set on the island on which Immalee lives, before Melmoth has met her or attempted to corrupt her. Immalee herself knows nothing of God or religion at this stage, having been washed ashore there as an infant, and is clearly a child of nature whose sympathy with and dependence on her surroundings demonstrate her purity. Though Maturin gives many pages of descriptions of the island, with its luxuriant foliage and abundance of wildlife, unlike the novel Rossetti's sonnet names specific plants and animals. When Immalee finally speaks in the novel, her first words are 'God made me' (Maturin, 2000, p. 313). She also shows an instinctive inclination towards religion. It is arguable that Rossetti's specific naming in her sonnet is indicative of her recreation of Immalee's Christian nature. Tractarianism emphasizes the significance of typology and the understanding of symbols in the natural world, which link to higher parallels as signs given by God to increase human understanding.[18] In Tract 80 in 1837, Isaac Williams states:

> There appears in God's manifestations of Himself to mankind, in conjunction with an exceeding desire to communicate that knowledge, a tendency to conceal, and throw a veil over it, as if it were injurious to us, unless we were of a certain disposition to receive it.

It is this understanding of typological readings, also shared with Evangelical theology, which the Tractarians extended from traditional Old Testament foreshadowings to include symbolism in nature which pointed to God. Using it to link the corporeal to the sublime, Rossetti employs it in her poems throughout her life. Indeed the sublime seems to be the antidote to Gothic, lifting humanity away from the fears and threats of the world and glimpsing the alternative situation of heaven, though not reaching it until after death.

This Edenic, natural landscape depicted by Rossetti in her poem is as far removed as possible from the Gothic landscapes of gloomy interiors and treacherous terrain which feature in Maturin's novel, and thus contrast starkly with 'Isidora', set in a prison cell. The animals that appear do not include the guard of peacocks with which Maturin endows her, but instead birds, deer, goats, squirrels and hares: less exotic animals but ones with a common cultural significance. The deer is used in Psalm 42 as a symbol of the soul's longing for God, which is appropriate since Immalee is also described as a young deer by Maturin. She declares herself to be longing to know about God, while in Song of Solomon the deer or gazelle is the soul for which Christ longs. According to the book of Leviticus, 'the goat shall carry all their iniquities', as depicted in Holman Hunt's painting *The Scapegoat* (1854), thus perhaps implying Immalee's innocence at this stage and also that she will die as a result of her lover's actions.[19]

This use of specific natural symbols is common throughout Rossetti's work, but is particularly prominent in her poem 'Eve'. 'Immalee' foreshadows this later poem by translating the Gothic heroine of Maturin's novel into an emblem of unfallen womanhood. The innocence Immalee displays is not depicted in Rossetti's vision of Eve, though Immalee is presented as a convincing cipher for prelapsarian Eve; but instead, as Eve struggles with her responsibility for the fall, the animals around her take pity on her. This pathetic fallacy is not only significant for the demonstrable sympathy of the natural world, but also because Rossetti carefully chose the animals.

By claiming sympathy with nature and God's symbols, Rossetti is implying sympathy for Immalee's and Eve's situations while simultaneously allowing them both to shoulder responsibility. 1 Corinthians 15.21–22 states: 'For since by man [came] death, by man [came] also the resurrection of the dead. For as in Adam all die, even so in Christ shall all be made alive.' 'Eve' makes little mention of Adam, instead allowing Eve to take responsibility for her actions, and admit that she is culpable, though there is a hint that Adam had the opportunity to refuse the fruit and save mankind. Elizabeth Barrett Browning's *A Drama of Exile* (1844), by contrast, rewrites the traditional versions of the Fall to give Eve the upper hand, and celebrates the knowledge gained by the Fall rather than condemning women for it, closing with the line 'exiled, but not lost!' This provides a more theologically radical narrative than Rossetti; yet even here, Adam supports and comforts his wife, while in Rossetti's poem, the solitary figure of the grieving woman who has transgressed presents a much stronger picture of femininity than the tradition of women's poetry usually allows.

The suffering which results from the Fall is enacted for the reader in 'Isidora'. Both 'Immalee' and 'Isidora' are closely linked with certain moments in *Melmoth the Wanderer*, with 'Isidora' depicting the heroine's death, as in typical Rossettian style she attempts to come to terms with the events that have led her there. That Isidora talks for several stanzas to an apparently sleeping child becomes much more sinister in the context of the novel, when it becomes clear that the child is not sleeping but dead, possibly murdered by his father – and yet the unlucky mother envies her child's peace. Maternal feeling, usually so strong in the poetess tradition, is virtually absent here. Maturin aimed to produce terror in the reader, at the fate of Isidora and at the loss of one's soul. Terror 'activates the mind and imagination [. . .] enabling the subject to move from a state of passivity to activity', while horror produces the opposite effect, freezing or stupefying the subject or reader (Botting, 1996, p. 48). Rossetti depicts Isidora at such moments of stasis, yet her activity is apparent in her spirituality.

Isidora is represented as a 'fallen woman' in this poem, though not in the conventional sense. Her sin is to have loved Melmoth, though her love of God is paramount, and she does not give in to his call to take his place. It is in loving the wrong man that she falls; when she leaves her Eden and becomes Isidora instead of Immalee, she represents a postlapsarian Eve. Her secluded island, which represented a liminal space in which she was innocent, is replaced by the world, and in crossing the threshold to other lands, she unwittingly transgresses. A truism of the Gothic genre is that it both transgresses boundaries itself and also represents transgression as an act of defiance against God; Immalee's transgression is made in innocence, but in leaving her island where she was secure, and entering the world, she has committed herself to a path from which she cannot turn back, similar to the depiction of the figure in 'Shut Out', forever looking back on a cherished place of peace and safety.

While Maturin's concern is with the blasphemy and superstition of religion, in 'Isidora' Rossetti subverts this. By assuming the inherent goodness of Christ and his ability to save, the element of despair is removed. In its place, the boundaries of female responsibility are extended beyond contemporary cultural definitions of femininity. This engenders a sense of female autonomy which strengthens the heroine, in some cases beyond the character of the hero or anti-hero. Rossetti's Eve goes so far as to suggest that if Adam had declined the fruit she offered him, he might have stayed in Eden while she alone was exiled. The argument that, as her husband, Adam was therefore compelled to eat of the fruit as she did and thus not share but take on her responsibility for the transgression is negated. Self-sacrifice for a potentially unworthy man is a shared characteristic of Rossetti's Eve and Isidora. While Isidora says: 'I would gladly give my soul | So that thine might dwell in bliss' (ll. 14–15), Eve, similarly, suggests:

I might have pined away;
I, but none other:
God might have let thee stay
Safe in our garden,
By putting me away
Beyond all pardon. (ll. 20–5)

While both women consider taking the responsibility for their husbands' souls, they are taking on a Christ-like image of a saviour, and contravening contemporary assumptions about their place in the gender hierarchy by even contemplating the possibility that they might be in a position to do this.

'I must choose 'twixt God and man' ('Isidora', l. 7) is often quoted as a biographical note to Rossetti, who broke off two engagements on religious grounds. However, in both these poems, women transgressed not through their choice of man rather than God, but through the desire for knowledge. Immalee's fall is initially brought about, not by her love for Melmoth, but rather through her desire for knowledge, since she, who knew nothing of life other than that observed on the island and in nature, begged him to increase her knowledge of 'the world of answers' (p. 315), and even after Melmoth's diatribes about the corruption of civilization she still desires knowledge more than happiness. It is this same choice which Eve makes.

The end result of their transgression, for both women, is death: for Eve it causes the death of mankind; for Immalee, however, her own death counts as nothing since her soul is saved, but the uncertainty over her husband's fate wracks her as she dies, asking in Maturin's words, 'Paradise – will he be there?' (l. 72). However, Rossetti exposes the fallacy of the Isidora plot of *Melmoth the Wanderer* with the lines 'Thy life is not in my death' (l. 30), adding: 'By the loss of my salvation | To increase thy condemnation' (ll. 35–6). Isidora, despite admitting she is prepared to exchange places with her husband, knows that by allowing him to die she will not be giving him peace, since death will not release him from the grasp of Satan, and that if he allows her to give up her soul, he will be additionally culpable for the loss of her salvation. To receive God's blessing is the best gift Isidora and Eve can give to their husbands, yet the impossibility of it means that their peace can only be found in resigning Adam and Melmoth to the care of God. The women's own repentance is not mentioned in the poem; the implication is that repentance has already occurred before the poems take place, and consequently the women are by this stage struggling to overcome their grief instead.

Both poems appear to be about transgression and punishment, significant thematic concepts in both biblical and Gothic terms. At the point at which Rossetti has set 'Isidora', the heroine is imprisoned by the Inquisition on suspicion of being an heretic. While Isidora (in the novel) remembers sadly her freedom on her island, Eve is shown as still in Eden, surrounded by the natural world from which she takes comfort, although biblically she is soon to be banished from there. Since Eve's sin is against God, her anguish is related to (and supported by) the natural world, while Isidora's sin, which is against society as much as God, and being innocent in her heart, is confined within man-made prison walls, which Rossetti does not describe. However, with the contrasting of heaven above and hell below, and her child on one side and her husband on the other, these spiritual confinements alone provide the prison walls.

Rossetti's poem 'Shut Out' has similar implications. This can be read as also relating to Eve; it is a narrative of grief after leaving Eden, in which the banished woman cannot enter the garden but can see into it, thus increasing her misery for what she has lost:

> The door was shut. I looked between
> Its iron bars; and saw it lie,
> My garden, mine, beneath the sky. (ll. 1–3)

Repeated enjambments force a sense of claustrophobia on the reader, as though it is the world which is a prison, keeping Eve from the freedom of Eden. This notion of the world as a prison, with the threshold of heaven a barrier to be crossed, is one which Rossetti repeats and explores throughout her writing life. Eve's sense of imprisonment increases when the sinister 'spirit' which 'kept the gate' (l. 9) will not give her even a twig to remind her of her home. Instead:

> The spirit was silent; but he took
> Mortar and stone to build a wall;
> He left no loophole great or small
> Thro' which my straining eyes might look: (ll. 16–20)

The fallen, corrupted and essentially Gothic world in which Eve (and, by implication, the reader also) is imprisoned can provide no delights to compensate for the loss of Eden. Instead, only the joys of heaven can await Eve.

Methods of discipline such as prisons, Foucault argues, 'dissociate power from the body' (1991, p. 138). For Rossetti's heroines, their bodies are virtually absent; by this stage in their development it is only their souls that are at stake, and the 'discipline' of their beliefs has in fact freed them. Modern feminist criticism would argue that gender itself becomes their prison, since a heroine in a Gothic novel is doomed to the fate of existing within the framework of a patriarchal culture. If, as Auerbach argues, we 'imprison what we adore', then it is the physical confinement, whether inside a prison or outside of Eden, and the contrasting spiritual freedom of these women, which Rossetti is emphasizing and asking us to admire in her characters (1986, p. xi).

Through God, there is an escape for these women, and the poem strengthens the religious element in order to provide no doubt of an escape. Botting describes *Melmoth* as a novel that does not, 'like conventional Gothic texts, restore a moral order or explain a mystery, but suggests that the human condition is as inescapable as the narrative labyrinth itself, a relentless chain of cruel events without purpose, unity or meaning' (1996, p. 108). This moral order is usually superficial, however; the Gothic world is invariably complex and chaotic. For Rossetti, the reverse is true, at least in terms of the 'inescapable' human condition.

Both Eve and Isidora have given up freedom for knowledge, yet they become free through a combination of their own beliefs and God's grace. When Isidora says 'I have conquered; it is done' (l. 61), Rossetti is stressing the power of the heroine's will to trust in God over her desire to save her husband. The final lines even indicate that she maintains a hopeless belief that her husband may yet be forgiven and redeemed as she will be. Equally, while Eve mourns that she has eaten the forbidden fruit, and the earth mourns with her, she remains certain she is the 'sad mother of all who must live' (ll. 26–7) – that is to say, although she has brought death into the world, future generations will be born, while the mourning of nature highlights the life that continues around her. Like Isidora, she has transgressed, but with her knowledge, despite its fatal results, she has also conquered through the power of God. Where the Gothic novel highlights the dangers of the notion of the decentring of the self, by the projection of anxieties onto the chaotic world, Isidora and Eve, through Rossetti's rewriting of them, become recentred in their monologues through their acceptance of their sin and the possibility of their redemption.

In her devotional prose work *The Face of the Deep*, Rossetti considers this redemption of Eve:

> And yet, even as at the foot of the Cross, St. Mary Magdalene, out of whom went seven devils, stood beside the 'lily among thorns,' the Mother of sorrows: so (I humbly hope and trust) amongst all saints of all time will stand before the throne, Eve the beloved first Mother of us all. Who that has loved and revered her own immediate dear mother, will not echo the hope? (*FD*, p. 310)

Without doubt, both women maintain their trust in divine love and grace to forgive them and overcome their transgression. Maturin, however, implies no forgiveness or peace, and instead conforms to the pattern of the death of a transgressive woman, though not without some pity for the innocent Immalee who brought about her own fall by desiring knowledge of the world when her demonic lover offered her the choice to stay alone on her island. 'Eve' does not indicate God's forgiveness, but arguably the sympathetic natural world represents the divine love that supports mankind after death has entered the world as well as associating Eve with life rather than death. Isidora, by contrast, in contemplating the potential loss of her salvation, accepts that she will be saved, by 'the heart's death for the soul's life' (l. 42). Her monologue ends:

> Blessed Saviour, take my soul
> To thy Paradise and care:–
> Paradise, will he be there? (ll. 70–2)

If Gothic provides 'an analysis of the limits of rationality' (Smith, 2000, p. 1), then this and her other Maturin poems end, like faith itself, just beyond the confines of our understanding – 'Isidora' with her contemplation of divine forgiveness and Paradise, and 'Eve' with the gloating of the snake, which precipitated the Fall. From Rossetti's earliest poems, it is possible to trace a strand of Gothic which is concerned primarily with the supernatural and unknowable, which points to God; the shadow of the fallen world of the Gothic novel serves only to indicate the eternal glories of heaven. Rossetti's engagement with Maturin's Gothic demonstrates her ability to reshape and transform aspects of the Gothic novel, and, in the *Melmoth* poems in particular, her interest in the contrast between the fallen world and the perfection of heaven. As the next chapter will explore, this postlapsarian world is peopled with grotesques which serve specific purposes in Rossetti's poetry, and complicate the aesthetic relationships of the Gothic.

Rossetti, Ruskin and the Moral Grotesque

Rossetti's aesthetics are, like those of many of her contemporaries, often complicated and contradictory. In many poems, Rossetti does not refer to the appearance of her characters, instead relying on an aesthetics of interiority, in which the mind of the speaker is given primacy over the external appearance. In some earlier poems, however, particularly the ballads and 'fallen women' poems, she refers to the conventionally beautiful appearance of the speaker. For Rossetti, beauty can be indicative of purity of soul and goodness of character, but can also be deceptive, hiding an inner evil. It can also be complicated by other issues: for example, the speaker of 'Cousin Kate', with her 'flaxen hair' (l. 6), is portrayed as beautiful, but her beauty has been her downfall. Despite this, she retains a moral strength which sets her above her still more beautiful cousin. As Harrison points out, 'for Ruskin the perception of the beautiful is contingent upon the perception of the divine', and the same is true for Rossetti (1988, p. 54). For both Rossetti and Ruskin, appearances are complicated by use of the grotesque, a category which falls between the beautiful and the hideous, but contains meanings unique to itself. The grotesque is largely absent from critical studies of Gothic, but not only does Ruskin identify it as a part of the genre in *The Stones of Venice* and *Modern Painters*,[1] it also appears in Gothic novels in their elements of distortion and excess. This is reflected in Rossetti's poetry. This chapter argues that the Rossettian grotesque has much in common with that of Ruskin, particularly in the relationship between internal truths and external appearances, and the emphasis on the moral purposes of the grotesque. This chapter will argue that Rossetti uses the grotesque as Ruskin described it throughout much of her work, emphasizing a mode of moral Gothic in which an internal beauty or grotesqueness of character is depicted as more significant than external appearance.

There are of course many contrasting and complex aspects of the grotesque, which, like Gothic, is fractured and diffuse. As Harpham has noted, it raises questions such as:

> What can possibly be 'in' all these things? How can 'it' be strained out so it can be observed by itself? And what is to be made of the fact that the grotesque is by no means confined to art, but can be experienced as a psychological event for which a work of art may create a favourable climate, but which can occur outside their sphere of influence altogether? (1982, p. xv)

As this suggests, the grotesque can appear in multiple forms and arenas, which art can depict to a certain extent, but which act upon the writer and the reader in diverse ways, and depends upon the mind of the reader as much as that of the writer. That which is not intended to be grotesque may appear so to the reader, and the emotional and psychological impact can be intense. Harpham suggests a kind of solution to the issues presented by a study of the grotesque, by acknowledging the very presence of the issues. As he explains, 'it is up to the culture to provide the conventions and assumptions that determine its particular forms' (p. xx). The implication, then, is that in order to establish a logical notion of Rossetti's use of the grotesque, some contextualization is necessary. This chapter will consider issues such as these. Primarily, in the case of Rossetti, I will argue that Ruskin's theory of moral Gothic, relating to the grotesque as giving access to the sublime, is the most appropriate response to her use of grotesquerie, and also provides a historical and conceptual framework in which to situate it.[2]

The grotesque

Scholarly work on the grotesque generally agrees on certain aspects of grotesquerie in art and literature, such as that the grotesque must appear in an apparently realistic setting, which provides a normative mode against which to contrast aberrations. The material grotesque body is thus presented in literature as part of a familiar world. As Mary Russo suggests, quoting Bakhtin's *Rabelais and His World*: 'The grotesque body is not separated from the rest of the world; "it is blended with the world, with animals, with objects"' (1994, p. 8). Ruskin's argument is similar, that the best examples display 'a true union of the grotesque with the realistic power' (1996, V, p. 137).

Writers on the grotesque have traced the development of the term in detail, considering its original application to art and tracing its history through the works of Continental writers such as Schlegel and Wieland.[3] There have been many attempts to define the grotesque concisely, such as Thomson's attempts to sum up the word: 'Disharmony', 'comic and terrifying', 'extravagance and exaggeration', 'abnormality' (1972, p. 9). These are expected terms which appear frequently in discussions of the grotesque, but there are serious problems with such categorizations. As with Gothic, it is difficult to distinguish clear features of the grotesque. As Kayser suggests, by the nineteenth century the word had been 'debased', and became much more open to interpretation. Kayser writes that '[t]he word thus covers an exceedingly wide range of meanings and seems to have been shorn of its essential qualities' by the time it was defined in a German–French dictionary in 1771: 'Figuratively speaking, grotesque means odd, unnatural, bizarre, strange, funny, ridiculous, caricatural, etc' (1957, p. 28). Thus, although the grotesque is considered here as a mode of Gothic, its history is as eclectic as that of Gothic itself.

In 1820, Hazlitt accorded the grotesque a literary status which separated it from the historical artistic category into which it had previously fallen, and equates it with Gothic. Discussing English literature in particular, he states:

> We may be accused of grossness, but not of flimsiness; of extravagance, but not of affectation; of want of art and refinement, but not of a want of truth and nature. Our literature, in a word, is Gothic and grotesque; unequal and irregular; not cast in a previous mould, nor of one uniform texture, but of great weight in the whole, and of incomparable value in the best parts. It aims at an excess of beauty or power, hits or misses, and is either very good indeed, or absolutely good for nothing. (Hazlitt, 1820, p. 36).

For Hazlitt, then, the grotesque is a by-product of an excess of *gravitas*, of good intentions often overstated and misplaced in enthusiasm. His explanation of the grotesque uses descriptors which appear frequently in discussions of grotesquerie: grossness, extravagance, truth, nature, 'unequal and irregular'. Hazlitt combines the abstract with the aesthetic, suggesting that these aspects are the redeeming characteristics of English literature, which is as a whole grotesque. Unlike other aesthetic categories, it is the abstract, such as 'grossness' or 'exaggeration', which marks it out, rather than specific visual features or techniques. To attempt to define the grotesque in specific terms is often to curtail its meaning considerably.

Instead, the grotesque is best approached with an open mind, examining its broader meanings. Victor Hugo emphasizes the importance of Christianity in the use of the grotesque in poetry:

> Christianity leads poetry to the truth. Like it, the modern muse will see things in a higher and broader light. It will realise that everything in creation is not humanly *beautiful*, that the ugly exists beside the beautiful, the unshapely beside the graceful, the grotesque on the reverse of the sublime, evil with good, darkness with light. It will ask itself if the narrow and relative sense of the artist should prevail over the infinite, absolute sense of the Creator; if it is for man to correct God. (2001, para. 31)

Hugo seems to be interested in a form of realism, a kind of Pre-Raphaelite 'truth to nature' which, as Ruskin said, sees the world and reproduces it 'rejecting nothing, selecting nothing and scorning nothing; believing all things to be right and good, and rejoicing always in the truth' (1996, IV, p. 624). This acceptance of the coexistence of the sublime and the grotesque in the natural world, and the duty of the artist to render it, complements Rossetti's beliefs about the existence of a reflection of the divine in the natural world and in human beings. Indeed, the grotesque provides a framework which measures the distance between the ideal of Christian perfection and the reality of fallen mankind. Hugo goes on to suggest that it is in its ability to depict such contrasting aspects of the world that poetry, like Christianity, can permit one to see clearly; in fact he suggests that this ability of poetry can itself change the world:

> [P]oetry will take a great step [. . .] which, like the upheaval of an earthquake, will change the whole face of the intellectual world. It will set about doing as nature does, mingling its creations – but without confounding them – darkness and light, the grotesque and the sublime; in other words, the body and the soul, the beast and the intellect; for the starting-point of religion is always the starting-point of poetry. All things are connected. (para. 31)

There can be no doubt that for Rossetti all things were connected through God, and that she endeavours to represent them as such. For the reader, however, the poems may produce a somewhat different, and distorted, view. To read the grotesque and the beautiful, or the normative, as two aspects of nature rather than as a binary opposition, provides a useful way into Rossetti's work, since for her these characteristics link directly to the body and soul.

Walter Bagehot, writing in 1864, uses the grotesque more or less as a term of abuse for the poetry of Browning, and suggests that it is ugly, demanding, 'jagged', and the product, he seems to suggest, of a poet who desires to hide himself in obscure references:

> Good elements hidden in horrid accompaniments are the special theme of grotesque art, and these medieval life and legends afford more copiously than could have been furnished before Christianity gave its new elements of good, or since modern civilization has removed some few at least of the old elements of destruction. A *buried* life like the spiritual medieval was Mr Browning's natural element. (Bagehot, 1911, I, p. 344)

Bagehot appears to see in the grotesque an aesthetics of ugliness which need not correspond to sublimity, or point to higher truths, though there may be 'good' elements contained within. Certainly Bagehot suggests that the grotesque is largely Christian, yet not 'pleasing' (p. 345), though he admits that it pleases the 'half-educated' public (p. 350). However, it is clear that for Bagehot as for G. K. Chesterton, Browning's grotesque relates to nature. As Harpham points out, 'By the end of the nineteenth century it was more common than not to speak of the "naturalness" of the grotesque' (p. xix). Certainly for Ruskin, both 'naturalism' and the grotesque were aspects of Gothic. Ronald Paulson argues contrary to this, suggesting that by the early nineteenth century, 'the term grotesque carried both connotations of deviance from nature (the monstrous) and of a breakthrough to a higher art' (1983, p. 171). To a certain extent, Bagehot's views clash with those of Ruskin, whose notions of the grotesque relate not only to the medieval but to the sublime, linked more closely to Hugo than to Bagehot in his preoccupation with realism in nature as giving access to the divine. As Thomas Mann was later to say:

> The grotesque is the supratrue and the exceedingly real, not the arbitrary, false, antireal, and absurd. And an artist who would deny all obligation to life, who would carry disgust for the impression so far that he practically divests himself of all obligation to real forms of life, and who allows only the dictatorial emanations of some kind of absolute art demon to hold sway: such an artist may well be called the greatest of all radical fools. (1983, p. 417)

The grotesque is more than truth, Mann suggests, and it is certainly more than art. Clearly the grotesque exceeds the boundaries once placed upon it in antique art, but most importantly, Mann implies that use of the grotesque is an indication of an artist's commitment to truth. Not unlike Ruskin, Mann seems to be indicating that through the grotesque one might be able to view a portion of the writer's soul, as well as illuminating the mind of the reader.

It is Walter Scott, writing on the 1817 tales of E. T. A. Hoffmann, in 1827, who first suggests explicitly that the grotesque can be 'noble', representing a higher plane.[4] With reference to Hoffmann, however, he objects to the lack of moral content, and suggests that a moral purpose in Hoffmann's work would produce a noble grotesque. In his review of the stories of Hoffmann, Scott defends 'the existence of the most extravagant fictions', including *Frankenstein* and *Gulliver's Travels*, since they permit the reader 'to extract from them philosophical reasoning and moral truth' (1878, VI, p. 292). In this review, where he deals harshly with Hoffmann's flights of fancy for their lack of moral basis, Scott appears to be setting an agenda for literature, in which all events, symbols, plots and discussions should relate to the provision of a moral purpose which 'our mental faculties are too obscure to comprehend' without the aid of fiction (p. 270). Scott relates his discussion of the use of the grotesque specifically to British literature. Hoffmann, as a European, is less kindly dealt with, and Scott goes so far as to suggest that his mind is 'diseased' by the events which have occurred in his life, which caused him to resort to 'grosser means of diverting the paroxysm' than would a morally stronger man (p. 302). Hoffmann himself is not 'corrupt' but 'ill-regulated', with an 'undue tendency to the horrible and the distressing' (p. 306). Hoffmann's grotesques, therefore, are the product of a mind under wicked influences, and as such cannot be what Ruskin would term 'the noble grotesque'.

Like Ruskin, Scott sees no value in or even possibility of divorcing the creator from his work, and therefore the work itself has dubious value when measured by moral standards. Tellingly, Scott continues by comparing Hoffmann's grotesques to the arabesque mode:

> In fact, the grotesque in his compositions partly resembles the arabesque in painting, in which is introduced the most strange and complicated monsters, resembling centaurs, griffins, sphinxes, chimeras, rocs, and all other creatures of romantic imagination [. . .] while there is in reality nothing to satisfy the understanding or inform the judgement. (pp. 306–7)

The implication is that Hoffmann's lack of moral character caused his writing to produce an ornamental effect of superficial grotesquerie, which does not correspond to an underlying morality. Hoffmann's figures, such as the Sandman, are purely decorative, and serve no useful purpose. The grotesque without morality is simply ugly or bizarre, certainly pointless, and this is crucial to understanding both Ruskin's and Rossetti's use of it. It is the moral imagination which not only makes it meaningful, but also makes it effective in artistic terms.

Unlike Ruskin, Scott does not link the grotesque with the sublime, either as binaries or as related aspects of nature, stating instead that '[t]he grotesque, also, has a natural alliance with the horrible; for that which is out of nature can be with difficulty reconciled to the beautiful' (p. 324). Scott commends Hoffmann's observations of nature, but condemns the human weaknesses on display. Idealizing nature, perhaps, Scott implies that the grotesque is too divorced from the natural world to reflect it truly. This contrasts with Mann's views, as well as Ruskin's, and conflicts with Rossetti's presentation of the grotesque as a facet of nature.

The Ruskinian grotesque

These views, with emphasis on the relation of aesthetics to morality, and the power of the imagination, are discussed by Ruskin in considerable detail. For the purposes of understanding the nineteenth-century grotesque, particularly in relation to Rossetti, it is most helpful to consider Ruskin's discussions on the grotesque in *The Stones of Venice* (1851–3) and *Modern Painters* (1844–60). The Ruskinian grotesque is particularly significant for the consideration of a Rossettian grotesque since Rossetti's poems, like Ruskin's criticism, consistently link the earthly and the divine, the deformed and the beautiful, and assume that the natural world provides an index of the spiritual world.

In *The Stones of Venice*, Ruskin's chapter on 'Grotesque Renaissance' sets out his views on the grotesque as a category, not just in architecture or even art, but as a more abstract concept which covers all areas of human endeavour, and reaches far beyond the aesthetic. According to Ruskin, the grotesque period of Venice succeeded its high Gothic Renaissance, and represents its fall from grace, which he links to the moral fall of its citizens. That fall was further reflected in the dilapidated state of the buildings he visited, and he presents Venice as a moral warning to Britain, with 'recognition that Venetian stones announced a larger message of human history; modern disregard for Venice's heritage was only a continuation of the greed and luxury that the Renaissance introduced and which destroyed its Gothic Eden' (Dixon Hunt, 1998, p. 196).[5] The aesthetic alone is not enough for Ruskin's discussions of art and architecture, influenced by his reading of Hazlitt: the moral message is paramount, and gives force to his arguments. In examining his extensive discussions on the grotesque, I shall focus on what he considered to be successful, or 'noble', grotesque.

In 'Grotesque Renaissance', Ruskin suggests that the grotesque is 'composed of two elements, one ludicrous, the other fearful' (GR, p. 151). The grotesque may be produced with these two elements in the artist's mind, and may combine them to a greater or lesser degree. That Ruskin initially takes no account of the emotive effect of the grotesque upon the viewer, incidentally, suggests that here as in other areas of his criticism, he leans towards the artist, rather than the viewer, as being of ultimate significance in the generation of meaning for any work of art, despite his role as critic. He continues to discuss these states of mind, while explicitly linking the 'nobleness' of humanity with nobility in art. Later in life, after *The Stones of Venice* was published, Ruskin was to change his views on this subject, perhaps in part due to his discovery of some of Turner's vices, writing to Elizabeth Barrett Browning that 'nobody can be a great painter who isn't rather wicked – in a noble sort of way' (Cited in Dixon Hunt, 1998, p. 262). Even at this stage he qualifies his description of 'wickedness' to include nobility; possibly the 'wickedness' also relates to the need for play with which he was concerned in 'Grotesque Renaissance'.

Looking at the idea of playfulness which leads to the 'ludicrous' side of the grotesque, Ruskin suggests that only a certain kind of healthy playfulness can produce healthy work: that playfulness which is resonant of laughter and recreation rather than 'excitement of the energies' (GR, p. 152).[6] Play is subcategorized as 'men who play wisely; who play necessarily; who play inordinately; and who play not at all' (GR, p. 152). The first two of these exist in those whom Ruskin terms 'thinkers' and 'workers' (GR, p. 154), who are best placed by pre-existing temperament to produce art. Indeed, in a Ruskinian utopia only these two types of people would exist. The third category, inordinate play, forms the conditions which led to the post-Renaissance 'fall' of Venice, and Ruskin avers that '[t]he greater portion of the misery of this world arises from the false opinions of men whose idleness has physically incapacitated them from forming true ones' (GR, pp. 154–5). Those who 'play not at all' receive little attention, being dismissed as 'morose' and 'dull' (GR, p. 155).

'Necessary play', according to Ruskin, is that of the working man seeking relief from his daily labour. Satire rather than beauty in art should be the aim in this instance, he posits, but 'it is not in recreation that the conditions of perfection can be fulfilled' (GR, p. 157). Perfection, however, is not called for in the grotesque, as he proceeds to explain in a paragraph which draws together his strands of discussion on that playful element of the grotesque which leads to the 'ludicrous' or even humorous:

> Now all the forms of art which result from the comparatively recreative exertion
> of minds more or less blunted or encumbered by other cares and toils, the art
> which we may call generally art of the wayside, as opposed to that which is the

business of men's lives, is, in the best sense of the word, Grotesque. And it is noble
or inferior, first, according to the tone of the minds which have produced it,
and in proportion to their knowledge, wit, love of truth, and kindness; secondly,
according to the degree of strength they have been able to give forth; but yet,
however much we may find in it needing to be forgiven, always delightful so long
as it is the work of good and ordinarily intelligent men. And its delightfulness
ought mainly to consist *in those very imperfections* which mark it for work done
in times of rest. (GR, pp. 157–8)

The grotesque is testament to man's frailty, though growing out of what is best
in men's hearts. This passage seems to suggest that it develops at moments of
relaxation rather than concentration. Since W. M. Rossetti stated that his sister
barely worked at her poems, instead dashing them off in moments of inspiration,
one might infer that her circumstances of writing fit Ruskin's conditions
perfectly. However, her brother's comments are not to be taken at face value,
and, as a painstaking poet, Rossetti's effects of grotesquerie are often deliberate
and considered. For Ruskin, the viewer of grotesque art is responding not so
much to the physical characteristics of the work as to the spiritual dimension
of the artist's mind, thus combining the significance of artist and critic in the
production of meaning. This 'sympathy' between the artist and viewer suggests
a much deeper significance to the grotesque than more recent writers on the
subject tend to imply; it leads to the sublime, an understanding of minds on
a spiritual rather than a physical plane, and related to the (wholesome) mind
rather than the (deformed) body.[7] In this respect, Rossetti's personal beliefs as
well as her work appear to fit more closely with Ruskin's views. It is, of course,
'wise play' which produces the highest and most serious works of art. The jest in
such work will be only a passing moment, yet:

[w]e find them delighting in such inventions, and a species of grotesqueness
thence arising in all their work, which is indeed one of its most valuable
characteristics, but which is [. . .] intimately connected with the sublime or
terrible form of the grotesque. (GR, p. 156)

The moral seriousness of the 'jest' is perhaps unfamiliar to the modern reader,
though traditionally it would make a serious point, but it provides a helpful
entrance into the poems of a writer such as Rossetti. Later, Freud understood
the significance of play, and how it permits both writer and reader to access
deeper 'truths' than one might assume. Indeed, Freud's comments on the work
of Kuno Fischer suggest that 'the comic is concerned with the ugly in one of its

manifestations', which is reminiscent of the grotesque (1976, p. 40). Further on, Freud discusses the joke in relation to the world of dreams, where he posits that the joke provides a 'relief of psychical expenditure' not unlike that of dreams; further, the dream, like the joke, may provide the originator with a form of wish-fulfilment from which one can dissociate oneself (p. 211). This complex web of issues forming around the grotesque – dreams, comedy, the id – culminate in the possibility that the grotesque may also provide access to the sublime.

That the sublime can be linked with the grotesque goes some way to explain its value. In 'Grotesque Renaissance', Ruskin discusses the sublime and its relation to the grotesque, and suggests that to understand sublime truths, the human mind requires the grotesque; as we see 'through a glass, darkly' (1 Corinthians 13.12), our vision of the sublime can only be dim. This dimly perceived sublimity, combined with fear, produces a grotesquerie that, Ruskin posits, is seen often in the Bible, particularly in dreams such as those of Jacob, Joseph, Pharaoh and Nebuchadnezzar. For example, he says that: 'Jacob's dream revealed to him the ministry of angels; but because this ministry could not be seen or understood by him in its fulness, it was narrowed to him into a ladder between heaven and earth, which was a grotesque' (GR, p. 181). This passage has particular implications for reading Rossetti's work in the light of the grotesque. First, it implies that this grotesque was inspired by or even created by God, not unlike typological methodology, using symbols and oblique references for the benefit of flawed human understanding. Secondly, it proposes that the ladder itself was grotesque, not, presumably, in itself or its aesthetics, but in its representation of a higher truth. This is what Ruskin terms the 'symbolical grotesque': the presence of an object which is perhaps unexpected or even absurd, but which represents a sublime truth in a symbolic manner.

The Rossettian grotesque

Ruskin's explanation of the grotesque is especially helpful for examining one of Rossetti's more cryptic poems, 'My Dream', which, as she later commented in an MS note, was 'not a real dream' (WMR, p. 479). Critics have been uncertain whether this poem was written as a joke or an allegory, particularly given its unlikeness to her other works. 'My Dream' seems most obviously parallel with Pharaoh's first dream in the book of Genesis, which Joseph interprets. Here, seven well-fed cattle are devoured by seven lean kine, and Joseph offers an interpretation of the dream, which was sent by God. Pharaoh's dream is strangely inverted in 'My Dream': one crocodile eats many others; the fat crocodile eats the smaller ones rather than the reverse, and in the end the 'prudent crocodile' (l. 47) seems to repent, wringing his hands and shedding 'appropriate tears' (l. 48), that is, crocodile tears.[8] 'My Dream' seems to owe its provenance in part to de Quincey's *Confessions of an English Opium-Eater* (first published in *London Magazine* in 1821), which contains a passage in which the narrator recounts his 'dreams of Oriental imagery and mythological tortures', in which 'The cursed crocodile became to me the object of more horror than almost all the rest' (de Quincey, 2003, p. 82). De Quincey's *The English Mail Coach* shows an even more grotesque figure, however: that of a coach man with a marked resemblance to a crocodile. The narrator comments on the horror this provokes in him:

> This horror has always been secretly felt by man; it was felt even under pagan forms of religion, which offered a very feeble, and also a very limited gamut for giving expression to the human capacities of sublimity or of horror. We read it in the fearful composition of the sphinx. (p. 209)

De Quincey's description of this sublime horror is a vital description of the human response to the grotesque, in which an encounter with a true grotesque seems to be as much cathartic as horrifying in the accepted sense. Such a response seems appropriate to Rossetti's poem.

Rossetti's poem is linked by writers such as Marsh to Thomas Lovell Beddoes's grotesque poem 'Song by Isbrand' in his *Death's Jest Book* of 1850, which Marsh calls 'a Rossettian favourite' (Rossetti, 1994, p. 432). Like Beddoes's poem, which incorporates a variety of grotesque, hybrid animals, Rossetti's poem features 'young crocodiles' (l. 7), each 'girt with massive gold' (l. 13). One grows stronger, and devours the rest of them. The poem is framed as a dream, in the manner of *The Dream of the Rood* (eighth century) and *Piers Plowman* (fourteenth century), and thus set up, appears allegorical; reader expectations based on allegorical tradition are that a dream-sequence must contain a deeper meaning. Like Ruskin's discussion of the symbolic grotesque which appears in dream-form, it seems to have a deeper meaning not immediately apparent on the surface. However, Cora Kaplan argues that 'the dream-form [. . .] release[s] the poem from a conventionally moral conclusion', adding that 'The "dream" itself is overloaded with symbols – heathen, phallic and patriarchal – but they are as elusive as a gnomic folk tale' (1986, pp. 34–5).

The concluding lines tantalizingly add, 'What can it mean? you ask. I answer not | For meaning, but myself may echo, What?' (ll. 49–50). Like 'Winter: My Secret', 'My Dream' seems to pose an unanswerable question, which critics have attempted to answer in a variety of ways, many by suggesting that it is not possible to answer it.[9] Simon Humphries, however, posits that the poem relates to the book of Revelation; that the setting, the Euphrates, recalls Babylon, and thus moral corruption, and, further, links it to the Crimean War and Rossetti's own distress at these violent events (2008b, p. 57). This is a convincing argument, though as Humphries points out, 'Rossetti's application of the apocalyptic is always open, always tending towards generalization' (p. 57). Like so many of Rossetti's poems, it loosely fits many interpretations, and is closed to few. This is particularly appropriate for Rossetti's Tractarian approach to reading and writing; a significant aspect of Tractarian poetics is its highly developed theory of reader-response, which Keble extrapolates in his *Lectures on Poetry* (1832–41). In his opening lectures, he discusses the importance of poetry's effect on its readers, uplifting them and appeasing their sorrows. Believing that everyone has an innate desire for poetry, Keble sees poetry as the ideal vehicle for influencing readers. Further, it is a divine gift, to both writer and reader, as an outlet for directed and controlled emotion, with its 'prime and peculiar function of healing and relief' (Keble, 2003, I, p. 66). In the response of the reader the poet's worth can be measured, he argues. For example, Shakespeare's work inspires 'nobility of mind' – 'not that nobility merely which by a certain attractive and enthusiastic quality excites youthful minds, but the more austere qualities of purity, integrity, strenuousness, goodness' (I, p. 70). Reserve, he suggests, is vital, so that the poet does not appear to be moralizing, but rather allows the reader to draw from the poem conclusions only hinted at:

> Judicious writers [. . .] lightly touch the special points to be impressed on the reader; and an author, like a host, shows his ability most surely if his readers are dismissed with an appetite whetted but not satisfied. (I, p. 77)

Keble also suggests, however, that authorial intention is irrelevant, since it is the uplifting moral value which the reader may gain from the work which signifies.[10] The text, it seems, must stand alone, in order to be treated fairly and to fulfil its purpose.[11] The potent space between writer and reader, which is filled with spectres, is also where meaning is generated. Ricoeur suggests that 'the book divides the act of writing and the act of reading into two sides, between which there is no communication. The reader is absent from the act of writing; the writer is absent from the act of reading' (Ricoeur and Valdes, 1991, p. 45). What communication there is between the two is through the act of creation, with the reader becoming the producer of the text; it is the act of reading that constitutes a threshold, and a means to crossing this divide between reader and writer. The author may indeed be dead, but the text itself becomes her proxy, haunting the reader and interacting with the culture in which the text is read. This is an appealing theory in the light of the Tractarian desire for moral influence, allowing an author to haunt a text as a reader interprets it, using signposts such as biblical references and typology.

In its details, 'My Dream' seems to be purely ornamental. The 'kingly' crocodile himself is an example of grotesque, arrayed in human adornments yet thoroughly animal:

> But one there was who waxed beyond the rest,
> Wore kinglier girdle and a kingly crown,
> Whilst crowns and orbs and sceptres starred his breast.
> All gleamed compact and green with scale on scale,
> But special burnishment adorned his mail
> And special terror weighed upon his frown; (ll. 15–20)

Certainly Ruskin's combination of the ludicrous and the fearful seem present here, yet the moral purpose which he emphasizes is apparently absent. This crocodile devours the lesser beasts, yet appears to escape judgement, and exhibits only a mockery of repentance. His very appearance is perhaps a sufficient moral; readers might recoil at the image of his consumption of the other crocodiles, with 'The luscious fat distilled upon his chin, | Exuded from his nostrils and his eyes' (ll. 29–30): perhaps the terrifying ugliness is a warning in itself of the perils of excessive greed.

Despite the obvious yet baffling parallels with the book of Genesis, it is possible that this may be Rossetti's attempt at a poem which is purely fanciful, composed of an ornamental grotesque. It is a deliberate challenge, baffling and teasing the reader who seeks 'meaning' where none is intended. This early example of Rossettian grotesque may have no moral at all – apart from the suggestion that to look for the moral too hard may be a pointless exercise. If indeed she was influenced by Beddoes's poems, 'The Crocodile' and 'Song by Isbrand', she may also be imitating his ornate form of grotesque mischief, in which meaning seems lost to the overwhelming visual descriptions; and the poetry is none the less for it, causing Robert Browning to describe *Death's Jest Book* as 'fine as fine can be: the power of the man is immense and irresistible' (1872, p. 52). 'My Dream' seems part of a different milieu to Rossetti's other poems which manifest the grotesque; as with other of her earlier works which cannot easily be encompassed in a general survey of the trends of her poetry, it seems rather to be part of an experimental thread as the young poet began to explore the workings of her craft. Kaplan comments, reasonably, that the poem is 'a joky lesson to critical head-hunters tracking either phalluses, patriarchs or oppressors', though an intention to baffle critics suggests a calculation which is unlikely to have occurred to Rossetti (1986, p. 110). What the poem does successfully achieve, however, is an open dialogue with the reader.

Ruskin's chapter on 'Grotesque Renaissance' has thus far concentrated on the mental and spiritual state of the artist. Ruskin next discusses the more precise elements of what the grotesque might involve. With particular reference to landscape – though with a potentially wider application – Ruskin painstakingly distinguishes the picturesque from the grotesque. In *The Seven Lamps of Architecture* (1849) he described the picturesque as 'parasitical sublimity': that is, where the sublime is attached to the picturesque object but is not an intrinsic part of it (1996, VIII, p. 236). He suggests that the picturesque adds 'to the pleasurableness of grotesque work' while remaining a discrete element of it (GR, p. 160). The grotesque is produced 'exclusively by the fancy of man' (GR, p. 160), while the picturesque develops through the workings of nature. These two elements combined lend a grandeur and dignity to the work which depicts them.

The Ruskinian grotesque, one can infer, is a human-focused concept. Unlike other categories used for art, and the subjects of art, the grotesque is a depiction of human work, which only makes sense with the considered thought of its viewers. This might suggest that it is an unnecessary or self-seeking idea, created simply to draw attention to itself, and indeed Ruskin describes it as 'an elaborate and luscious form of nonsense' (GR, p. 162). *The Stones of Venice* considers its highest, most sublime configurations and usage, however, as well as its debased and 'disgusting' forms. Yet where the grotesque depicts debased humanity, Ruskin regards it as unacceptably corrupt and immoral. This is, of course, not the view of all writers on the grotesque; Russo, for example, sites the grotesque entirely in the human body, suggesting that while '[t]he classical body is transcendent, and monumental, closed, static, self-contained, symmetrical and sleek', by contrast '[t]he grotesque body is open, protruding, irregular, secreting, multiple, and changing' (p. 8). Although Russo implies that her definition of grotesque fits a masculine construction of the female body, I suggest that these contrasts are exemplified in the 'classical body' of the unfallen sisters in 'Goblin Market', and the grossness of the 'grotesque body' of goblins. Ruskin's reluctance to permit that noble grotesque can feature the human form could be read as a biographical distaste, but also suggests his idealization of the human body – an idealization upon which Rossetti places limits, since the fallen sister in her poem becomes herself a grotesque.

Rossetti shows little of Ruskin's impatience with grotesque in human form; instead, she uses character as a clear indication of the grotesque, as much as physical appearance. In 'Brother Bruin', written in the 1880s, the anti-vivisectionist Rossetti reverses the accepted notion of the physical grotesque. Rossetti felt strongly about the morality of the treatment of animals; the title implies brotherhood between humanity and the animal world, and the poem is a child-like tale which uses emotive language to emphasize its point. In the poem Rossetti neatly reverses the expected norms of the grotesque to demonstrate a form of natural justice against the wrongdoer. The dancing bear of the title is the obvious grotesque, as the opening lines suggest: 'A dancing Bear grotesque and funny | Earned for his master heaps of money' (ll. 1–2). The bear, in fact, initially is hardly grotesque at all in its appearance or character; it is described as being 'good-natured', 'fond of honey' (l. 3) and it 'danced contented anywhere' (l. 12). As it grows older, however, and 'scarce could prance' (l. 16), the master becomes angry, goading it on with 'hard blows' which 'battered his ears and poor old nose' (ll. 19–20). It is this harsh treatment which causes the bear to become increasingly grotesque in his antics: 'From bluff and gruff he waxed curmudgeon; | He danced indeed, but danced in dudgeon, | Capered in fury fast and faster' (ll. 21–3). Eventually, the bear dies, and, angry at his loss, the master sells the bear's skin. The bear, the poem suggests, may appear to be the grotesque of the poem; but the nature of the bear's master has become morally deformed into that of a true grotesque. His treatment of the animal in his care marks him out as a morally deficient character – similar to the dog's master in Dora Greenwell's poem, 'Fidelity Rewarded' (1889). Eventually he is old and alone, akin to Dickens's Ebenezer Scrooge in *A Christmas Carol* (1843), with no friends and no money left, becoming increasingly physically grotesque himself in age:

> All doors stood shut against him, but
> The workhouse door which cannot shut.
> There he droned on – a grim old sinner
> Toothless and grumbling for his dinner,
> Unpitied quite, uncared for much. (ll. 46–50)

Years of wickedness have caused him to die alone and penniless, himself a grotesque version of the animal he once maltreated. Rossetti seems to have intended a clear moral in this poem. Finally, his grotesqueness of character is manifested in his outward appearance as well as his behaviour. Physical appearance and grotesquerie are closely related in this poem; though the bear is figuratively speaking a grotesque, initially both his character and appearance are pleasant. As he is badly treated, this declines until he becomes fully grotesque. His master demonstrates a grotesque character, and as this develops it affects his physical appearance in a precisely balanced shift of positions.

Rossetti appears to adhere to the nineteenth-century belief that character is manifested in physical appearances, though she complicates this in many instances, and it is not a straightforward association. Certainly readings of Victorian novels emphasize this belief: examples of Dickens's grotesques such as Fagin or Miss Havisham have similarly warped personalities, and in the work of the Tractarian novelist Charlotte Yonge this is particularly pronounced. One nineteenth-century writer describes the science of physiognomy thus:

> [I]t may be defined as the art of decyphering the human face, and of reading in those living characters the inward faculties and emotions of the soul [. . .]. The discerning physionomist contemplates these with the eye of a philosopher, and the understanding of a moralist. He judges, from those parts which are visible, of certain others, not perceptible till called into action; and from the whole forms his estimate of the natural, or constitutional, character of the individual. (Cooke, 1819, pp. 28–9)

For Rossetti's contemporary readers, versed in the ways of physiognomy and phrenology, the correlation between appearance and character would have been instantly noticed and understood, though Rossetti's poems frequently complicate this.[12]

Further into the chapter on 'Grotesque Renaissance', Ruskin explicitly states the role of fearfulness in the grotesque:

> Thus there is a Divine beauty, and a terribleness or sublimity coequal with it in rank, which are the subjects of the highest art; and there is an inferior or ornamental beauty, and an inferior terribleness coequal with it in rank, which are the subjects of grotesque art. And the state of mind in which the terrible form of the grotesque is developed, is that which in some irregular manner, dwells upon certain conditions of terribleness, into the complete depth of which it does not enter for the time. (GR, pp. 165–6)

These states of mind, he explains, depend on the concentration of the mind of the creator: if they fully understand and appreciate the fear, which is ultimately always of sin and death, then their grotesque will be 'noble', and thus presumably allied to the sublime. If the mind '*plays* with *terror*' (GR, p. 166), this mockery can only produce an ignoble grotesque. It is straightforward, according to Ruskin, to distinguish the noble from the ignoble grotesque, since the ignoble will be lacking 'Nature', 'Horror' and 'Mercy' (GR, p. 176). Fear is a necessary part of Christian existence, since its absence implies a lack of understanding of God and the horrors of sin and death. This sentiment accords with Rossetti's own beliefs, particularly manifested in her devotional poems which plead with God for mercy. Further, Rossetti equates outward beauty with a Christian spirituality in *Called to be Saints*, where she says 'How beautiful are the arms which have embraced Christ, the hands which have touched Christ, the eyes which have gazed upon Christ, the lips which have spoken with Christ, the feet which have followed Christ' (*CS*, p. viii). This beauty bears no relation to physical appearance, instead referencing a spiritual beauty which can be perceived by the attuned eye.

Ruskin states that 'the tendency to delight in fantastic and ludicrous, as well as in sublime, images, is a universal instinct of the Gothic imagination' (NG, p. 239). However, in *Modern Painters* he expands upon this, dividing grotesques into categories. It becomes clear in *Modern Painters* that all art, and in particular that in the Gothic mode, has a moral element for Ruskin because it derives from the imagination, which is closely linked to the moral character and personality of the artist. It is the mind of the creator, rather than his hand, which creates; and it is the morality of the mind which assures the success, or otherwise, of the work of art. 'The imagination is *always* right', he claims, but in order to succeed as true art, it must be the 'right' imagination, imbued with an ideal morality (Ruskin, 1996, VI, p. 145). Of his three proposed models of grotesque, the first implies indolence, the second an element of wickedness; the third, he posits, is the 'true' or 'ideal' grotesque. Rossetti's grotesque, particularly in 'Goblin Market', appears to contain elements of each of Ruskin's types. The second form, stemming from 'contemplation of terrible things', may seem unlikely in the case of Rossetti, yet the extent of her use of Gothic, as manifested in her later prose works on the apocalypse, for example, makes this a possible prospect. Ruskin's comments on this second type suggest that the first type would become dull and moralizing in most cases, and that therefore the 'taint of [. . .] evil' is unintentionally introduced:

> It hardly ever is free from some slight taint of the inclination to evil; still
> more rarely is it, when so free, natural to the mind; for the moment we begin
> to contemplate sinless beauty we are apt to get serious; and moral fairy tales,

and such other innocent work, are hardly ever truly, that is to say, naturally, imaginative; but for the most part laborious inductions and compositions. The moment any real vitality enters them, they are nearly sure to become satirical, or slightly gloomy, and so connect themselves with the evil-enjoying branch. (GR, pp. 131–2)

Indeed, given Rossetti's close family connections with Ruskin, and her known enjoyment of, and interest in, his work, it seems highly likely she would have been aware of these comments prior to commencing her own 'moral fairy tale', 'Goblin Market'. His comment that such works are 'hardly ever [. . .] imaginative' is surely belied by her work, which combines the grotesque and the familiar in a distinctly Gothic blend, and which Ruskin himself commended.

In fact it is Ruskin's final category of grotesque which to him represents the 'noble' grotesque, the apotheosis of the form. In this 'confusion of the imagination', overwhelmed by the extent of spiritual truths, the grotesque as a mode of allegory comes into its own, and may serve to point humanity towards God. George Landow (2005) explicitly links Ruskin's symbolical grotesque to his Evangelical 'theories of allegory', in which man, in his fallen state, can only understand divine truths through allegorical means. Landow cites Ruskin's comment in *Modern Painters* as evidence of this, since Ruskin unequivocally says: 'what revelations have been made by humanity inspired, or caught up to heaven, of things to the heavenly region belonging, have been either by unspeakable words, or else by their very nature incommunicable, except in types and shadows' (Ruskin, 1996, IV, p. 208). For Rossetti these 'types and shadows' were part of a framework of Tractarian beliefs, in which Old Testament typology expanded to provide all earthly objects and events with a heavenly counterpart. This is discussed in Tract 80 of *Tracts for the Times*, 'On Reserve in Communicating Religious Knowledge', in which Isaac Williams discusses the use of 'figurative expressions' as an intrinsic part of the use of reserve and typology. There can be no doubt that Rossetti makes extensive use of typology in 'Goblin Market', but, in the case of the grotesques of the poem, this index linking the physical with the spiritual world is complicated by Rossetti's extensions to Ruskin's theories.

In his short story for children, 'The King of the Golden River' (1851), Ruskin utilizes his own theories of grotesque. In line with traditional fairy tales, there are three brothers who differ in physical appearance as well as character traits. The 'ugly' brothers, Schwartz and Hans, are carefully described to present a vivid picture of ugliness: 'the two elder brothers, were very ugly men, with overhanging eyebrows and small, dull eyes which were always half shut, so that you couldn't see into *them*, and always fancied they saw very far into *you*' (*KGR*, p. 314). Hans and Schwartz are equally deformed in temperament: '[T]hey never went to mass, grumbled perpetually at paying tithes; and were, in a word, of so cruel and grinding a temper, as to receive from all those with whom they had any dealings, the nickname of the "Black Brothers"' (*KGR*, pp. 314–15).

Gluck, the youngest brother, provides a contrast: 'Gluck was as completely opposed, in both appearance and character, to his seniors as could possibly be imagined or desired. He was not above twelve years old, fair, blue-eyed, and kind in temper to every living thing' (*KGR*, p. 315). Gluck provides the normative contrast which sets up the conditions for the grotesque to operate. However, it is not enough that a character should be ugly in order to be grotesque, as Ruskin's criticism discusses. The combination of the internal and external grotesque, encompassing the playful and the fearful, and to a certain extent the human and the animal, provides the element of grotesquerie. It is their ugliness of spirit as well as appearance which makes the wicked brothers into grotesques, as it does with Charles Perrault's Ugly Sisters.

Ruskin's model of the grotesque provides three key possibilities for reading Rossetti. His discussion of the playfulness of the grotesque, with the implication that it need not be taken quite seriously, and the detailed discussions of the state of mind in which such works are successfully created, have implications for many of Rossetti's poems, particularly those which are often termed inscrutable, or those with a multiplicity of interpretations. Closely related to this, Ruskin's insistence on the moral implications of the grotesque, in the mind of its creator, and in its effect on the reader or viewer, alongside the concept of the moral jest, sheds light on Rossetti's poems.[13] His discussion throughout his work notes identifying features of the grotesque, many of which correlate with those identified by other critics, but notably adding some such as Horror, Nature and Mercy in the noble grotesque. Finally, Ruskin links the grotesque to the sublime – or, rather, suggests that the grotesque can provide a way of accessing the sublime. Particularly taking Ruskin's (and Rossetti's) view of nature as a divinely inspired book, which contains many natural grotesques, this route to the sublime is the most pertinent aspect of Ruskin's discourse. The relationship between the natural world, the grotesque and the divine is discussed in detail in David Williams (1996); here, it is made clear that the natural world, to the medieval mind, should consist of the four elements, earth, air, fire and water, and each element should be contained within its natural state or shape. Consequently, 'The transgression of the order or physical nature was the source of a seemingly limitless number of monstrous forms' (p. 178). Williams makes it clear that it is the transgressing or exceeding of boundaries which forms the grotesque, and this contravention of natural laws had theological, often moral, consequences. Ruskin's constructions of the grotesque lead to a primarily moral form of grotesque, in which the mind of the craftsman, artist, writer or stonemason, determines the potential effects of the grotesque. Moreover, the morality of the mind is manifested, usually unintentionally, in the work. The best grotesques give access to the sublime, and yet can present a straightforward moral, as in the cautionary tale of the 'fall' of Venice. For Rossetti's work this moral is especially applicable.

A comparable moral stance towards the grotesque is demonstrated in many of Rossetti's early poems, such as 'The Dead City', written in 1847. This poem, which has been related to *Melmoth the Wanderer*, as well as to Dante's *Inferno*, details a visit to a city where the inhabitants have become statues, which are grotesque parodies of humans. The poem demonstrates the morality later indicated in 'Goblin Market', that moral decline leads to 'spiritual petrifaction' (Rossetti, 1994, p. 441). Rossetti further explores this metaphor by illustrating a physical result of immorality. Marsh suggests that Rossetti's poem betrays the influence of Tennyson's poem 'The Sleeping Palace' in 'The Day-Dream', which takes a similar setting, but largely precludes the moral view which the young Rossetti emphasizes. An apposite comparison might also be made with Shelley's 'Ozymandias', a ruined and grotesque statue of a figure who was once great: 'Half sunk, a shattered visage lies, whose frown | And wrinkled lip, and sneer of cold command' (ll. 4–5). The moral is obvious, though ironic: '"Look on my works, ye Mighty, and despair!"' (l. 11). Though Rossetti extends the tale, her moral is similar. Ruskin uses examples of Venetian architecture to make a similar point: the lowest grotesques to be found in Venice are those which are *'entirely destitute of every religious symbol, sculpture or inscription'* (GR, p. 146, original emphasis), and serve as a monument to human endeavour rather than to God, even in ecclesiastical architecture. Ruskin adds drily: 'Throughout the whole of Scripture history, nothing is more remarkable than the close connexion of punishment with the sin of vainglory [. . .] the forgetfulness of God, and the claim of honour by man, as belonging to himself, are visited at once [. . .] with the most tremendous punishment' (GR, pp. 146–7). While Venice still stands, though scarred, Ruskin suggests that its architecture remains as a warning to those who see it to avoid the 'insolent atheism' (GR, p. 148) of the past.

'The Dead City' opens with a carefree ramble through a forest, with lush descriptions of the natural world which catch the narrator's eye, and which are related to the spiritual world: 'Where the woods are ever vernal, | And the life and joy eternal | Without Death's or Sorrow's rest' (ll. 38–40). From a seemingly deathless natural world, the narrator moves into a place where the trees are sparse, and the birds have vanished, and 'the pale sun | Shone with a strange lurid sheen' (ll. 64–65). Entering a ruined city, with remnants of its former beauty, she walks on noting the deserted place until encountering a palace, gilded and bejewelled. It is interesting to consider this city in the light of Ruskin's Venice; he describes the Renaissance Venetians as immoral, occupied in the 'unscrupulous pursuit of pleasure', and posits that consequently their standards of architecture fell as did their virtues. Consequently their architecture became 'the worst and basest ever built by the hands of men, being especially distinguished by a spirit of brutal mockery and insolent jest, which [. . .] can sometimes be hardly otherwise defined than as the perpetuation in stone of the ribaldries of drunkenness' (GR, p. 135). Ruskin gives two examples of grotesque consequent to this: the noble and the ignoble. The noble is a fourteenth-century griffin; the ignoble a debased human face from Renaissance Venice. The implication seems to be that it is the debasing of humanity which spoils art. Similarly, Ruskin suggests that grotesque ornaments which represent grotesque humankind are the most unnecessary and unpleasant, comparable to 'the most disgusting types of manhood and womanhood which can be found amid the dissipation of the modern drawingroom; yet without either veracity or humour, and dependent for whatever interest they possess, upon simple grossness of expression and absurdity of costume' (GR, p. 162). Later in the same chapter he explains his reasons for this, stating that if one can 'draw the human head perfectly' (GR, p. 170), one has no right to ruin it by turning it into a grotesque. The human form is closely allied to nature, and thus to God, being in God's image, and should not needlessly be malformed because of its theological significance.[14] In 'The Dead City', the architecture is ornate, the objects bejewelled and glistening, a grotesque parody of beauty in themselves; ironically, the inhabitants become no more than a part of that stone city themselves, and less allied with nature and natural beauty than with the stones of the architecture.

Rossetti's extensive description of the man-made and natural beauties of the palace and its grounds pre-empts the disclosure of the moral purpose of the poem:

> Then the breezes whispered me:
> Enter in, and look, and see
> How for luxury and pride
> A great multitude have died. (ll. 161–4)

Though the moral is clear, that indulgence turns life to death, what caused this petrifaction is never disclosed; one assumes it to be the judgement of God – or, perhaps, the beginning of a fairy tale, as Tennyson's poem is. At a great banquet table, the revellers are seated, turned to stone. Their fate seems that of the supplicant in 'A Better Resurrection', who says 'I have no wit, no words, no tears; | My heart within me like a stone' (ll. 1–2), and whose life 'is like a frozen thing' (l. 13). Yet that speaker had hope through Christ; these statues have none, like the object of the poem 'Dead before Death', whose physical appearance reflects death as does his spiritual state, though he is still alive.

Though many of the figures in 'The Dead City' are portrayed as beautiful, in their form of petrified flesh they are grotesques, as Rossetti emphasizes:

> Here a dead man sat to sup
> In his hand a drinking cup;
> Wine cup of the heavy gold,
> Human hand stony and cold. (ll. 241–4)

Rossetti describes the guests – children, lovers, mothers, the elderly – and suggests that their eyes are stonily staring. A moment later, the palace has vanished, and the narrator is returned to the wood where she began, and kneels to pray. It is an apparently straightforward moral tale, yet it demonstrates Rossetti's belief that the moral state will, in time, be reflected by the physical. These statues are grotesque in their very life-likeness; it is what they are, or represent, that is repulsive, rather than their bodies.

This chapter seeks to suggest, then, that for Rossetti as for Ruskin, it is the morality of the grotesque which is its strongest characteristic; the appearance is secondary to moral character. Several of Rossetti's poems suggest that the grotesque surrounds us, yet she subverts expectations neatly in a poem such as 'The World'. Once again, there is an attempt at seduction with natural objects such as fruit and flowers, while beauty and ugliness are starkly contrasted.[15] It is 'the world' which attempts to seduce the righteous from their sight of heaven, seeming lovely by day but hideous by night:

> By day she woos me, soft, exceeding fair:
> But all night as the moon so changeth she;
> Loathsome and foul with hideous leprosy
> And subtle serpents gliding in her hair.
> By day she woos me to the outer air,
> Ripe fruits, sweet flowers, and full satiety:
> But through the night, a beast she grins at me,
> A very monster void of love and prayer.
> By day she stands a lie: by night she stands

In all the naked horror of the truth
With pushing horns and clawed and clutching hands.
Is this a friend indeed; that I should sell
My soul to her, give her my life and youth,
Till my feet, cloven too, take hold on hell? (ll. 1–14)

What seems real, beautiful, and wholesome to many people is here transformed into an object of disgust, where Ruskin's concept of grotesque fear certainly prevails over the playfulness. Rather than fear of death, it seems here that Rossetti depicts a fear of life.[16] This is complicated by the world's symbolic representation of sin: 'Loathsome and foul with hideous leprosy', which leads to eternal death. To simplify Rossetti's theology, rejecting earthly life leads to eternal life; this poem personifies the world which leads one astray as beautiful, but deceitful in its beauty. Like a fairy-tale creature whose appearance is designed to mislead, the beauty of 'sweet flowers' hides 'a very monster' with wicked intentions.

It is clear that one of the reasons that the grotesque fits into Rossetti's work is because her poems maximize visual content in the way she liberally uses image and symbol in her poetry; her aesthetics thus lend themselves to the grotesque, which still is essentially understood as a visual category. Like Fuseli's *The Nightmare*, or the engravings of Dürer, 'The World' appears to be a poem of apparitions in dreams, yet the logical voice of the speaker in the final three lines shows the grim rationale of the poem. One might go so far as to argue that Ruskin's picturesque and grotesque are both represented in this poem as oppositional forces combined in one concept. The beauty of the natural world which Ruskin deems picturesque is present in the fruits and flowers, while the grotesque, horrifying creature which haunts the narrator is Sin, made by man at the Fall. The grotesquerie is not only in the appearance but in the very existence of the creature, a kind of Frankenstein's monster, created by the Fall of humankind. This creature, 'the world', is a caricature of grotesque, however. The beauty with which it is contrasted fades in comparison with the horror of its ugliness, which breathes moral corruption, and in its explicit moral, that no appearances, whether beautiful or ugly, can be trusted, this appears to be the least subtle of Rossetti's grotesques examined here.

Rossetti's grotesque, then, contains many of the elements which for Ruskin are required in order for a grotesque to be noble, as opposed to debased and ignoble. Her grotesque figures, with the possible exception of the crocodile, are grotesque for a reason, appearing designed to lead the reader to a moral conclusion. Though her poems incorporate the necessary elements of the humorous and the fearful, the balance of the two varies considerably, and the fearful overtakes the ludicrous as her work matures. There can be no doubt that Rossetti herself did have the serious understanding of the Christian fear of sin which Ruskin impresses upon his readers. However, many of her poems which do not seem to fit in with stereotypical notions of Rossetti as a devout and moralizing writer, for example, 'Goblin Market', and the ballads of 'fallen women', suggest that she also had a deep understanding of the 'wickedness' which Ruskin admired. Yet in the moral aspects discussed by Ruskin, and also Scott, Rossetti's work certainly manifests an ennobling grotesque which is tailored to her own religious and poetic ends. She maintains a sympathy between reader and writer which is testament to the efficacy of Ruskin's commentary on architecture, requiring her readers to work to understand the moral, and to appreciate her restrained poetics.

However, it is of course not possible to map Ruskinian grotesque neatly onto Rossettian poetry. There are modes of grotesque, in landscape and architecture, a visual mode, which are Ruskin's preoccupation; and in poetry, as an element of the wider Gothic mode of literature, and also associated with the sublime and the fantastic. It appears that both visual and literary modes seem to concentrate on morality, and especially in the poetry of Rossetti, an inclination to exaggerate her fears leads the frightening to become terrifying, and the threat to the virtue of her readers to be intensified. Ruskin's construction of the grotesque provides a framework in which it is helpful to situate Rossetti's work, yet she sometimes evades that framework. Her inclination towards the 'monstrous' discussed by Paulson is a step away from Ruskin's more restrained notion of the ideal or noble grotesque, particularly in such poems as 'The World'. The Rossettian approach to nature is more complicated than Ruskin's appears to be, seeing it both as the face of the divine, and a temptation to mankind. The corruption secreted in the most beautiful images of the world is sensed and feared by Rossetti, and this strengthens her approach to the grotesque, and to the Gothic, an approach seen clearly in her most famous poem, 'Goblin Market'.

'Goblin Market' and Gothic

'Goblin Market' has for many years occupied a central position in studies of Rossetti, both poetical and biographical. According to a reviewer of 'Goblin Market', writing in 1863, it is:

> one of the works which are said to 'defy criticism'. Is it a fable – or a mere fairy story – or an allegory against the pleasures of sinful love – or what is it? Let us not too rigorously enquire, but accept it in all its quaint and pleasant mystery, and quick and musical rhythm – a ballad which children will con with delight, and riper minds may ponder over [. . .]. (Norton, 1863, pp. 401–2)

Since it appeared in Rossetti's first published volume in 1862, 'Goblin Market' has engaged critics in debate more than any of her other works, largely for the multiplicity of critical ideologies to which it opens itself. W. M. Rossetti suggests in his notes to Rossetti's poems that his sister said 'more than once' that she 'did not mean anything profound by this fairy tale – it is not a moral apologue' (WMR, p. 459). The poem has been read as a discussion of a marketplace economy, a critique of the paternalistic construction of Victorian society, an allegorical representation of the redemptive Anglican Eucharist and an exploration of anorexia, to name a few theories.[1] Since Rossetti wrote the poem while working at the Mary Magdalene Penitentiary for Fallen Women, the moral tale has also been considered as a warning to women, as well as offering them hope for redemption. There has also been an historical tendency to read the poem biographically: Violet Hunt, in her colourful book on Elizabeth Siddal, suggests that Maria Rossetti saved her sister from the dreadful fate of an affair with a married man, and is therefore represented as the self-sacrificing sister in 'Goblin Market' (1932, p. xiii). This reading of the poem was extended in a biography of Rossetti in 1963 in which Lona Mosk Packer postulates that

Rossetti had a romantic relationship with the painter William Bell Scott. These speculative biographical theories have now mostly been discounted.

By far the most extensive work on the poem, however, has taken a feminist angle. In 1971, in *Sexual Politics*, an overtly feminist text, Kate Millett added a footnote suggesting that 'For some glimpses of female sexual fantasy, the reader is recommended to Christina Rossetti's "Goblin Market"' (1977, p. 149). From then onwards, the poem has frequently been read as dealing with repressed female sexuality. The following year, a detailed analysis of 'Goblin Market' examined in terms of the 'faery' or supernatural, continued this trend. *The Erotic World of Faery* considers the history of fairy creatures as an aspect of sexuality, able to manifest a sexuality otherwise repressed by society and the church. Maureen Duffy's approach centres on eroticism, and she relates this specifically to a sexual reading of 'Goblin Market', also reading the poem biographically (1972, pp. 271–3). Isobel Armstrong warns against too literal interpretations of the poem, however (1993, pp. 347–52), focusing on the 'ambiguities at work in the poetics of expression' (p. 351).

An edition of 'Goblin Market' published in 1975 included a foreword by Germaine Greer, in which Greer appears hostile to Rossetti's religious beliefs, dismissing them as 'sentiment' rather than 'intellectual' (1975, p. xvi). Further, Greer claims that the poem is notable for its 'godlessness' (p. xvi), a questionable judgement given readings of the poem as a Christian allegory. Greer's foreword seems to have coloured subsequent criticism, and certainly brought 'Goblin Market' to the forefront of Rossetti's poems. She suggests that:

> Now and then critics hint at what might be the poem's theme, but more often they are content to let it lie enveloped in mystery, for fear that to unravel it would be to reveal more of the psychology of the unraveler than it would of the meaning of the poem itself. (p. ix)

Such scruples on the behalf of critics certainly faded during the 1970s, and criticism of 'Goblin Market' blossomed, which, if Greer's supposition here is right, perhaps tells us as much about the changing state of literary criticism as the history of Rossetti's poem.

Notoriously, in *Slipshod Sibyls* Greer includes a chapter titled 'The Perversity of Christina Rossetti', in which she first suggests that Rossetti was responsible for popularizing the Pre-Raphaelite school of poetry with 'Goblin Market', quoting Swinburne's comment that she was 'the Jael who led our hosts to victory' (1992, p. 359). Greer goes on to demonstrate that, having been classed as a religious poet, Rossetti has now become 'if not a feminist poet, a poet important for feminists'

(p. 359), which is certainly true. However, Greer's criticism rather sacrifices Rossetti's religious poems, which she dismisses as 'minor' and 'sentimental', on the altar of her earlier 'poems of rebellion' such as 'Goblin Market' (p. 359). Moreover, in her edition of 'Goblin Market', Greer suggests that women poets are indulged by feminists, and consequently she is severe with Rossetti, stating that 'Wilfully, she set out to waste her life' (1975, p. xix). Other critics are less severe, but frequently take issue with or ignore her religion, with the underlying assumption that it muted her poetic voice or held her back. Leder, for example, suggests that 'Goblin Market'

> expresses one of the nineteenth century's most vivid nightmares of female violation in the marketplace and one of the most brazen fantasies of the redemptive powers and pleasures of sisterly love. [It] reveals Rossetti's sharp and modern insight into women's dual role in the marketplace as both objects and perpetually unfulfilled consumers. (Abbott and Leder, 1987, p. 125)

This provides a comparatively mainstream reading of the poem, which most Rossetti scholars would not dispute, but naturally focuses on a few aspects to the detriment of others. Rosenblum (1986), however, synthesizes the feminist readings of 'Goblin Market' with a religious, though not specifically Tractarian, interpretation. Her claims that 'there *is* no friend like a sister, there is no power like that of the female community' and that '"Goblin Market" represents a rediscovery of true female origins and a rejection of the patriarchal quest myth' (p. 83) both reject readings of lesbian sexuality and reinforce a potential reading of female Gothic in the suggestion that female strength can outwit masculine cunning.

Marsh, in her comprehensive examination of 'Goblin Market' in her biography of Rossetti, states firmly that 'erotic readings of "Goblin Market" are our creations, not Christina's. [. . .] But the poem's cadences are nevertheless erotic' (1994, pp. 232–3). Despite this, Marsh's reading of 'Goblin Market' owes more to Tractarianism than it does to theories of sexuality. She interprets the poem convincingly as 'Tractarian exegesis' (p. 235), and as a work about 'temptation, resistance and redemption' (p. 229) with unmistakable typological overtones which relate to but are not dominated by issues of sexual misdemeanour. Indeed, in Rossetti's approach to the longings of Laura in 'Goblin Market', it is helpful to consider G. B. Tennyson's comment on Rossetti's poetry in general:

> Christina Rossetti's most Tractarian element is her very approach to poetry itself as a way of seeking the Deity. Keble's bedrock principle that poetry is the

expression of intense religious longing finds no more complete exemplification than in the poetry of Christina Rossetti. The biographical approach to her poetry, the strange, modern view that all longing must be sexual, especially if it is the longing of an unmarried Victorian woman, has obscured the extent to which Christina Rossetti's poetry illustrates not Freud's theory of art but Keble's. Much has been made of Christina Rossetti's yearnings in psychological terms, but not enough has been made of them in religious terms. (1981, pp. 202–3)

However, in all of these readings and the various interpretations to which 'Goblin Market' is open, few critics identify the inherent and familiar landscape of Gothic which haunts it. The psychosexual approach to the poem has been popular with critics, though there have been many attempts to produce a final, or at least potential, meaning for 'Goblin Market', particularly in essays which concentrate on a specific aspect of the poem. An interesting point which Marsh raises sheds some light on interpretations of 'Goblin Market'. Commenting on the way subsequent generations have reinterpreted Siddal, she examines what twentieth-century critics bring to any critical or creative interpretation of a historical figure such as Elizabeth Siddal, comparative to Greer's comment on the 'psychology of the unraveler'. Consequently, Marsh says that:

> in the 1960s, Elizabeth Siddal lost her virginity [. . .]. Once again, this altered perspective owed more to contemporary attitudes than new historical information. The new versions were constructed from existing source materials, however, and in many ways, of course, the sources supported a permissive view, for the Pre-Raphaelite circle can legitimately be seen as the counter-culture of its time: iconoclastic, unconventional, progressive, and self-confident in its artistic affairs. (1989, p. 131)

In the 1960s and 1970s, reinterpretations, Marsh suggests, owe more to a new permissiveness of society which sought a reflection of itself in earlier periods, and may in part account for the renewed interest in Pre-Raphaelitism during this period. The act of interpreting 'Goblin Market' critically is growing in complexity as trends in criticism are brought to bear on it. Indeed, it has been noted that the range of interpretations of 'Goblin Market' is already 'disconcerting' (Edmond, 1988, p. 170).[2]

Gothic, Ellen Moers claims, is engaged with fear, fantasy and the supernatural, and so it is interesting that she was also one of the few critics to assign the label of 'Gothic' to 'Goblin Market', though not to Rossetti's other poems, including it in her chapter on 'Female Gothic' (1978, pp. 100–6). She discusses the possibility of a Rossettian Gothic, though within the context of sexuality, which she considers as 'the night side of the Victorian nursery – a world where childish cruelty and childish sexuality come to the fore' (p. 105). The idea of the female Gothic has been developed since Moers's initial labelling; Ghislaine McDayter claims that both 'eighteenth century moralism' and 'twentieth century feminism' attempt to explain Gothic in terms of 'female readers' fixation with their own suffering, their own oppression' (1995, p. 58). However, she goes on to suggest that the aesthetic element of fantasy is what gives rise to the sublime pleasures of Gothic, not reader identification with the heroine, because 'there is no stable identification between subject and fantasy' (p. 61). The subjects become a vehicle for fantasy, and the situations which test the heroines fill the void, in just such a way as the moralists originally feared, but for different reasons.

While Ellen Moers was the first to label the poem 'Gothic', other critics have also done so, including Rosemary Jackson, who suggests that 'Goblin Market' is written in a Gothic tradition, though she offers no explanation of this (Jackson, 1981, p. 103). Susanne Waldman similarly frames the poem as Gothic (2008, pp. 62–5). These references to this poem as Gothic tend not to qualify such categorization; this chapter will therefore address the potential Gothic nature of the poem, exploring Rossetti's use of the tropes and aesthetics, as well as atmosphere, of Gothic in her most successful work. 'Goblin Market' is, in its simplest form, a fairy tale of the moral fall of a young girl, Laura, and her subsequent rescue by her sister, Lizzie. The seducers of the poem are goblins, popular with illustrators, who appear as anthropomorphized animals, swarming around the girls and offering them fruits. The parallels with the temptation and fall of Eve in Eden are clear; there is also an emphasis on 'consuming', which has been interpreted in a variety of ways by critics. Chapman, for example, comments on 'consumption as a multiple trope' in the poem, pathological, moral and economic (2000, p. 132), while Marina Warner, writing on fairy tale, points out that 'the metaphor of devouring often stands in for sex' (1994, p. 259), particularly in relating the consumption of the apple by Eve in Eden to sexuality. The narrative lends itself to exploration of tropes such as the double and the fallen woman, as well as vampires and monsters. These provide the main themes of this chapter.

The grotesque in 'Goblin Market'

There are elements of the poem which can be categorized as grotesque, in the Ruskinian mode discussed in the previous chapter. Rossetti's grotesques, like Ruskin's, serve a moral purpose, which critics have sensed since the first publication of her poems. For example, in 1893 a review of 'Goblin Market' in the *Century* magazine suggested a link between the grotesque and the moral in Rossetti's work:

> It is one of the very few purely fantastic poems of recent times which have really kept up the old tradition of humoresque literature. Its witty and fantastic conception is embroidered with fancies, descriptions, peals of laughing music, which clothe it as a queer Japanese figure may be clothed with brocade, so that the entire effect at last is beautiful and harmonious without ever having ceased to be grotesque. I confess that [. . .] I dimly perceive the underlying theme to be a didactic one. (Gosse, 1903, p. 149)

Edmund Gosse's review casts 'Goblin Market' as a poem of contrasting moods, 'beautiful and harmonious' on the surface yet remaining disturbing in its grotesquerie. His comments underline surprising elements of the poem: that a poem may be in the 'humoresque' tradition, and at the same time be both beautiful and grotesque. Beauty is not a generally accepted attribute of the grotesque, yet Gosse is not the only critic to have emphasized the unsettling tone and apparently contrasting aspects of the poem. Moreover, he relates the beautiful and grotesque characteristics of the poem to an underlying morality.

Ruskin's commentary on the significance of play has particular resonance for 'Goblin Market'. In this poem, the poet herself appears playful, creating figures of imagination in the goblins, and developing a visual world of ostensibly carefree nature. In its very excesses the poem seems playful, with descriptive catalogues of fruits, and light-hearted descriptions of the goblins.[3] This world is then invaded by moral danger, as what appeared harmless becomes a threat to play. A grotesque form of play is an intrinsic part of the structure of this poem. Aesthetically, this is a playful poem, however; it may be a moral tale, but its strength and appeal are formed by its surface effects, such as its uneven rhythm which breaks into passages with a regularity which becomes almost a chant: 'Crab-apples, dewberries, | Pine-apples, blackberries, | Apricots, strawberries' (ll. 12–14). The metre lurches between iambic and dactylic feet, from binary to ternary with many variations and substitutions in between; it is impossible to determine a single prevalent rhythm, just as the critic cannot pin down a final meaning. Furthermore, the poem is markedly packed with rhymes and pararhymes, with some cross-rhymed couplets among mono-rhymed and non-rhyming lines. It is a poem whose playfulness of style engages the reader's attention by its changefulness, and in its irregularity forms of itself a grotesque artefact.

'Goblin Market' provides one of the most obvious examples of the Ruskinian grotesque in Rossetti's work, particularly in relation to the goblins themselves, yet the issues are more complicated than in other poems. The poem is framed to project the goblins as the centrepiece, not only in the title but with the opening lines, which concentrate on the goblins and their fruits up to line 31. In the next stanza, Lizzie and Laura's introduction into the poem provides a normative function, since they are recognizable as figures which permeate Victorian fiction: young girls anxious to avoid wrongdoing, and living in a familiar domestic space. They serve as a contrast to the exotic descriptions of fruit which precede them. The otherness of the goblins and their wares is emphasized by the sisters' words:

> We must not look at goblin men,
> We must not buy their fruits:
> Who knows upon what soil they fed
> Their hungry thirsty roots? (ll. 42–5)

Not only the fruits but also the goblins themselves seem included in these lines, merging animal and vegetable forms, which suggest grotesque images without any physical description. Their exoticness is contrasted with the 'blushes' and 'golden head' of the girls, and presents a sharply defined danger, setting up the goblins as a grotesque element in the poem and delineating clear boundaries between the girls and their would-be seducers. Rossetti's description of the goblins initially depicts them as half-animal, though not yet frightening:

> One had a cat's face,
> One tramped at a rat's pace,
> One crawled like a snail,
> One like a wombat prowled obtuse and furry,
> One like a ratel tumbled hurry skurry. (ll. 71–6)

The true nature of the goblins is revealed when their desire to force their fruits on Lizzie is thwarted, and their appearance as well as their behaviour becomes threatening:

> No longer wagging, purring,
> But visibly demurring,
> Grunting and snarling [. . .]
> Their tones waxed loud,
> Their looks were evil. (ll. 391–7)

This contrast is emphasized by the illustrations which have accompanied the poem, from Dante Gabriel Rossetti's to Arthur Rackham's. In these, the girls are familiar fairy-tale figures, as are the goblins. They occupy an expected and traditional role, a facet of the Beauty and the Beast tale which sets virtuous young women against male evildoers. The goblins of 'Goblin Market' and their function as seducers in the poem are superficially clear-cut: they are described as bestial, at first, yet with voices 'kind and full of loves', and the girls have no fear of them. When Lizzie refuses to eat the fruit, however, the domestic animals become savage; they attack her, and eventually they run away. Illustrations of the goblins bring out these different elements, with most showing the goblins as they attempt to cajole the girls into eating their fruit, rather than as the vicious creatures they are to become. Nevertheless these visual depictions of the goblins are grotesques, albeit more in the arabesque mode than the true grotesque – they seem powerless, and are considerably smaller than the sisters, but they are deformed, leering and supernatural. Dante Gabriel Rossetti's illustrations play down the grotesquerie of the poem, producing a bland fairy-tale scene which normalizes the content of his sister's poem, portraying the goblins as small furry creatures rather than as a genuine threat to their safety.

For Christina Rossetti, therefore, physical appearance can be misleading, and to read the grotesque status of the goblins as a simple opposition to the normative and virtuous appearance of the sisters is to oversimplify the poem. Though much is made of the girls' appearance by illustrators, drawn from lines such as 'Laura stretched her gleaming neck' (l. 81), and 'Golden head by golden head' (l. 185), Rossetti provides relatively little physical description of the sisters, instead concentrating on heightening the grotesque appearance of the goblins. After Laura has sampled the goblin fruits, there is no more description of the goblins' appearance, but only of their behaviour. This suggests that no physical descriptions were needed, even in their worst excesses, since their behaviour towards the girls demonstrates what the reader needs to know. Of course, goblins were also familiar fairy- or folk-tale creatures, already familiar to Victorian readers, and thus their grotesqueness and wickedness, as well as immorality, would be expected.

The girls may have an expected natural beauty, but they have other attributes too, especially 'curious Laura' (l. 69). Arguably there is a grotesquerie in the girls' behaviour which is not entirely divorced from physical appearance. While Lizzie restrains her feelings, demonstrating no curiosity, perhaps surprisingly, but only fear of the goblins, Laura's succumbing to temptation creates a grotesque figure of excess. In her curiosity, Laura is presented as a figure verging on the grotesquely beautiful:

> Laura stretched her gleaming neck
> Like a rush-imbedded swan,
> Like a lily from the beck,
> Like a moonlit poplar branch,
> Like a vessel at the launch
> When its last restraint is gone. (ll. 81–6)

Here, she appears as allied to the natural world as the goblins are; the images Rossetti uses are unexpected, and imply a kinship with the goblins, as though salvation comes through a dissolution of boundaries that should not be crossed in the normal course of events. This is in stark contrast with Laura's appearance as she falls into a decline after tasting the goblin fruit. Duffy discusses the possibility that, having tasted forbidden fruits with the goblins, Laura afterwards exhibits what William Acton in 1857 described as the classic hallmarks of the habitual masturbator: 'The pale complexion, the emaciated form, the slouching gait, the clammy palm, the glassy or leaden eye, and the averted gaze, indicate the lunatic victim to this vice' (cited in Duffy, 1972, p. 272). This description of this supposed grotesque outcome of a grotesque 'vice' corresponds with Laura's behaviour and appearance; she 'sat up in a passionate yearning, | And gnashed her teeth for baulked desire, and wept' (ll. 266–7). 'Her hair grew thin and grey' (l. 277), and she has 'sunken eyes and faded mouth' (l. 288). She is becoming a grotesque herself, after her experience with the goblins, yet her longing for the fruit still appears symbolic; it is not the fruit itself which destroys her, but her longing for it. Lysack (2008) suggests that the poem 'affirms female desire within [. . .] a marketplace' (p. 18), commenting on the pleasures of such anticipated consumer spectacles; essentially, she ultimately equates sex and shopping in a discussion which validates female consumer desire. Laura's changed nature is due to her succumbing to temptation, not necessarily to the effects of the fruit she had 'purchased'. In her desire for the forbidden, Laura is a grotesque, both physically and mentally, as well as a moral example, and yet not one beyond redemption.[4]

The goblins, grotesque though they may be, are closely allied with nature, not only in the fruits they sell but also in their appearance, as animal–human hybrids. They appear only in the glen, devoid of any man-made setting, and their attributes are described in terms of the natural world. While nature may be a face of the divine, it can also be a source of temptation and evil. Rossetti seems to be suggesting that the forces of evil, of temptation, are simply an aspect of the postlapsarian world. Moreover, one could extrapolate the moral that in the eyes of God, all humanity is grotesque in its changed and fallen state.

Fallen women

A significant way in which the influence of Gothic manifests itself in Rossetti's work is through the depiction of women, specifically transgressing or 'fallen' women, frequently treated severely in Gothic novels. Rossetti, however, undermines this traditional approach by offering redemption to her female characters, depicting them as 'more sinned against that sinning'. Many critics have dealt with 'Goblin Market' as a parable of sexual sin, referring to Jeanie 'in her grave, | Who should have been a bride; | But who for joys brides hope to have | Fell sick and died' (ll. 312–15), or arguing that the 'precious golden lock' which Laura offers the goblins as payment is in fact pubic hair (Duffy, 1972, p. 272).[5] The tone of the poem is undeniably sensual, but it seems probable that Rossetti's depictions of fallen women centre on the idea that they have suffered, not necessarily a carnal lapse, but one in the original sense, of Eve's sin of disobedience to God. The girls know they must not consort with the goblins; the implication is that they are wicked tempters and must be avoided, but no detailed explanation is given; they simply know that it is a line they must not cross. Consequently, one could argue that many of Rossetti's devotional poems also reflect the fallen state of the speaker, on behalf of womankind. For example, 'A Better Resurrection' depicts the speaker as a broken vessel: 'My life is like a broken bowl, | A broken bowl that cannot hold | One drop of water for my soul', echoing Ecclesiastes 12.6, 'the golden bowl be broken, or the pitcher be broken at the fountain'.

Some of her poems reflect the experience of Eve, such as 'Shut Out' and 'Eve', while others use the contrast of innocence and experience in a representative manner.[6] 'Goblin Market' can be read in this way, particularly with reference to typological readings, as D'Amico does:

> The list of similes in which Lizzie is compared to a lily, a rock, a beacon, a blossoming fruit tree, and a royal town can all be read within the context of Christian symbolism [. . .]. The obedient maiden, who first knew when to flee evil, now also proves herself to be a maiden who can face and resist evil for another's sake. In other words, she becomes a figure of self-sacrificing love, and thus she becomes a figure of Christ Himself. Rossetti underscores Lizzie's

Christ-likeness, in her call to Laura, which recalls Christ's words to his apostles at the Last Supper. (1999, pp. 74–5)

Such readings seem convincing in the context of Rossetti's beliefs, but they also permit a consideration of her use of Gothic. The fall of Laura is indeed described in sexual terms, but the fact that she is tempted by luscious fruits proffered by subhuman species clearly allies her temptation to that of Eve. In succumbing, Laura's fall is moral, not sexual. When Lizzie exposes herself to the same temptation to save her sister, the goblins attack her in a scene which can be compared to rape, but it is the attack on her morality and senses which is paramount here. It would be convenient to read Laura as the weaker side of Lizzie, to see them as two sides of one character, but to do so would negate the implication behind the poem, that salvation is both external (through Christ) *and* internal (through repentance). Rossetti is thus doubling the fallen and the unfallen, and the inner and the outer person, linked to the dual nature of women which is also underlined in the novels and poems, since the virtuous woman is frequently only half of the whole; the fallen woman with her different attributes completes the picture.

In 'A Triad', for example, Christina Rossetti suggests that earthly love may lead one astray, and that, despite apparent respectability, intemperate affection may cause a different kind of fall:

One shamed herself in love; one temperately
Grew gross in soulless love, a sluggish wife;
One famished died for love. (ll. 9–11)

Though some critics have suggested that Rossetti was personally inclined against marriage, manifested in poems such as this, it seems more probable that her argument is against marriages that she felt to be corrupt.[7] Like Lady Montrevor's daughters in *The Wild Irish Boy*, marriage for financial gain is, to Rossetti, comparable to prostitution, as is irreligiosity, or a depraved mind. Mulock Craik also suggests this in *A Woman's Thoughts About Women* (1857):

Such a one cannot be too fiercely reprobated, too utterly despised. However intact her reputation, she is as great a slur upon womanhood, as great a bane to all true modesty, as the most unchaste Messalina who ever disgraced her sex. (Rossetti and Craik, 1995, p. 190)

Despite such indictments against women who were immoral in other sins than sexual sins, the fallen woman continued to haunt nineteenth-century society and culture, with institutions being set up for their reformation. Since Rossetti worked in one of these, her attitude towards them may have been tempered by her intimate understanding of these women, but her position might have been developed long before, in the reading of the novels of Maturin. Yet there is little rivalry between the fallen and unfallen women in Rossetti's poems; instead, as with Zaira and Eva, the connections lie much deeper and contain more sympathy than jealous rivalry.

The association with fallen women in the poem stems primarily from the section of the poem telling of Lizzie's redemption of Laura, and also from the warning the girls have had from the fate of a friend, Jeanie. These sections hint at the threat to the girls' morals, souls and home. In 'Goblin Market', the domestic centre of the poem is in the sisters' house, and it is the safety of this which is disrupted by the temptation of Laura, which takes place in the 'mossy glen' (l. 87). The threat thus comes from outside the home – and yet it operates, taking effect on Laura's body and mind – inside the house (as well as inside her body). The internal physical space becomes the physically internal, and it seems likely that this is Rossetti's intention: the temptation to 'fall' may come from external sources, but the fall itself is internal and self-instigated, stemming from lack of self-discipline and the wilful transgressing of boundaries. Nonetheless, when Laura recovers, although the poem is still situated within the domestic space, the imagery is of the natural world outside, referring to 'dew-wet grass' (l. 533) and 'new buds with new day' (l. 535). Conversely, in 'Cousin Kate', a very different tale of a fallen woman, the speaker, initially an innocent girl 'Hardened by sun and air' (l. 2),[8] is 'lured' (l. 9) inside by the man who precipitates her fall, only to be supplanted by Kate, whom he also met outside and brought into the enclosed space of his 'palace home' (l. 9), while the speaker is this time left outside, shut out because fallen. The redemption in this poem, however, which reconciles the speaker with her 'outcast' life (l. 28), is her son: the implication is that she may be shut out of the palace, but her place in the world is with her child.

Rossetti's poems are generally consistent, however, in their sympathetic treatment of fallen women, and their criticism of the moral code by which such women are condemned. 'Noble Sisters' has two female characters, one apparently rescuing the other from her lover by lying to him and thus presumably saving her from sexual sin. The poem is thus structurally similar to 'Goblin Market', and yet very different in its approach, its tone and its outcome. Both sisters seem to be cloistered and looking on the world with sadness and envy. The sister who did not want to be saved, however, states her intention of leaving home to look for him, to which she receives the reply:

Go and seek in sorrow, sister,
And find in sorrow too:
If thus you shame our father's name
My curse go forth with you. (ll. 57–60)

The reader's sympathy is undoubtedly with the woman who will leave her home to travel the world looking for her lover, even though it may precipitate her fall. The world outside, it seems, which intrudes on the domestic in natural imagery, represents many opportunities for women, and not necessarily to be avoided. Poems such as 'An Apple-Gathering' see the woman's fall in terms of natural imagery; here, the speaker picks her blossoms to wear in her hair and thus has no apples. She defends herself, saying 'I counted rosiest apples on the earth | Of far less worth than love' (ll. 19–20), and implies that the fault is the man's, for being fickle, rather than her own for her vanity and haste. Even in 'Shut Out', the speaker (Eve) is excluded not from a palace or house, but a garden – the Garden of Eden. The domestic interior, then, may be a safe place for a woman, but is not necessarily the best place for her. The exception to this is 'The Convent Threshold', in which a woman who has renounced her lover accepts that her only escape from the convent is 'the stairs that mount above, | Stair after golden skyward stair, | To city and to sea of glass' (ll. 4–6). The woman who is cloistered, such as the temporary confinements of Emily St Aubert in the castle of Udolpho, and Ellena di Rosalba in *The Italian*, forced into a convent to prevent her from marrying into a wealthy family, usually seems to escape. The speaker of 'The Convent Threshold', however, has already fallen, and is accepting of her fate, and believes her escape from the convent, and her lover's escape from damnation, can only be effected through repentance. She speaks longingly of the outside world, but this confinement is a punishment, though a self-chosen one, it seems, and she anticipates her redemption through a spiritual salvation by equating it with freedom:

When once the morning star shall rise,
When earth with shadow flees away
And we stand safe within the door,
Then you shall lift the veil thereof. (ll. 141–4)

As a Tractarian, Rossetti placed a high importance on the imagery of nature, and clearly aligns her female characters with it, but also seems to accept that women, when escaping confinement into the less controlled environment of the natural world, present a greater threat to patriarchy than when enclosed in the home.

Williams argues that one of the primary concerns of Gothic is with history, in the form of lineage – the 'house' in the sense of family and ancestry – and thus Gothic's preoccupation with the fallen woman makes sense. Feminist critics have long argued that patriarchy is threatened by female capacity for reproduction, and this concern is embodied in the figure of the sexually wayward woman. However, Rossetti's approach subverts this, by divorcing the woman from the lengthy narrative and family background in which Gothic novels swathe her, and instead portraying her as an isolated figure, often embracing her own fallenness, such as the speaker in 'Cousin Kate' who has a beloved son as a result of her sins. In this poem, in fact, the speaker seems to taunt the 'respectable' woman with her son, saying:

> Yet I've a gift you have not got
> And seem not like to get:
> For all your clothes and wedding ring
> I've little doubt you fret.
> My fair-haired son, my shame, my pride,
> Cling closer, closer yet:
> Your father would give lands for one
> To wear his coronet. (ll. 41–8)

The speaker here exploits the uncertainty of succession to her own ends, reversing the fallen and unfallen relative positions of the women. The possible harm this could cause to a respectable family is not stated here, though the significance is clear, but Rossetti shifts blame from the women onto the male unheroic figure, and thus places the blame for the potential collapse of patriarchy onto the patriarch himself. The sisters in 'Noble Sisters' and 'Maude Clare' who act to save a sister from erring, and emphasize the need to preserve the family name, act in the interests of patriarchy, it seems, and Rossetti shows little sympathy for their viewpoint, despite also suggesting that the usual happy ending, of marriage such as Cousin Kate has, is only another kind of fall.[9]

One of Rossetti's favourite novels, *The Italian*, concentrates on a young woman locked away in a convent by the wealthy family of the man she loves for fear that a connection with her will weaken their house since she is poor and from an obscure family. The threat she poses to the patriarchy is unfounded, Radcliffe suggests, and yet she remains cloistered and unmarried until it transpires that she is descended from a much more prominent line than supposed. This restoration appears to reinforce the patriarchal elements of Gothic tradition, which is possibly why Rossetti stops short of this, and concentrates on those who are not well-born but have other traits; for example, in 'Maude Clare', the roles appear reversed: 'His bride was like a village maid, | Maude Clare was like a queen' (ll. 3–4). That this as well as others poems take place at weddings is significant for Rossetti's rearrangement of Gothic. Wedding vows as legally binding language serve as a cultural index of the authority of the family within Gothic, legitimizing relationships and extending dynasties. In these poems of Rossetti's, the vows either do not take place, or are seen as destructive rather than constructive.

Doubles

Critics have long noted the frequency of the trope of doubling in Gothic literature. In many Gothic novels, characters often appear doubled, reflecting two facets – usually good and evil – of one character. In Radcliffe's *The Mysteries of Udolpho*, for example, Valancourt and Montoni, hero and villain, frequently manifest similar characteristics or appearances despite their oppositional natures. In the Gothic novel, '[i]ndividuals were divided products of both reason and desire, subjects of obsession, narcissism and self-gratification as much as reasonable, responsible codes of behaviour' (Botting, 1996, p. 12). The duality or fragmentation of human nature itself is seen as a Gothic subject here, in which the instability of the psyche is manifested as split entirely. One character which may be both good and evil is separated into two, a hero and a villain, emphasizing the contrast between the two and enacting the struggle that ensues, as well as simplifying characterization.[10] Furthermore, in 'The Uncanny', Freud sees the double as a portent of evil:

> From having been an assurance of immortality, he becomes the ghastly harbinger of death. [. . .] The quality of uncanniness can only come from the circumstance of the 'double' being a creation dating back to a very early mental stage, long since left behind, and one, no doubt, in which it wore a more friendly aspect. The 'double' has become a vision of terror, just as after the fall of their religion the gods took on daemonic shapes. (1949, pp. 387–9)

If the double can refer to the childhood of an individual or character, this returns again to the childhood stories which impact on writers' and readers' understanding of Gothic as containing familiar yet uncanny elements of fairy tale. In her book of poetry for children, *Sing-Song*, Rossetti draws on the apparent simplicity of childhood to create a dual atmosphere of realism and fairy tale. For example: 'A pin has a head, but has no hair; | A clock has a face, but no mouth there;' (ll. 1–2). The effect of poems such as this is often to superimpose strange or comic images onto the everyday object.

The polarities which exist in human consciousness, and their representation in fiction as a 'device for articulating the experience of self-division' are clearly expressed in the doubling which forms the structure of many of Rossetti's poems (Herdman, 1990, p. 1). 'Goblin Market' provides one of the clearest examples of this, in which the two characters work in unison to solve the 'problem' of fallenness. Similarly, Dante Gabriel Rossetti uses the trope of the double in 'Jenny', where the narrator musing over the archetypal fallen woman twins her in his mind with his cousin Nell, 'the girl I'm proudest of' (l. 191). This is a device Christina Rossetti uses in her poems which consider the state of fallen women, such as 'Maude Clare', where a respectable woman and a dishonoured one are compared, with the morality of the fallen woman bearing scrutiny better than might be expected. It might be argued that the fallen woman was herself a spectre in nineteenth-century society, being both a focus for moral outrage and also for attempts at reform.[11]

Many biographers of Rossetti have concentrated on her ostensibly dual nature, in which her preadolescent temperament was lively and rebellious, but a nervous breakdown in her early teens led to a more subdued and religious character.[12] Rossetti's biographers frequently assume that illness and anxiety created a more reflective and deeply religious young woman than the wayward child might otherwise have become. Whether this personality trait manifested itself in her writing is debatable, but there is no doubt that she appears aware of the potential dualities in human nature, writing contrasting or doubled characters in many poems. She expanded this idea in *Time Flies*, where she writes:

> The gas was alight in my little room with its paperless bare walls. On that wall appeared a spider, himself dark and defined, his shadow no less dark and scarcely if at all less defined. They jerked, zigzagged, advanced, retreated, he and his shadow posturing in ungainly dissoluble harmony. He seemed exasperated, fascinated, desperately endeavouring and utterly helpless.
>
> What could it all mean? One meaning and one only suggested itself. That spider saw without recognizing his black double, and was mad to disengage himself from the horrible pursuing inalienable presence.

I stood watching him awhile. (Presumably when I turned off the gas he composed himself.)

To me this self-haunted spider appears a figure of each obstinate impenitent sinner, who having outlived enjoyment remains isolated irretrievably with his own horrible loathsome self.

And if thus in time, how throughout eternity? (*TF*, pp. 121–2)

Like the Coleridge's Ancient Mariner and his dead albatross, to Rossetti the double can represent man's 'horrible loathsome self', as a harbinger of death, since sin brings death, and also as retribution for wrongs. In 'Goblin Market' it is made clear that Jeanie died for her sins, and Lizzie escapes that fate only due to the intervention of Laura. Akin to the spectre, the double is a creation of the mind which serves to emphasize what we already know, be it the coming of death or the guilt of sin.

This is especially pertinent to 'Goblin Market', in which Rossetti explores doubles in a variety of ways, such as doubling the 'fallen' woman with her 'unfallen' counterpart. Here, Laura and Lizzie are similar in every respect, sleeping 'golden head by golden head' (l. 184), yet only one succumbs to the charms of the goblin fruit, and must be rescued by her more virtuous sister.[13] That the two girls are a representation of two sides of one character is a possible interpretation in a psychological reading of the poem which credits the same, dual character with both fall and redemption. Doubling is a form of fragmentation of the self, if one assumes that the unconscious mind is doubled with the conscious. Where Laura and Lizzie are doubled, two characters with a single destiny, they remain indistinct in appearance according to Rossetti's poem. The self has its good and evil aspects, which Gothic novels represent frequently, and this is explored here as a struggle between the two sides of one nature. When Laura accepts the goblin fruit, her fate seems sealed, like Jeanie. If one assumes that Lizzie is not merely a good sister but an aspect of Laura, then the redemption of Laura owes more to transference or self-interest than to sisterhood. The possibility of saving oneself therefore appears paramount in 'Goblin Market', but must be facilitated – that is, it is dependent on someone else. By confronting the goblins with a manifestation of her better nature, Laura can save herself. The struggle between good and evil is here suggestively personified as two characters rather than one, an internal struggle which features in many of Rossetti's poems.

Marsh uses this example to align Rossetti with Aestheticism and Decadence, and submits that 'this dark side *is* Christina Rossetti, both in literary terms and in devotional terms' (Liebregts and Tigges, 1996, p. 28). I am suggesting that this image of the 'self-haunted spider', or the literary double, appears throughout much of Rossetti's work, but to greatest effect in 'Goblin Market'. As Laura wastes away after her taste of the goblin fruit, she becomes a shadow of Lizzie, no longer 'Like two pigeons in one nest' (l. 185). This notion of the spectre-sister which is both other and the same emphasizes the spectral, ever-present nature of sin. The ghost of Jeanie, whom Chapman describes as a 'precursor' who is 'associated with diminishment and depletion', serves as a reminder of the fate of the fallen woman, an 'other' who haunts the text (2000, p. 148).

In 'The Uncanny', Freud suggests that the very notion of the *unheimlich* or uncanny is doubled with the *heimlich*, the familiar. In the doubling of Laura and Lizzie, where Laura becomes the spectre of her sister, this is exactly what Rossetti has done. Freud goes on to suggest that the double becomes the 'harbinger of death', and to accept this is to conclude that the redemptive element of 'Goblin Market' is its central theme:

> For the 'double' was originally an insurance against the destruction of the ego, an 'energetic denial of the power of death', as Rank says; and probably the 'immortal' soul was the first 'double' of the body [. . .]. Such ideas, however, have sprung from the soil of unbounded self-love, from the primary narcissism which holds sway in the mind of the child as in that of primitive man. (1949, p. 387)

Where the fallen woman is concerned, if 'the wages of sin is death' (Romans 6.23) then the doubling of the character only emphasizes what the reader already knows. D. G. Rossetti also uses this trope in 'Jenny', where the speaker reflects upon the fallen woman, Jenny, and his 'pure' cousin, saying 'Of the same lump (it has been said) | For honour and dishonour made, | Two sister vessels' (ll. 203–5). The image of the fallen woman asleep 'Just as another woman sleeps' (l. 176) is reminiscent of the sisters of 'Goblin Market' asleep side by side; and yet to read too much into the links between these poems is to ignore their differences. While D. G. Rossetti may be pitying Jenny and considering the wrongs inflicted by society, he is nonetheless implicated by his presence in her room. The doubled figure in 'Jenny' might appear similarly constructed to those in 'Goblin Market', but their meanings are very different. As Lawrence Starzyk asks, 'Is her [Jenny's] charm, he wonders, affected to waylay the convert from his noble "aims"?' (2000, p. 231). Starzyk points out the implicit concept in 'Jenny' that it is potentially the woman here who is the seducer, being suspect by her very fallenness. For the speaker of 'Jenny':

> Salvation in a world devoid of the divine must depend on the only pure thing among men – a 'woman's heart' (250). [. . .] The real reason for the hopelessness

of the human condition is not the inability of the pure woman to read the text
of life, but rather the innate compulsion of man to corrupt any text he attempts
to read. (p. 233)

In 'Jenny', hope of salvation is destroyed by the man's presence, Starzyk suggests,
yet in 'Goblin Market' salvation comes through Lizzie's pure heart, contradicting
the essence of D. G. Rossetti's poem.

Gothic and fairy tale

Gothic and fairy tale are closely linked in 'Goblin Market', sharing many of the
same characteristics. If, as McDayter argues, it is the fantastic with which readers
identify in readings of Gothic, it would be logical to assume a similar aspect
in the reading of fairy tale. This is borne out by other analyses of the primary
qualities and functions of fairy tale. For example, Swann Jones (2002) suggests
four of these:

> fairytales depict magical or marvellous events or phenomena as a valid part of
> human experience. (p. 9)
>
> the confronting and resolving of a problem, frequently by the undertaking of a
> quest, [is] essential to the fairy tale. (p. 14)
>
> This happy ending is such a basic and important aspect of the genre, it may be
> regarded as a third definitional feature. (p. 17)
>
> A fourth quality of the fairytale is that the audience is encouraged to identify
> strongly with the central protagonist, who is presented in an unambiguous way.
> (p. 17)

These criteria are all met in 'Goblin Market', which may be why the poem is
frequently identified as a poem for children. These aspects, however, are also an
intrinsic part of the traditional Gothic novel, such as those of Radcliffe. Warner
(1994) notes the absent mother, the happy ending and the presence of magic as
intrinsic to the fairy tale, and these aspects are shared with Gothic writing.

The use of the supernatural, or 'magic', is common in Gothic. Though many
writers, such as Radcliffe, provide human explanations for the apparently
supernatural (yet without dispelling the air of mystery), many, including Maturin
and Matthew Lewis, do not. The supernatural aspect of the Gothic appears in
the form of the goblins, and the enchanted fruit, as well as its occult effect on
Laura. The liminal space of the 'glen' where the goblins operate provides an area

for magical discourse not unlike the wood in *A Midsummer Night's Dream,* where magic may happen and is contained. A particularly threatening aspect of 'Goblin Market' is that the magic is not contained within its designated space, but invades the home of the girls. This is significant, since it demonstrates a penetration of boundaries, a threat which reaches inward to a sacred space, and is representative of the central theme of violation in the poem: of the girls' bodies, their minds and their home.

Arguably, 'Goblin Market' can be situated at a point where Gothic and fairy tale intersect, where the supernatural threat is real, crossing the threshold into the apparently safe and domestic space: but the quest can be resolved from within the heroine. Moreover, the poem's plot contrasts two dominant strands of nineteenth-century literary thought: realism (in the girls and their domestic centre) and fairy tale or the fantastic, in the goblins and their fruit. It is this juxtaposition of the everyday with the supernatural that provides the appearance of Gothic, as well as emphasizing the presence of the grotesque.

Like early Gothic novels, the poem appears to offer a moral to young, female readers, which allies the genre to fairy tale. The closing couplets of 'Goblin Market', with a more regular rhythm and rhyme than hitherto, provide a neat moral ending to the more disorderly tale:

> Then joining hands to little hands
> Would bid them cling together,
> 'For there is no friend like a sister,
> In calm or stormy weather,
> To cheer one on the tedious way,
> To fetch one if one goes astray,
> To lift one if one totters down,
> To strengthen whilst one stands.' (ll. 560–7)

This closure seems so final, as if the past can be easily dispelled and even laughed at. Such a dismissal of the events of the poem seems problematic, as though trivializing the troubling story, although some critics take a more positive message from the moral:

> The pragmatism of Rossetti's message would have been particularly empowering to the Victorian woman, stemming from the kinds of experience that made up the greater part of her life. The volume is the fulfilment of Rossetti's early appeals to sisterhood, the reassurance that 'there is no friend like a sister' from 'Goblin Market'. (Palazzo, 2002, p. 103)

Equally, however, it is possible to argue the reverse: that sisterhood is less significant to the poem than the sensual aspects, and that the goblins and their fruit provide the central focus, rather than the salvation of one sister by another, thus largely negating the moral, which seems a hasty addition in its different measure. If the aphoristic closure of the poem seems at odds with the rest of the text, this implies that Rossetti wished to emphasize one aspect of the poem above the others, elevating the importance of sisterhood above the threat, the fall and the salvation the poem depicts. Arguably this is a characteristic of many fairy tales, however, in which a moral closure places a stress on one, pious attribute of the text, but without managing to eliminate the terror which may have preceded it.

As Freud points out, many of the issues of Gothic, the spectral and the uncanny in literature are motifs which are familiar in fairy tales, and which are therefore both familiar, and assumed to offer a kind of childhood morality. His example from Hoffman's tales illustrates this, and there are many other examples throughout the tales of the Brothers Grimm, for example. This is an idea still popular in current pop-psychology, with books such as *Spinning Straw into Gold* (Gould, 2005). Gould suggests that fairy tales provide an early training for adulthood, but of course this training includes warnings. Similarly, Schiller states that 'Deeper meaning resides in the fairy tales told to me in my childhood than in the truth that is taught by life' (*The Piccolomini*, III, p. 4, cited in Bettelheim, 1991, p. 5). The popular understanding is that morality is often gleaned unconsciously from the tales of childhood, and as a consequence extensive work has been done on the psychology of fairy tales, by scholars such as Bruno Bettelheim. Yet Rossetti's poem does not seem to fit the model of morality tale, despite the desire of early readers to fit it to this pattern; its concentration on disobedience and the sensual seems to override the potential moral.

Knoepflmacher highlights the rationalism of the eighteenth- and nineteenth-century women writers for children, concentrating on good behaviour above all else, commenting on Charles Lamb's 'derision of writers such as Anna Barbauld and Sarah Trimmer as malignant censors of the child's unreason' (1998, p. 19). A dynamic of male Romantic writers against female Utilitarian writers is set up by Knoepflmacher's discussion. This, he posits, is in part due to the female writers' resistance to the idealization of motherhood and children due to their proximity to these apparently hallowed states. Rossetti conflates these two inherited positions, adopting, if not the Romanticist view of childhood, at least the idealization of nature which accompanies it. For example, Rossetti writes in *Sing-Song*:

> When a mounting skylark sings
> In the sunlit summer morn,
> I know that heaven is up on high,
> And on earth are fields of corn.
> But when a nightingale sings
> In the moonlit summer even,
> I know not if earth is merely earth,
> Only that heaven is heaven. (ll. 1–8)

Rossetti here appears to take a Wordsworthian aesthetic approach in permitting the natural world to indicate the sublime. However, rather than describing scenery with lofty grandeur, as does Wordsworth, she takes a homely approach which is more likely to appeal to children, rooting her spiritual meaning in familiar sights and sounds.

This approach is not only an extrapolation of Romantic ideals. It is also particularly embedded in Tractarian thought, with its emphasis on the natural sublime as a motif emblematic of God's creation. Though Rossetti's approach to nature is by no means unproblematic, as is demonstrated by the seduction of Laura by the tainted fruit in 'Goblin Market', she broadly follows the comments of Keble in Tract 89, *On the Mysticism Attributed to the Fathers of the Church*, in which the relationship between the natural world and the spiritual is explained through 'a particular set of symbols and associations, which we have reason to believe has, more or less, the authority of the Great Creator Himself'. The path from earthly to spiritual is laid out here as a typological explanation for human understanding. It is precisely this form of extrapolation of the spiritual from the apparently mundane which Rossetti employs in many of her poems, not only in *Sing-Song* but throughout her work. These 'familiar Tractarian evidences of God in Nature' form the fundament of Rossetti's beliefs, and in particular provide her with ample material for Christian teaching (Tennyson, 1981, p. 151).

In order to consider Rossetti's treatment of fairy tale in more detail, I propose to examine 'Goblin Market' in the light of Jack Zipes's analysis of fairy tale in *Fairy Tales and the Art of Subversion*, in which he considers the social significance of fairy tales, and their retelling, from Perrault through to the Grimm Brothers. Zipes discusses how the fairy tale operated as a form of social control, a discourse from which children (in particular, though not exclusively) learned not so much morality as social conformity to the patriarchal norms. Zipes's analysis states that, as a general rule:

> Initially the young protagonist must leave home or the family because power
> relations have been disturbed. Either the protagonist is wronged, or a change in

social relations forces the protagonist to depart from home. A task is imposed, and a hidden command of the tale must be fulfilled. The question which most of Grimm's tales ask is: how can one learn – what must one do to use one's powers rightly in order to be accepted in society or recreate society in keeping with the norms of the *status quo*? [. . .] The female hero learns to be passive, obedient, self-sacrificing, hard-working, patient, and straight-laced. Her goal is wealth, jewels, and a man to protect her property rights. Her jurisdiction is the home or castle. Her happiness depends on conformity to patriarchal rule. Sexual activity is generally postponed until after marriage. Often the tales imply a postponement of gratification until the necessary skills, power, and wealth are acquired. (1983, p. 46)

In the light of this it seems as though 'Goblin Market' begins where a traditional fairy tale ends: two girls are living alone in a house without parental control. In fact there are no authority figures against which to rebel in this tale; throughout, the girls are responsible for their own and each other's destiny, reliant on their sense of right and wrong. Of course, a place to live free of parental restraint is a childhood fantasy, free of duties and responsibilities, though Rossetti sets up the girls' home as a domestic idyll, with each doing her share of the tasks. Yet the domestic centre, the home the girls share, does not appear in the poem until after Laura has succumbed to the goblins' temptation. Before this, the setting of the poem relies on natural imagery as the girls appear to wander 'among the brookside rushes' and 'up the mossy glen', in a setting familiar from William Allingham's 1850 poem 'The Fairies', which opens 'Up the airy mountain, down the rushy glen, | We daren't go a-hunting for fear of little men' (ll. 1–2). After Laura eats the fruit, she returns home, and this is the first mention in the poem of the girls' domestic arrangements. Clearly as the sisters sleep side by side, and fetch honey, milk cows and bake bread, their home is their own – as though they are children playing at 'house'. However, the evil that has occurred works on Laura in their home; the taint of the goblin fruit has crossed the threshold with her, corrupting their sanctuary where it begins to seem that she will die. It is when Lizzie leaves the house to subject herself to the goblins as her sister did that restoration begins. The relationship between 'inside', or the domestic world, and 'outside', the natural world, is complicated here, and the domestic ending, does not provide a convincing solution. The house provides no sanctuary, the boundaries are blurred, since evil can enter so easily; in order to exterminate the threat of the outside world, it appears that one must remain outside the domestic sanctuary.

Nature therefore does not appear innocent; the threat posed by the goblins and their seductive fruit is one of which the girls are clearly aware. I would suggest that the power of the fruit is subtly indicated in 'Goblin Market' by echoes of the fruit with which Titania feeds Bottom, seducing him into the dangerous world of fairyland: 'Feed him with apricots and dewberries, | With purple grapes, green figs and mulberries' (*A Midsummer Night's Dream*, Act III, scene ii, ll. 158–9). Like the bewitched Bottom in the liminal space of the wood, knowledge of the threat posed by the goblins does not prevent Laura's 'fall'. This corresponds exactly with Zipes's analysis of Perrault's *Little Red Riding Hood*, in which the author reinvents the heroine to suit his audience:

> Instead of really warning the girls against the dangers of predators in forests, the tale warns the girls against their own natural desires which they must tame. The brave little peasant girl, who can fend for herself and shows qualities of courage and cleverness, is transformed into a delicate bourgeois type, who is helpless, naïve and culpable, if not stupid. In the folk tale the little girl displays a natural, relaxed attitude towards her body and sex, and meets the challenge of a would-be seducer. In Perrault's literary fairy tale Little Red Riding Hood is chastized because she is innocently disposed towards nature in the form of the wolf and woods, and she is raped or punished because she is guilty of not controlling her natural inclinations. (1983, p. 29)

It is therefore possible to read 'Goblin Market' as a warning that one must control one's natural desires, particularly curiosity. Warner discusses the moral fairy tale as 'in line with cautionary tales about women's innate wickedness: with Pandora who opened the forbidden casket as well as Eve who ate of the forbidden fruit' (1994, p. 244). Unlike the Gothic novel, in which curiosity is usually rewarded, if not lauded, Warner implies that the fairy tale seems to condemn the inquisitive female in tales such as 'Bluebeard'. The girls of 'Goblin Market' learn a salutary lesson, but, it seems, are none the worse for it, concluding with an apparently idyllic future, and, like the women of Gothic novels, bearing only traces of memory of their experiences.

There are some illuminating issues to consider about the intersection of fantasy and the Gothic. Jackson posits that fantasy must be understood in the light of historical and social context, rather than considered as transcendentalist, in part because fantasy operates on the borders of social convention, 'characteristically attempt[ing] to compensate for a lack resulting from cultural constraints: it is a literature of desire, which seeks that which is experienced as absence and loss' (1981, p. 3). Moreover, and most apposite for 'Goblin Market', Jackson describes the literature of fantasy as 'expressing desire':

> [F]antasy can operate in two ways (according to the different meanings of 'express'): it can *tell of*, manifest or show desire [. . .] or it can *expel desire*, when this desire is a disturbing element which threatens cultural order. (p. 3)

Rossetti's poem clearly comprises a poetics of desire and repression, quest for satisfaction, and eventual resolution (which is the loss or suppression of that desire), figured as a politics of redemption and salvation. Jan Marsh reads the poem as a reworking of the Anglican Eucharist, in which the consumption of the fruit via the body of Lizzie may be likened to the bread and wine which reflects the consumption of the body of Christ. This aspect is particularly pertinent to the Tractarian Rossetti, since the Tractarian arguments for the real presence in the bread and wine were collapsing the boundaries between the spiritual and physical just as the allegorical poem itself does. Marsh's arguments are convincing; however, there are other, secular parallels in fairy tales which also deal with redemption, of a physical rather than spiritual kind. One such is *Cinderella*, where a heroine falls from favour to become the 'Ash-girl' and is rescued and restored to her rightful place by a prince.[14] Laura's 'fall' is of course as much spiritual as physical, and moreover the redeemer is Lizzie, the sister who is quite unlike the spiteful, jealous sisters of many fairy tales. The trial of Cinderella, the fitting of the shoe, which in many older tales was a sexual trial, equates to the attack of the goblins upon Laura; in effect, both Laura and Lizzie fill the role of Cinderella, both falling and effecting their own salvation. Rossetti's take on the fairy-tale prince as rescuer can be seen in 'The Prince's Progress', a tale which is manifestly an allegory of human life based on *The Pilgrim's Progress*, but which owes as much in its fairy-tale telling to *The Sleeping Beauty* – only the Prince dallies on the way and arrives 'Too late for love, too late for joy, | Too late, too late!' (ll. 481–2).

A final parallel in the motifs of fairy tale may be found in *Beauty and the Beast*. The goblins of 'Goblin Market' and their function as seducers in the poem are superficially clear-cut: they are described as animalistic, at first, yet with voices 'kind and full of loves' (l. 79), and the girls have no fear of them. When Lizzie refuses to eat the fruit, however, the domestic animals become savage ones; they attack her and eventually run away. The illustrations of the goblins which have accompanied various editions of the poem bring out these different aspects. Zipes suggests that the beast in *Beauty and the Beast* and also in traditional folktales of animal bridegrooms is an agent of sexuality which must necessarily remain disgusting to children for as long as sexual behaviour is associated solely with the parent. Once the bride is ready to accept a bridegroom, symbolized in *Beauty and the Beast* by a kiss, the beast becomes a handsome prince. It is therefore possible to read Rossetti's goblins as men who desire the girls before they are ready to explore their sexuality. In support of this argument, Zipes quotes Heide Gottner-Abendroth, 'Matriarchale Mythologie', in which the man is:

> a wild, roving beast [. . .] in most of the animal bridegroom tales, and this condition represents his homelessness and undomesticity. That is, in the eyes of the matriarchal woman, who created a cultivated environment for herself, he has never developed beyond the condition of a predatory animal that roams the woods. He is still covered by fur or feathers, while she wears human clothes which she herself has made. The male condition as human is not yet extant, or it is one of 'death', which is the meaning of the state of 'enchantment' as beast. (1983, p. 49)

By the closing lines of 'Goblin Market', however, the girls have become wives and mothers, though there is no mention of their husbands. As Sharon Smulders says, sisterhood pushes these 'husbands and fathers into the margins of the poem's conclusion' (1996, p. 41). These unobtrusive men, following Zipes's argument, could be the very goblins who once attacked them, civilized and tamed by their contact with the sisters. Fanciful as this seems, it is the premise of fairy tale. Rossetti's work complicates the issues of fairy tale, however, by manifesting a latent eroticism. It is perhaps this complication which has discouraged serious consideration of the poem as an aspect of fairy tale. As early reviewers identified, Rossetti's poem defies genre and boundaries, and even makes readers uncomfortable.

In writing 'Goblin Market', Rossetti draws on a number of literary antecedents whose attributes offer much to the fantastic and to fairy tale, as well as early aspects of Gothic. For example, the Rossettis read the works of Milton, and it is possible to link 'Goblin Market' to the fall of Adam and Eve as depicted in *Paradise Lost*, and also to *Comus*, a play which Vevjoda (2000) claims may even have inspired 'Goblin Market'.[15] Like Rossetti's poem, it takes place in a liminal space in which magic may happen, and represents a kind of 'fall' and redemption. Milton's play offers a fairy-tale story in adult form; if Milton's poem is a precursor to Rossetti's, then readings which relate the poem to threatened virtue seem correct. In *Comus*, the action takes place in the liminal space of an enchanted wood, much like Rossetti's poem, and in a castle which serves as Comus's den of iniquity. The natural world is seen as an excuse for licentiousness in *Comus*, although the Lady refutes blame for 'innocent Nature' (l. 762), shifting the blame entirely onto his character. The Lady is ultimately saved by her own arguments and her faith in her own chastity; she tells her would-be seducer that 'Thou canst not touch the freedom of my minde' (l. 662). Like Lizzie, she is able to remain above her attack because her mind is free and pure, despite the physical indignities she may suffer. The Lady, however, remains immobilized until Sabrina undoes the charm put upon her by Comus; the nymph rescues the Lady because 'maid'nhood she loves, and will be swift | To aid a virgin such as was herself' (ll. 854–5). The Lady's circumstances may not be her fault, but still she requires a rescuer.

Monsters and vampires

The threat to the girls in 'Goblin Market' derives primarily from the goblins, who, despite their apparent smallness, seem to be of the same vicious race as the vampiric cannibal savages of *The Faerie Queen*, which Rossetti had read.[16]

> The damzell wakes; then all attonce upstart,
> And round about her flocke, like many flies,
> Whooping and hallowing on every part,
> As if they would have rent the brasen skies. (Book VI, Canto viii, stanza 40, ll. 352–5)

These monsters attack Serena after she has been caught in a compromising position in Book III and attacked by the Blatant Beast. The poem thus continuously links a sexual fall to a vampiric masculine attack, and only virtue can save the fallen from their fate. The overtones of cannibalism and of lust are unmistakable in both poems, and in fact the language of the two poems is surprisingly similar. The attack on Serena, like that on Lizzie, makes uncomfortable reading:

> The preparations for the sacrifice are narrated in great detail, as are the reactions of the cannibals to the sight of the naked Serena, creating a voyeuristic spectacle which has distressed (and fascinated) numerous readers owing to its graphic, pornographic, lingering over the helpless female body, making the connection between sex and male violence explicit. (Hadfield, 1997, p. 179)

Like the goblins, Spenser's cannibals group themselves around their victim, although in *The Faerie Queene* they do not have the opportunity to attack her before she is rescued, instead stripping her and placing her before their altar.

Both poems offer a spectacle of helpless women, and this sacrifice of female flesh, as retribution for 'fallenness', seems extreme, but supplies a situation for redemption and renewal which both poems provide. The significant difference is that in Rossetti's poem the figure who is attacked is innocent, taking on the sins of her sister; Spenser's poem offers a more conventional rescue of a lady by a knight.

It is possible to read into the discourses of 'Goblin Market' the existence of a specific monster: the vampire. Moers points out that the central verb is 'to suck', and, while emphasizing that she is not suggesting that this is 'a Victorian celebration of oral sex', she posits that it is about the 'erotic life of children' (1978, p. 102). Indeed, the women of many illustrations of the poem seem to be offering their necks for 'sucking', surrendering in what appears to be sexual ecstasy rather than resisting as the noble Lizzie of the poem. However, other critics discuss this possibility more seriously. Nancee Reeves has suggested that Rossetti is likely to have equated the fallen woman with the female vampire, in a femme fatale figure which owes much to Coleridge's 'Christabel'. Another critic, David Morrill, takes the concept of vampirism further by aligning 'Goblin Market' with Polidori's *The Vampyre*. Whether or not one agrees with this argument, the concept of vampirism as an aspect of the poem is convincing; he points out Polidori's footnote that 'The universal belief is that a person sucked by a vampyre becomes a vampyre himself, and sucks in his turn' (Morrill, 1990, p. 3), again emphasizing the 'sucking' or consuming aspect of the poem. Morrill's argument centres upon Rossetti's use of 'certain details of the vampiric myth – acts of biting and sucking, enervation, and death without grace' (p. 1). Significantly, he suggests that Rossetti takes what is a 'scientific [. . .] footnote' in Polidori's story and transforms it into an 'erotic' narrative (p. 3). While this may be true, the underlying sensuality of Polidori's tale, particularly contained in the apparent physical magnetism of Lord Ruthven, created a similarly seductive atmosphere.

The vampire, like the goblins, causes potential victims 'the most fundamental anxiety about boundaries of the self: fear of physical violation' (DeLaMotte, 1990, p. 29). The vampire, of course, can violate not only the body but the soul, a source of ultimate fear for Rossetti. In Polidori's tale, Aubrey knows the vampire's secret, and this alone is enough to contaminate his mind and consequently affect his body, as the description of him demonstrates: 'There he would often lie for days, incapable of being roused. He had become emaciated, his eyes had attained a glassy stare' (2001, p. 65). This description is comparable to Rossetti's Laura, who 'dwindling | Seem'd knocking at Death's door' (ll. 320–1), who sits inert and unable to participate in life after her experience with the goblin fruit.

Yet Rossetti's poem ultimately redeems and subverts Polidori's narrative. While, as Morrill points out, 'Lord Ruthven and the goblins function as a symbol for all that is corrupting in the world' (p. 10), in 'Goblin Market' that corruption of innocence can be subverted, as one sister offers salvation to the other; in 'The Vampyre', innocence and sibling love are helpless against the threat of the monster. Morrison, whose 1997 article builds on the work of Morrill, demonstrates how the innovations to the vampire tale which were instigated by Polidori are muted or modified by Rossetti, most notably in the focus on femininity and sisterhood. While there are parallels to be drawn between the two texts in terms of the figures of the monsters, and their effects on their victims, ultimately it is difficult to provide convincing equivalencies in the potential allegorical meanings of the works.

The poem has become known as a children's classic despite these monsters, an issue which became further blurred when, in 1972, the poem was published in *Playboy* magazine alongside illustrations by Kinuko Craft. Clearly setting out to shock, *Playboy* drew heavily on the fairy-tale aspect of the poem, writing an introduction which paired the sensual aspects of the poem with its supposed infant audience. The introduction suggests that Rossetti, disappointed at the end of a romance:

> sublimated her distress by writing a poem for children – a long poem called 'Goblin Market' [...] the poem became a Victorian nursery classic, still reprinted and read to this day. Ostensibly, it is a scary narrative about two beautiful maiden sisters who get mixed up with a sinister tribe of goblins. How really sinister and scary it is, given just a Freudian glance, has never been openly discussed. (*Playboy*, 1973, p. 115)

While *Playboy*'s intention is clearly both to amuse and to shock, the article serves the purpose of bringing such aspects of the poem to the fore, and emphasizing their apparent inappropriateness in conjunction with each other. In Craft's images there are considerably more goblins than in other illustrations, swarming over the bodies of the girls, seeming dehumanized, more animal than human, with lascivious eyes which are fiercer by far than the cunning slyness of Rackham's goblins. The nursery beasts which beset the girls in Rossetti's poem would be familiar to nineteenth-century readers from fairy tales and other works of the period, but *Playboy* transforms them into sexual predators. Craft makes it clear that against so many goblins, bent on having their way with the girls, there is no hope of escape for them. Her illustrations seem to suggest that the girls surrender themselves not only to a previously unthought-of sexuality, but to the possibility of sexual pleasure with creatures not of their own species. Kooistra, in her appraisal of illustrations of the poem, says that 'The lush sensuousness of the poem's imagery, coupled with its representation of gender relations as a predatory politics between grotesque, aggressive males and innocent, suffering females [. . .] has had inherent appeal for the post-Freudian imagination' (2002, p. 241). This appropriation of fantastic creatures is one of the most evident parallels between 'Goblin Market', Gothic and fairy tale. Bettelheim, writing in the vein of Freud, suggests that the 'monsters' in fairy tales are important to children and adults because they represent the unconscious, the other of which the child is afraid without recognizing that it is part of them. Fairy tales, he argues, permit children to learn to identify and exorcise the repression which has caused these monsters. By this logic, the defeated goblins provide a moral lesson for young readers.

Such references to supernatural monsters are crucial for the development of the atmosphere of threat and fear to which the poem owes much of its power. The concept of an ultimately safe domestic centre, where the girls 'both were wives | With children of their own (ll. 544–5) suggests the traditional conclusion to the novels of Ann Radcliffe, for example, in which the family, while a source of threat, is finally a place of security. The concept of an ultimate union which will dilute, if not negate, past terrors, is significant in the light of Rossetti's faith. Her late prose works, especially *The Face of the Deep*, follow in many ways a similar trajectory of threat, fear, horror, redemption, salvation and, finally, unity with a Bridegroom, rather than the threat of unity with a terrible other, spectre or vampire, long past. Yet in 'Goblin Market', despite the closing aphorism, and the sisters' dreamy recollections of 'The wicked, quaint fruit merchant-men' (l. 553), the threat is not quite negated, nor quite forgotten. Rossetti's goblins and their fruit leave a mark on the reader of a fear that remains on the margins, not quite dispelled – perhaps, in part, because of its very ambiguity.

Shadows of Heaven: Rossetti's Prose Works

There is one dangerous science for women – one which they must indeed beware how they profanely touch – that of theology.[1]

Late in her life, having already established herself as a poet, Rossetti produced six volumes of devotional prose, which combined biblical exegesis with poetry and excerpts from scripture. *Annus Domini: A Prayer for Each Day of the Year, Founded on Holy Scripture* (1874), *Seek and Find: A Double Series of Short Meditations on the Benedicite* (1879), *Called to be Saints: The Minor Festivals Devotionally Studied* (1881), *Letter and Spirit: Notes on the Commandments* (1883), *Time Flies: A Reading Diary* (1885) and *The Face of the Deep: A Devotional Commentary on the Apocalypse* (1892) must be Rossetti's least-studied works today, despite their publication in facsimile in 2003.[2] Yet as Maria Keaton points out: 'Recovering Rossetti's religious prose allows the reader of her poetry to understand some of the foundations of her poetic experience, because these prose texts are largely devoted to correlating her spiritual and philosophical ideas with her aesthetics' (*CS*, p. vi). Keaton's comment relates to Rossetti's tendency to demonstrate spiritual truths by reference to the natural world, and to her deep absorption in biblical texts. This chapter will suggest that it is in her faith that the roots of Rossetti's Gothic lie, and that these Gothic threads can be traced in her prose works. For this purpose, the most significant volumes are *Letter and Spirit* and, particularly, *The Face of the Deep*, which will be discussed in detail in this chapter. These two texts demonstrate the way in which Gothic interacts with the Christian faith in Rossetti's works, particularly with reference to some of the topics that have been discussed in previous chapters. It is through these later devotional works that the source of Rossettian Gothic becomes apparent.

This chapter will therefore examine Rossetti's prose works in the light of the aspects of Gothic covered in earlier chapters, particularly with reference to her depiction of women and the use of thresholds and boundaries to denote the crossing or transgressing of a barrier, be that literal, as is often the case in Gothic novels, or social or spiritual. For example, particularly in this latter instance, I suggest that it becomes clear on reading *The Face of the Deep* that Rossetti locates the often rather vague and generalized Gothic trope of the threshold specifically in the book of Revelation, where the final crossing of the barrier between earth and heaven is achieved. As this chapter will discuss, this crossing of thresholds is further reflected in the reading experience offered by Rossetti's texts. Throughout the prose, moreover, her aesthetics, from the grand sweep of the mountains to the tiny decomposing body of a mouse, appear to refer to the Gothic genre, when in fact they relate most closely to biblical sources. From this, it is possible to infer the extent to which Gothic may derive from the Bible, especially the book of Revelation, with its grandeur and fear, its deployment of the grotesque and the spectral, and its details of the Apocalypse.

Although the prose works tend to be considered as a homogenous group, in fact they are remarkably different in many ways, though a range of similarities emerges. Rossetti's departure from writing mostly poetry to producing such extended works of theology was in many ways due to the strength of her faith, but also to her desire to write in prose, and experiment in different genres. One might argue that, while her theology alters little, if at all, over time, her writing is increasingly impacted by her faith. *Called to be Saints*, for example, examines saints of the Christian year, offering biographical detail, scriptural reference, a relevant prayer and a commentary on a living creature, semi-precious stone and a plant associated with each of the 21 saints. Tractarianism revived Anglican interest in the lives of the saints, such as those by Tractarian writer J. M. Neale, whose book *Annals of Virgin Saints* (1846) Rossetti is likely to have read, and, later, Sabine Baring Gould's 16-volume *The Lives of the Saints* (published 1914). Neale's work in particular considers the devotional benefits for his readers of an understanding of hagiography. In our falls, he implies, we are comforted by the saints. Yet Neale's text is clearly aimed at women, not only in his choice of female 'virgin saints', but also in his discursive prose, which addresses women directly:

> [Y]ou are, in a double degree, indebted to her [the Holy Church]. To woman she has given even more than to man; – more in a spiritual sense she could not; more in a temporal sense she could and did bestow. Before that Blessed above woman had been privileged to reverse the curse of Eve, so that as death came by a woman, by a Woman should also life come. (1846, p. xxxii)

Addressing unmarried women in particular, Neale is clear about the benefits of Christian faith, and the examples of this set by the martyrs. Clearly Rossetti also intended scriptural readings and reflections on their lives to serve as a devotional aid to her readers, yet her work is far less gender-specific than Neale's. In this volume, she also defends her exegetical work:

> But if one object that many of my suggestions are exploded superstitions or mere freaks of fancy without basis of truth; and that if I have fancied this another may fancy that, and another again that, till the whole posse of idle thinkers puts forth each his fresh fancy, and all alike without basis; I frankly answer, Yes: so long as with David our musings are on God's works, among the chief whereof is His sinful Saint made perfect; and so long as with St. Timothy our meditations are on charity, faith, purity, which array the Saints of Christ in a robe more excellent than the glory of Solomon or the loveliness of a lily. (*CS*, p. xiv)

Only a few years before Dean Burgon's 1884 sermon against the admission of women to Oxford colleges, in which he expressed some doubt about the advisability of educating women to the same level as men, Rossetti's erudite published discussions of scripture demonstrate the validity of women's religious writings.[3] Her stalwart defence of her work in *Called to be Saints* affirms the significance of exegetical writing with no reference to gender, but rather to the necessary purity of the heart which writes, a theory familiar from Ruskin's earlier writings. This defence not only evades the gender debate, but opens the way for Rossetti to discuss aspects of Christian life and faith in her own idiosyncratic way. Many of the issues on which she touches in these volumes, including the Fall and the nature of evil, are controversial, yet, couched in Rossetti's careful prose and scrupulously linked with biblical references, controversy appears to have been largely avoided. Although contemporary reviews of her prose are scarce, the sales were good, and, as D'Amico points out, 'Certainly, both men and women were buying and reading these works. Possibly, Anglican vicars read Rossetti and occasionally drew upon her teaching for their sermons' (1999, p. 148). Unlike many of her contemporary female writers of Christian prose, Rossetti does not choose to concentrate upon advice on Christian life for women, but rather exercises her interest in theology much more widely, and indeed much more boldly, despite the apologies for her work which she offers in several of these volumes.[4] Roe argues that, in its structure and form, 'her devotional prose work was written with a Christian female audience in mind, and much of its content is geared toward the female experience of reading the Bible' (p. 97). Yet when reading Rossetti's prose it is rarely evident that she aimed primarily at a purely female readership due to her inclusive language and subject matter.

Indeed, Julie Melnyk makes a clear distinction between religious and theological prose produced by women in the nineteenth century, arguing that 'Women's writing on religious topics – those related to devotion, conduct, worship – was tolerated and even encouraged' while 'this encouragement of women's religious work and literature did not extend to theological writing. While Victorian religious discourse was gendered neutral or even slightly feminised, theology [. . .] remained a clearly masculine discourse' (p. xi). Yet, as Melnyk goes on to explain, clearly the theological activity among some women writers was seen as enough of a threat for Ruskin to comment vehemently upon it in *Of Queens' Gardens* (1865).[5] Despite such tirades, women including Rossetti felt drawn to write exegetical prose.

Called to be Saints

Called to be Saints draws upon the lives of the saints in the Anglican liturgical calendar, all of whom, with the exception of the Virgin Mary, are male. Though Rossetti had an interest in hagiography generally, it appears that she chose to focus expressly on the saints of the Anglican Church. Each saint is examined exhaustively: much scripture relating to each one is quoted, and some additional biographical material provided. Rossetti's narratives are generally fairly brief, due, she admits, to a lack of information in many cases. The book opens with a chapter titled 'The Key to My Book', in which she explains: 'Much of my material can only be drawn from uncertain traditions' (*CS*, p. xvi). Scrupulous as ever, she emphasizes that her work is based on the Authorized Version of the Bible, and that she will provide scriptural references so that her readers can trace the original sources, but the information about the saints may be based on legend: 'nor have I hesitated partly to construct my so-called "Memorials" on a legendary foundation' (*CS*, p. xvi). Her belief that legend, rather than fact, will suffice, points to the purpose of the book: it is not a history of the saints, but rather an exposition designed to aid the reader's devotions. Her free use of myth is perhaps a writerly trait which is prepared to favour a story, especially a moral tale, over facts obscured by time. The devotional aspect of the volume is emphasized by Rossetti's inclusion of prayers and, particularly, the natural imagery of gemstones, plants and animals associated with saints. As Keaton suggests in her introduction:

The use of natural objects as symbols for the spiritual is present in Rossetti's Christian tradition from its inception, but with the Tractarian movement and its revival of the use of many kinds of sensory symbols, the idea that nature itself provided the first and most available way by which human beings might both know and explain more about the divine gained considerable currency within the Anglican Church. (*CS*, p. x)

It is impossible to ignore the importance of natural imagery in the Bible, which may have secured its centrality in poetry in the Christian tradition. Tractarianism, however, restores a theological significance to the use of natural imagery, moving it away from the pantheistic poetry of the Romantics, for example. Certainly in Tract 89, *On the Mysticism Attributed to the Fathers of the Church*, Keble discusses the relevance of the natural world to the divine, as reminders in this world of the next:

> But the one great and effectual safeguard against such idolizing of the material world, or rather of our own minds acting upon it, is the habit of considering it in that other point of view, to which Christian Antiquity would guide us, as earnestly as it would withdraw us from the speculations of the mere natural philosopher. I mean the way of regarding external things, either as fraught with imaginative associations, or as parabolical lessons of conduct, or as a symbolical language in which God speaks to us of a world out of sight: which three might, perhaps, be not quite inaptly entitled, the Poetical, the Moral, and the Mystical, phases or aspects of this visible world.

> Of these, the Poetical comes first in order, as the natural groundwork or rudiment of the other two. This is indicated by all languages, and by the conversation of uneducated persons in all countries. There is everywhere a tendency to make the things we see represent the things we do not see, to invent or remark mutual associations between them, to call the one sort by the names of the other.

> The second, the Moral use of the material world, is the improvement of the poetical or imaginative use of it, for the good of human life and conduct, by considerate persons, according to the best of their own judgment, antecedent to, or apart from, all revealed information on the subject.

> In like manner, the Mystical, or Christian, or Theological use of it is the reducing it to a particular set of symbols and associations, which we have reason to believe has, more or less, the authority of the Great Creator Himself.

Keble indicates a precise trajectory of association from the earthly to the spiritual, ranging from the loose transcendence of the 'Poetical' to the ideal exactness of the 'Mystical'. It is difficult to pinpoint the use of natural imagery by individual writers on Keble's scale, and indeed each of these elements builds upon the previous, so that it is possible, in fact, to see all of these in Rossetti's work: all nature gives a 'poetical' image of the divine, a hint of the supernatural, yet the moral and Christian uses to which she puts her associations, especially in biblically derived work, are notable. Such reminders of the divine provide access to the sublime, and aim to uplift and transport the reader. This use of natural imagery features throughout Rossetti's work, and of course throughout many works of the period. Yet for Rossetti, it is clear that such signs of the divine in the earthly have specific meaning: not only do they relate to the theology of the Tractarians, but they also feature as a kind of access to the spiritual or sublime in many Gothic novels, especially those of Ann Radcliffe, where the heroines frequently reflect upon their awe-inspiring surroundings and connect these directly both to God and to a sense of earthly fear which reflects their coming trials in the novel.[6]

Time Flies

This aesthetic of Gothic and deployment of Gothic tropes and imagery characterizes *Time Flies* more than any structural incorporation of Gothic. The 'reading diary' is fragmentary in its nature, being a day-by-day book of devotional readings incorporating a wide range of styles, including poems, commentary, notes on saints' days and verses of scripture. It is, as such books tend to be, an aid to daily devotion and a source of solace in the trials of a fallen world. Its format thus permits Rossetti to vary the style and imagery of her writing and to employ diverse means of provoking the thoughts of the reader. As Roe points out, 'these "entries" are very intimate and personal, written in a plain, simple style, yet containing worlds of complexity' (p. 131). Once again the surface appears straightforward, but conceals a wealth of spiritual depths which the reader is expected to plumb. Rossetti uses personal anecdotes to provide insight, illustrating her points with descriptions of a variety of living creatures including a mole, earthworms, spiders, millipedes, jackdaws, frogs and a snake; all creatures associated with darkness or decay, and which she uses to suggest a moral. In addition, she employs scenery which is again reminiscent of the Gothic novels of Ann Radcliffe, for example, such as the 'mass and loftiness' of mountains,[7] a turreted bedchamber infested with insects, or a castle (*TF*, p. 111). The visual motifs of decay and enclosure create an atmosphere of Gothic, such as the entry for 4 October, in which a mourning narrator is inspired by a glimpse of the sublime:

> Life is a losing game, – with what to save?
> Thus I sat mourning like a mournful owl,
>   And like a doleful dragon made ado,
> Companion of all monsters of the dark:
> When lo! The light shook off its nightly cowl, (*TF*, p. 192)

Images which conjure the atmosphere of Gothic are packed into these few lines, where the contemplative and brooding narrator appears as a monster or 'doleful dragon', returned to human life by the light, adorned in a 'cowl'. Here Rossetti may use the language of Gothic, but she reverses its expectations: it is not that the narrator can hear an owl, but in fact is herself like one. Nor is she terrorized by monsters, but is their 'companion'. And while a ghostly monk, perhaps, might remove his cowl and frighten a Gothic heroine, here it is the beauty of daylight, dispelling the terror of night, which is revealed when the habit is displaced. *Time Flies* in this way both deploys the imagery of Gothic while undermining it, to a purpose which becomes clearer in *The Face of the Deep*. Similarly, the uncanny imagery of a room of waxworks is described, and the uncomfortable sensation which it inspired, yet Rossetti adds, 'looking back I laugh at my own absurdity' (*TF*, p. 36). Unlike Emily's response to the wax model of a decaying body in *The Mysteries of Udolpho*, Rossetti's instinctive reaction of fear is laughed off. Her anecdotes themselves are thus structured to demonstrate the passing of time, and the benefit of hindsight; unlike a Gothic heroine (except perhaps Catherine Morland), Rossetti projects herself as a narrator who can laugh at herself and demonstrate the wisdom of age.

Time, and its passage, is an obvious theme of the reading diary, embedded in its form. There are frequent reminders of the rapid passage of time and the need to use one's time wisely. The entry for 28 January concludes, 'From sudden death, Good Lord, deliver us' (*TF*, p. 23). Several entries indicate the problems of 'mortal frailty' and warn of the passing of time (*TF*, p. 90). Perhaps the most significant of these describes her own 'first vivid experience of death' in 'early childhood':

> I lighted upon a dead mouse. The dead mouse moved my sympathy: I took him up, buried him comfortably in a mossy bed, and bore the spot in mind.

> It may have been a day or two afterwards that I returned, removed the moss coverlet, and looked [. . .] a black insect emerged. I fled in horror, and for long years ensuing I never mentioned this ghastly adventure to anyone.

[. . .]

Only now contemplating death from a wider and wiser view-point, I would fain reverse the order of those feelings: dwelling less and less on the mere physical disgust, while more and more on the rest and safety; on the perfect peace of death, please God. (*TF*, p. 45)

Not only does the confessional tone of this entry vivify the moral tale, but the dual aspect of death is emphasized; the physical, relating to the memento mori of *The Mysteries of Udolpho*, or the crypt scene in *The Monk*, for example, and the fear which these are designed to engender; and the metaphysical, or spiritual, in which there is, for Rossetti, eternal hope. The appearance of the corpse, be it man or mouse, becomes irrelevant when compared to the soul's rest after death.

The Gothic novel has a complicated relationship with the symbiosis of inner and outer beings, or character and appearance, in repeated motifs. Examples of the misleading disjunction between the appearance and personality include the appearance of Melmoth, able to make Isidora fall in love with him despite his satanic secret; Zaira, in *Women*, is possessed of remarkable beauty but her soul is not as spotless as the equally beautiful Eva's. Beauty, in literature not only of the Gothic genre but of many kinds, is both an indicator of the pure heart and happy temperament, and simultaneously not to be trusted, being only a surface which may not match the depths. Perhaps the most striking example in Gothic literature of the untrustworthiness of appearance features in Hogg's *The Private Memoirs and Confessions of a Justified Sinner* (1824). Gil-Martin, whom the reader is expected to recognize as an incarnation of Satan, exposes the fallacy of appearance in the Gothic novel, in particular by his remarkable ability to change his appearance to suit his purposes:

'I beg your pardon, sir,' said I. 'But, surely, if you are the young gentleman with whom I spent the hours yesterday, you have the chameleon art of changing your appearance; I never could have recognised you.'

'My countenance changes with my studies and sensations,' said he. 'It is a natural peculiarity in me, over which I have not full control. If I contemplate a man's features seriously, mine own gradually assume the very same appearance and character. And what is more, by contemplating a face minutely, I not only attain the same likeness but, with the likeness, I attain the very same ideas.' (Hogg, 2009, p. 86)

The shape-shifting nature of the stranger alerts the reader to his evil status, but Hogg's nuanced depiction of Gil-Martin goes further than that. Not only can this personification of Satan take on the physical characteristics of a potential victim, but he can also assume their thoughts. Yet this is not to assume that he *becomes* another person. He may be able to read the mind of another man but he remains himself, essentially evil. The figure of Gil-Martin does not change in essence during the course of the novel, despite his remarkable abilities. Nonetheless, at moments of anger, Gil-Martin's appearance becomes too terrible to behold, suggesting that in some way his personality is reflected in his façade. This affinity, or disjunction, between the inner and outer person has been examined in the chapter on the grotesque, where the duality of body and spirit is discussed. In *Time Flies*, Rossetti instead constructs a dual space, of fallen and unholy earth and of pure heaven, with Christ as the intermediary. It is in human inability to comprehend God's truths that the fear and mystery of Gothic truly lies, partly through God's desire to protect our limited human minds from what we cannot comprehend, and partly through our own sin-obscured vision. How we best live on earth, with the celestial world in mind, is the true subject of her books.

Letter and Spirit

Letter and Spirit provides a very different reading experience. Unlike *Called to be Saints*, into which the reader may dip at random, Rossetti's exegetical discussion of the Commandments is a more sustained effort at theological writing, with fewer passages of scripture and more commentary. The title is presumably taken from the text 'Who also hath made us able ministers of the new testament; not of the letter, but of the spirit: for the letter killeth, but the spirit giveth life' (2 Corinthians 3.6). The phrase is familiar, with the most common usage referring to the 'letter and spirit of the law'; for example, in *The Merchant of Venice*, where Shylock, insisting on the letter of the law, is proved to be a mean-spirited villain. Similarly, Romans 2.29 reads: 'But he is a Jew, which is one inwardly; and circumcision is that of the heart, in the spirit, and not in the letter; whose praise is not of men, but of God.' The significance of the spirit, that is, of true obedience to God, rather than empty obeisance to a rule, is the implication of Rossetti's writing.

In *Letter and Spirit*, the meaning is made clear in its usage. Given Rossetti's extensive use of typology, it is likely that the 'letter' is represented by the Old Testament – that which sets examples, explaining the laws of Christianity, while the 'spirit' is the New Testament, in which the connotations of the Old Testament are carried forward and enacted or interpreted. *Letter and Spirit* aims to demonstrate the importance of interpreting the spirit of the Ten Commandments rather than becoming obsessed with the letter of the law, like the Pharisees in the New Testament, who observe ritual but discard true faith: 'Woe unto you, scribes and Pharisees, hypocrites! for ye pay tithe of mint and anise and cummin, and have omitted the weightier matters of the law, judgment, mercy, and faith: these ought ye to have done, and not to leave the other undone' (Matthew 23.23).

Rossetti examines the Ten Commandments closely, using the types of the Old Testament and the anti-types of the New Testament. Her text consists of a juxtaposition of the theological elements of the Commandments interspersed with a more devotional reading of scripture which encourages personal holiness in a manner typical of Tractarian writing. For example, Rossetti emphasizes the spiritual need to examine oneself for wickedness, selecting as her text what appears to be a conventionally Gothic image of a light shining in darkness.[8] Quoting Proverbs 20.27, she then writes: 'The spirit of man is the candle of the Lord, searching all the inward parts.' This verse provides an image of a tiny light in darkness, seeking out wickedness. Moreover, implicit in this verse (and Rossetti's discussion of it) is the notion of boundaries. The self – physically and metaphorically – contains this darkness. Rossetti's constructed self is thus inherently separate from the rest of the world, with an inner darkness but also potentially filled with the spirit of God. Christian faith provides for Rossetti's writing the possibility of an inner and outer unity. Notably, in the passage concerning the Pharisees in the Gospel of Matthew, it is the disjunction between the inner and outer being that is criticized:

> Woe unto you, scribes and Pharisees, hypocrites! for ye are like unto whited sepulchres, which indeed appear beautiful outward, but are within full of dead men's bones, and of all uncleanness.
>
> Even so ye also outwardly appear righteous unto men, but within ye are full of hypocrisy and iniquity. (Matthew 23.27–28)

The imagery is striking in these verses, which emphasize the problems of excessive concern with appearance while paying no attention to the cleanliness of the soul. The visual imagery, particularly of verse 27, is itself anticipatory of Gothic in its apparent macabre aesthetic appeal, concealing decay within. In *Time Flies*, with its exhortations to search oneself inwardly, and its insistence on the transitory nature of human life, this concentration on the permanence of God as opposed to the ephemeral existence of humanity becomes particularly prominent.

Unity and duality are matters which recur throughout Rossetti's religious prose, and are a particular concern of *Letter and Spirit*. The First Commandment, Rossetti states, 'is characterized by unity'. Moreover, 'within this unity is bound up the entire multitude of our duties; out of this one supreme commandment have to be developed all the details of every one of our unnumbered obligations' (*LS*, p. 8). Rossetti's conception of unity, therefore, is that it can encompass many aspects of one thing; there is no requirement to separate the multitudinous facets of one concept, but rather to understand them (in the spirit rather than the letter, perhaps) as being intrinsic to one another. The complexities of this argument are further problematized by the concept of the Trinity of Father, Son and Holy Spirit, consisting of three individual parts, separate yet indivisible. As biblical scholars have long pointed out, this is a concept which is beyond human understanding; the combined unity and separateness is not something fallen humanity can comprehend. Yet aside from its theological implications, the nature of the Trinity also usefully indicates shifting boundaries; the Trinity is both utterly one and yet quite separate, with no defined boundaries or sense of where one begins and another ends.

It is possible, therefore, through Rossetti's insistence on unity in *Letter and Spirit*, to trace an interest in boundaries and their dissolution. One way of crossing these boundaries is in fact through typological readings; Rossetti suggests in *Letter and Spirit* that it is because of the Trinity that God created humankind, and that therefore corresponding archetypes exist: 'If [. . .] God is not to be called like His creature, whose grace is simply typical, but that creature is like Him because expressive of His archetypal Attribute, it suggests itself that for every aspect of creation there must exist the corresponding Divine Archetype' (*LS*, p. 13). Such interpretations encourage reading back and forward through the Old and New Testaments, unifying the biblical text by considering it holistically. The boundaries between the earthly and the divine, therefore, are not where we might think; if not only the natural world but also humanity reflect God Himself, the boundary between the two is elided. Moreover, Rossetti adds that: 'And even as our God is One, so does He summon us to become one in His service. The powers and passions of our complex nature must be concentrated in one only love of Him alone: His many gifts to us must be returned to Him in one self-exhaustive gift of all we are and all we have' (*LS*, pp. 13–14). Not only the Trinity, but also humanity, are both separate and unified.

Following this assertion of unity, however, Rossetti immediately divides the self which must love God with an undivided heart into four aspects: heart, soul, mind and strength, and presents biblical examples of characters who have erred in each of these areas. These preoccupations with unity and division, with the dimly perceived crossing of boundaries both physical and spiritual, have resonance for a study of Gothic in Rossetti's work. As earlier chapters have discussed, Gothic is frequently preoccupied with issues of physical and emotional space, and the passage between them, which Rossetti translates into the spiritual. The perceived boundaries between earth and heaven, the spiritual and the material, represented in Tennyson's poem 'Crossing the Bar', are the concomitant thresholds in Rossetti's devotional works, but she indicates a surprising bridge:

> Looking back for a moment at what the Tenth Commandment seems to indicate as the wife's position, we observe that the clause which forbids coveting the house is repeated word for word on behalf of the wife; not so, as regards aught else specified; whence she appears to stand as connecting link, akin to both, between what the man is and what he has; even as Christ's sacred humanity, bridging over the severing gulf, unites the Godhead to the Church. (*LS*, p. 193)[9]

Rossetti is evidently concerned to remove any indication that the woman is the property of her husband, alongside his servants and animals. Yet the unexpected leap from the nature of the wife's position to the 'sacred humanity' of Christ demonstrates Rossetti's desire to place women at the heart of Christianity. Her Tractarian interest in the Incarnation constructs an image of Christ as a bridge between this world and the next, but she extends the metaphor to apply it in other circumstances. Like the heroine of the Gothic novel whose function as character is to move between the sheltered domestic world of home and the terrors of the unknown, the 'wife' figures as a character both possessed of free will and yet also bound by the cultural rules of the society in which she is placed, subject to patriarchal laws. Womanhood alone, it appears, provides sufficient power to cross thresholds, and, by implication, to do so for the benefit of others.

The Face of the Deep

Such concerns with thresholds and the 'place' of women are yet more evident in *The Face of the Deep*, a detailed discussion of the book of Revelation, taken verse by verse, combining the exegetical with devotional and reflective discussion, and interspersed with poems. Robert Kachur suggests that 'female devotional authors [...] were attracted to the Apocalypse precisely because it allowed them to begin to articulate arguments with controversial implications.'[10] Kachur's argument is that since it was more acceptable for women to write devotional works, a number of theologically minded women produced works that were ostensibly devotional but in fact contained a considerable proportion of 'original biblical exegesis' (p. 15). Though he gives only a few lines to *The Face of the Deep*, this comment is as pertinent to Rossetti's work as to other texts; Kachur's suggestion that the book of Revelation appealed to a few women as a subject for theological work is in part due to its diverse reception history, which permitted further works, even by women, particularly those which appeared to take a devotional line. Hassett posits that Rossetti's work may also have been inspired by Isaac Williams's devotional works (2005, p. 213). An examination of Williams's book *The Apocalypse, with Notes and Reflections* (1852) suggests that this is highly likely; for, at least in concept and construction, Rossetti's work is very similar to Williams's, using every verse of Revelation with exegetical discourse, though, as closer examination will demonstrate, Rossetti's content and analysis take a more personal approach. Like Rossetti, Williams also emphasizes in his introduction the 'divine simplicity' and 'deep and hidden analogies' of the book (1852, p. iii).

It is not within the remit of this book to consider in any detail the theology of Rossetti's extensive work on the Apocalypse, though it is worth noting that her approach falls into what Kachur determines the 'spiritual-allegorical' category, in which 'the Apocalypse must be approached as allegory', operating on the understanding 'that the book describes timeless spiritual realities rather than specific historical events' (p. 9). My consideration of *The Face of the Deep* is, however, predicated on the assumption that Rossetti was at least in part attracted to the book of Revelation for its Gothic affinities. In its depiction of the end of the world and the coming of a new world order, the book of the Apocalypse is saturated with endings and beginnings, depicted in grotesque visual imagery that is often violent and extreme. It is full of 'mysteries', in the Christian as well as the secular sense of the word, which many have attempted to unlock, though Rossetti's work tends to concentrate on a devotional and explanatory interpretation of the book rather than a literal or historical exegesis. Yet in the threat that the Apocalypse offers to the world as it exists, and its promise of a better world which will appear through suffering, Revelation's potential influence upon Gothic is remarkable. In terms of the Apocalypse, it is useful to note Julia Kristeva's suggestion that the 'horror of being' consists of 'the abyss of abjection' which is 'the other facet of religious, moral, and ideological codes'. It is, she states, the resurgence of repressed abjection which creates a human apocalypse (Kristeva, 1982, pp. 208–9).

It is notable that the threshold between heaven and earth will be dissolved upon the realization of St John's revelation, and that it thus predicts an end to the boundaries and thresholds which preoccupy Rossetti's work. Roe discusses the problem of contradiction in Revelation and Rossetti's response to it, suggesting that 'Rossetti posits God as the answer to contradiction, and heaven as the place where all contradictions will be resolved' (p. 176).[11] In the meantime, however, Rossetti's writing concentrates on 'man's fallen relationship to God' – that is, how one forms and maintains a relationship across the threshold between earth and heaven (Roe, 2006, p. 173).

The title *The Face of the Deep* itself suggests the existence of surface and depth and, significantly for a metaphoric reading of Revelation, the sign and its signified. The phrase is taken from Genesis 1.2, 'And the earth was without form, and void; and darkness was upon the face of the deep. And the Spirit of God moved upon the face of the waters.' The 'face of the deep' is the earth, covered with darkness before the creation of light. Rossetti emphasizes the necessarily superficial nature of her work, which can only hint at the spiritual depth, saying 'Only should I have readers, let me remind them that what I write professes to be only a *surface* study of an unfathomable depth: if it incites any to dive deeper than I attain to, it will so far have accomplished a worthy work' (*FD*, p. 365). This is significant not only for its theological implication that an exegesis of biblical work can still only remain on the surface, requiring further study, thought and prayer, but it also resonates with nineteenth-century devotional reading practices, particularly those of the Tractarians, who encouraged deep and thoughtful reading, and aimed to provoke further thought, relating writer and reader in a two-way relationship that was operative through faith.[12]

It is clear, therefore, that the metaphorical 'face' is what is presented and can be seen, while the 'deep' is what is hidden from view. Once again there are thresholds to be crossed, as the two are divided by a lack of understanding, though a glimpse of the divine presence is available in the Eucharist, or in prayer, which George Herbert refers to as 'heaven in ordinary' ('Prayer', l. 11). This is crucial to an understanding of Rossettian Gothic; we do not understand because we *cannot* understand, as fallen humans; yet we also do not understand because we are blinding ourselves by ignorance and lack of faith. Yet it is important to remember that for Rossetti, as Roe points out, it is heaven that is real, while earth is transitory (p. 170). It is the absence of human understanding which Rossetti, with her theological writing, intended to address.

Rossetti's theological Gothic examines and questions the nature of unity and division, and it seems probable that this may be related to concerns about the position of women. In her reflections on the nature of the book of Revelation, Rossetti necessarily considers the future for Christians, and her ultimate conclusion is regardless of gender. Kachur's interpretation of many women's theological writings on the Apocalypse is that 'its emphasis on the redeemed's unification as one body under God provided a way for women [. . .] to justify their vision of an egalitarian community' (p. 6). Such a view of future unity of the body of Christ, the Church, is reflected in the Anglican liturgy, deriving from 1 Corinthians 10.17: 'For we being many are one bread, and one body: for we are all partakers of that one bread.' The notion of faith promotes the concept of unity and division, of individuals which are part of a larger body, and of the oneness and separateness of Trinity. Rossetti provides a highly visual description of this:

> Multitude no less than Unity characterizes various types of God the Holy Spirit. Water indefinitely divisible, and every portion equivalent in completeness to the whole. Fire kindling unlimited flames, each in like manner complete in itself. Dew made up of innumerable drops: so also rain, and if we may make the distinction, showers. A cloud as a cloud is one, while as raindrops it is a multitude. And as in division each portion is a complete whole devoid of parts, so equally in reunion all portions together form one complete whole similarly devoid of parts: let drops or let flames run together, and there exists no distinction of parts in their uniform volume. (*FD*, p. 15)

Rossetti's construction of 'God the Holy Spirit' demonstrates a potential collapsing of boundaries, resonant of the future indicated in Revelation in which, post-Apocalypse, the boundaries and limitations currently imposed on fallen humanity will be dissolved and replaced with a unity between Christ and his Church.

It would perhaps be natural for nineteenth-century women to be drawn to a vision of an entirely equal society which makes no distinctions based on gender, which many theologians have seen as suggested by Matthew 22.30: 'For in the resurrection they neither marry, nor are given in marriage, but are as the angels of God in heaven.' This unification, in which all are equal, if not the same, is indicative of an idealized unity of believers reflected by the more specific unity of Christ with his Church. Such unity, of course, eliminates thresholds, representative of fear and danger as well as adventure and possibility in Gothic, and points to a New Jerusalem in which the complexities and latent evils of Gothic become redundant. For Rossetti, gender differences are not to be eliminated by the Apocalypse, but rather celebrated. Though much of her writing in *The Face of the Deep* does not appear to have a specifically gender-based appeal, she concentrates at times upon positive images of women, including the figure of the Church as the Bride of Christ.

The book of the Apocalypse presents issues which feminist theologians have struggled to overcome. It is in many ways an 'especially misogynist text' (Melnyk, 1998, p. 5). The figure of the prophetess Jezebel in Revelation 2 and the Whore of Babylon in Revelation 17–18 are viciously presented and suffer horrible fates, which, as Tina Pippin has suggested, 'would be totally unacceptable to biblical scholars' if this violence was perpetrated against a male (1999, p. 94), whatever the circumstances.[13] Rossetti's comments on Jezebel are restrained and, without emphasizing her womanhood, indicate that it is for her licentious and corrupting behaviour that she is condemned, since she was 'an abandoned woman and a witch, [. . .] a nursing mother of idolatry. But whatever witch she may have been, there appears about her no trace of the genuine prophetess' (*FD*, p. 76). However, Rossetti goes on to argue gender difference in favour of the masculine, which suggests that in fact Balaam's responsibility must therefore be the greater:

> As Balaam in comparison with Jezebel, so men in comparison with women may usually be expected to exhibit keener, tougher, more work worthy gifts. Therefore if Jezebel the woman, going about to establish her equality with Balaam the man, poses as *prophetess* to his *prophet*, nothing is more likely than that she will have to eke out and puff up her pretensions by a whiff of imposture, conscious or unconscious imposture. (*FD*, p. 76)

Hassett suggests that *The Face of the Deep* 'elides what terrifies' in Revelation, remarking that this may be due to the recent death of Rossetti's atheist brother, Dante Gabriel Rossetti (p. 200). In fact, Rossetti's result was to create an aid to devotion which does not require an elucidation of the threats hidden in Revelation; these are already explicit in *The Face of the Deep* through the inclusion of verses of scripture, thus allowing the apocalyptic terror to speak for itself. Rossetti uses Revelation as an aid to devotional life, but she does not ignore its implications or minimize the fear it may evoke. However, what she does endeavour to minimize is the negative treatment of womanhood. In her commentary on subsequent verses (Revelation 2.21–22) she writes of the need for repentance, describing it as a 'space' which cannot be neutral: 'Empty space, neutral space, is impossible; it must be occupied by accumulating guilt or by repentance unto progressive amendment' (*FD*, p. 76). This space, then, in which the reader can repent, is the liminal space of human life, in which sins occur and repentance must follow in order to obtain God's forgiveness. This repentance, theologically speaking, begins the process of dissolving the barriers between heaven and earth. In contrast, Isaac Williams's response to these same verses concerning Jezebel is more specific, and indeed harsher, though he comments that 'it is her sufferance, not her active participation, which is reproved.' Moreover, he posits that 'allusion is made not to any women, but to a heresy', taking the figure of a woman entirely as a metaphor for a heretical church (p. 35).

The Whore of Babylon, or the Great Harlot, of Revelation 17–18, receives rather different treatment at the hands of Rossetti and Williams.[14] While Williams concentrates on explaining what he understands to be the fate of Babylon, identifying the Harlot with 'a Christian Church', he is more concerned with facts than with extrapolating moral lessons (p. 314). Clearly he is comfortable with the identification of Babylon with a harlot, adding that the term 'adulteress' would be insufficient, since 'the impure Church barters and prostitutes her faith to Christ for the advantages of the world' (p. 315). Northrop Frye illuminates the biblical language used for this figure, suggesting that 'The word "whoredom" in the Bible usually refers to theological rather than sexual irregularity' (1982, p. 141). However, Williams, it appears, is keener to identify the figure of the woman with sexual than with religious sins. In *The Face of the Deep*, Rossetti, perhaps less comfortable with labels concerning women's morality after her work in the Mary Magdalene Penitentiary for Fallen Women, is vociferous concerning 'the vileness and ruinousness of idolatrous defection', thus clearly associating the 'harlot' figure with the city of Babylon rather than womanhood (*FD*, p. 396). Yet it is therefore surprising that she later advocates that this imagery is to be taken as a warning to women, specifically, for the penalties for female sins:

> As it seems possible to study the sun-clothed exalted Woman (ch.xii) as a figure of the all-glorious destiny awaiting the Virtuous Woman, so now I think this obscene woman may (on the surface) be studied as illustrating the particular foulness, degradation, loathsomeness, to which a perverse rebellious woman because feminine not masculine is liable. (*FD*, p. 400)

Scrupulously fair, if the best of women's destiny can be extrapolated from the positive images of woman, then the reverse must also be true; Rossetti is never an apologist for her sex. Indeed, she characterizes Babylon as a femme fatale, who 'proffers filthiness in a golden cup' (*FD*, p. 400). Not unlike her figure of 'The World' in a much earlier poem, this woman 'tyrannizes by influence', dissembling and hiding her true nature under her assumed beauty. Once again this Gothic figure of the dangerous woman – Madame Montoni, Zaira, Matilda de Villanges – poses a threat, though here it is a global rather than a personal menace. Furthermore, this woman is grotesquely united with a 'beast'; 'by a foul congruity [they] seem to make up a sort of oneness' (*FD*, p. 399). This grotesque image, half woman and half beast, is reminiscent of the Gothic heroine's fear of unity with an unknown other.

Rossetti provides an imaginative poetic illustration of Babylon, demonstrating the seductive beauty which comes with familiarity, and the face of evil hidden behind it:

> Foul is she and ill-favoured, set askew:
> Gaze not upon her till thou dream her fair,
> Lest she should mesh thee in her wanton hair,
> Adept in arts grown old yet ever new.
> Her heart lusts not for love, but thro' and thro'
> For blood, as spotted panther lusts in lair;
> No wine is in her cup, but filth is there
> Unutterable, with plagues hid out of view. (*FD*, p. 406)

The poem, opening with the incontrovertible 'Foul', attempts to reveal the hidden loathsomeness of the depiction of Babylon, which, as one becomes accustomed to it, may come to seem 'fair'. This woman's femininity is accentuated by her 'wanton hair', and her panther-like inexorable move towards her victim is reflected in the slow and steady pace of the alliterative consonants. As she seeks her prey and longs for blood, she is akin more to the vampiric Lucy Westenra than the typical femme fatale of earlier Gothic, although her 'plagues' are concealed beneath a dissembling exterior. The connection of the evil woman with a dangerous animal more than with humanity suggests both that she is beneath contempt and also that she poses a serious threat. Another poem, 'Standing Afar Off for the Fear of her Torment' again demonstrates the woman's 'pride' and 'foulness', yet here she is alone, in the flames as Babylon burns, indicating the consequence of her sins. As the wicked in the Gothic novel receive justice and are punished, so in Revelation, where the ultimate punishments, of which all others are shadows, are finally seen.

The Face of the Deep is also concerned with the positive images of women in the book of Revelation. The Church as the Bride of Christ receives less attention than might be expected, though the figure is clearly equipped with ideal feminine virtues in Rossetti's commentary.[15] Chaste and arrayed in splendour, the Bride and Bridegroom are depicted as the sun and moon, united in eternal love and glory. Such union, 'longed for, toiled for, Self-sacrificed for, bought with a great price' is the finale to the struggles for unity which are reflected on earth, in which journeys must be undertaken, thresholds crossed and fears faced (*FD*, p. 481). All earthly conception of unity, including the sacrament of marriage, which is a pale reflection of heavenly union, reaches its apotheosis for Rossetti in the vision of woman restored to her rightful place as the Bride of Christ.

The book of the Apocalypse is noted by theologians for its imagery of doubleness. The notion of the double incorporates both unity and division, as the two parts appear to form one whole, yet are divided, often by apparently insuperable barriers. For example, the structure of the book poses the earthly Babylon, represented by the 'Great Harlot', as the polar opposite to the New Jerusalem, depicted as the Bride of Christ. These two women, or cities, are divided by their places, in heaven and on earth, but also by the gulf created by their different characteristics. Theologian Richard Bauckham indicates the oppositional, yet parallel, characteristics of these cities, of which a few examples are cited below:

(1) The chaste bride, the wife of the Lamb (21.2, 9)
   v. the harlot with whom the kings of the earth fornicate (17.2)

(2) Her splendour is the glory of God (21.11–21)
   v. Babylon's splendour from exploiting her empire (17.4; 18.12–13, 16)

(3) The nations walk by her light, which is the glory of God (21.24)
   v. Babylon's corruption and deception of the nations (17.2; 18.3, 23; 19.2)

(1993, p. 131)

When the attributes of the Harlot and the Bride are placed side by side, the gulf between them, as well as the similarities, becomes increasingly apparent. The dividing line of the threshold of heaven cannot be crossed; these two characters are mirror images, one evil and one holy, a prototype for the figure of the doubled woman in literature, such as Una and Duessa in Spenser's *The Faerie Queene* (1590–6), Zaira and Eva in *Women*, and indeed Laura and Lizzie in 'Goblin Market'. As Tennyson suggests in 'Merlin', in *Idylls of the King*, 'For men at most differ as heaven and earth | But women, worst and best, as heaven and hell' (ll. 812–13). These extremes are repeated ad infinitum in both Gothic and Victorian literature. The unity as well as the separateness of these figures is emphasized by Auerbach, who suggests that 'The Victorian queen is not the anti-type of the Victorian victim, but the release of the victim into the full use of her powers' (1982, p. 39). The implication is that the unity of these two apparently oppositional figures – the 'good' and 'bad' woman – is stronger than one might expect. Certainly in Gothic literature these figures are often literally related or physically similar. In literary terms, the space between these women is minimal, though morally and theologically it may be an unbridgeable gulf. Auerbach's argument, unsurprisingly, is that the masculine is thus afraid of the hidden power of the feminine, perhaps hidden under a beautiful face, and consequently attempts to repress all feminine power. Such stereotypes have evolved from biblical sources such as Revelation, as Gothic may also have done.

Though Rossetti concentrates on the female virtues of both these figures, it is notable that, as with the Maturin characters, it is the 'wicked' figures about whom she writes poetry; the virtuous women are more highly prized, one senses, but seem to provide less poetic inspiration. The 'woman clothed with the sun' is described in intense language as:[16]

> weakness made strong and shame swallowed up in celestial glory. For thus the figure is set before our eyes. Through Eve's lapse, weakness and shame devolved upon woman as her characteristics, in a manner special to herself and unlike the corresponding heritage of man.
>
> And as instinctively we personify the sun and moon as *he* and *she*, I trust there is no harm in my considering that her sun-clothing indicates how in that heaven where St. John in vision beheld her, she will be made equal with men and angels; arrayed in all human virtues, and decked with all communicable Divine graces: whilst the moon under her feet portends that her some time infirmity of purpose and changeableness of mood have, by preventing, assisting, final grace, become immutable; she has done all and stands; from the lowest place she has gone up higher. (*FD*, pp. 309–10)[17]

This is the closest one can get to a form of Rossettian feminism; she will not entirely excuse Eve's weakness, but she sees that the grace of God can redeem womankind, and make her 'equal with men and angels'; she depicts this with confidence that it will come to pass, remaining convinced not only that women will be made equal to men, but that Eve herself 'will stand before the Throne', despite her sins.[18] For Rossetti, equality can only exist in a spiritual, not a social, sense. This is certainly not a possibility in Williams's commentary, in which he is somewhat grudging in his admittance of the feminine characteristics of these positive female figures.[19] Rossetti understands the nature of Eve's sin and Mary's purity, however, and sets them up against each other in a direct comparison:

> Eve exhibits one extreme of feminine character, the Blessed Virgin the opposite extreme. Eve parleyed with a devil: holy Mary 'was troubled' at the salutation of an Angel. Eve sought knowledge; Mary instruction. Eve aimed at self-indulgence: Mary at self-oblation. Eve, by disbelief and disobedience, brought sin to the birth: Mary, by faith and submission, Righteousness. (*FD*, p. 310)

The use of femininity as ciphers of such apparent strength of good and evil in Revelation reinforces the stereotypical dichotomy of woman as Madonna/whore, and Rossetti apparently does little to diminish this. Certainly not only nineteenth-century thought but also Gothic novels have a tendency to promulgate this split. However, she refuses to see femininity in such extreme terms, and instead problematizes traditional femininity in her discussions of Eve. Though in biblical tradition Eve is the opposite of the Virgin Mary, the originals of the dual images of women in the early church, and though Rossetti acknowledges this once throughout her body of work, quoted above, she otherwise refers to Mary relatively little, bypassing the elements of Mariolatry which appear in some Tractarian writings and instead focusing her attention on Eve, who, without Mary to throw her into relief, has the potential to appear as a more human and believable character. It seems that the dividing line between the 'good' and 'bad' woman is dissolved and united in the character of Eve, whom Rossetti refers to as 'Eve the beloved first Mother of us all. Who that has loved and revered her own immediate dear mother, will not echo the hope?' (*FD*, pp. 310–11). However, the position of the 'daughters of Eve' is made abundantly clear in her poem 'A Daughter of Eve', in which the narrator mourns her own foolishness:

> A fool I was to sleep at noon,
> And wake when night is chilly
> Beneath the comfortless cold moon;
> A fool to pluck my rose too soon,
> A fool to snap my lily. (ll. 1–5)

Rossetti's desire to inspire compassion for Eve is partially undermined in her work by her determination not to excuse her. Poems such as this relate to Rossetti's many fallen women poems and ballads, and to 'Goblin Market', as previously discussed.

Rossetti's preoccupation with the figure of Eve provides a useful point of reference in relation to her approach to the position of women. Rossetti demonstrates an interest in Eve in several of her poems and much of her prose, in particular, discussing the theologically complex problem of Eve. Her earliest work which seems to reflect the figure of Eve is 'Shut Out', which reverses the Gothic trope of the enclosed woman in a domestic space by configuring Eve in exile, mourning after her expulsion from the Garden of Eden. At first, Eve is able to look through the 'iron bars' (l. 2) of the door which excludes her from Eden, but there is a 'shadowless spirit' (l. 9) at the gate to prevent her from re-entering. Having once crossed that threshold, there is no return – and yet Eve retains hope that she will return, begging fruitlessly to 'bid my home remember me | Until I come to it again' (ll. 15–16). The spirit builds a wall to prevent any further sight of Eden, which places Eve in the position of being imprisoned in the world, locked out of Eden. Forced from her home, she becomes a figure for pity despite her sin, and she is forced into the situation of a Gothic heroine, facing an uncertain future in an apparently inhospitable world. The unspoken irony is that these threats derive from her own actions, yet the image of Eve 'Blinded by tears' (l. 22) anticipates Rossetti's hope in *The Face of the Deep* that Eve too will be redeemed. In 'Eve', the anti-heroine is placed upon the threshold:

> While I sit at the door
> Sick to gaze within
> Mine eye weepeth sore
> For sorrow and sin: (ll. 1–4)

It is noteworthy that Rossetti situates Eve on the brink of two worlds to speak her narrative in this poem; her act of eating the apple is barely past as we see her grief for what she has lost. The abbreviated lines give a sense of disjointed emotion which the speaker can barely control; this emotion, one suspects, is exacerbated by passing through the gate which will exile her from her home. As the chapter on Maturin has discussed, the image of Eve in 'Shut Out' and 'Eve' is foreshadowed by Rossetti's early poem, 'Immalee', in which the innocent island girl of *Melmoth the Wanderer* can be read as a cipher for prelapsarian Eve. The sympathy of nature with Eve's plight as she gazes into a lost Eden presupposes that Eve's sin which precipitated the Fall was a 'natural' sin, of curiosity as well as disobedience, which paves the way for Rossetti's unusual exegetical approach in her devotional prose.

Rossetti exploits verbal ambiguities in her interpretation of scripture to present an unusual case for Eve; for example, in *Letter and Spirit* Rossetti considers the Fall, and her conclusion suggests that language may be at the root of it, similar to Milton's argument in Book IX of *Paradise Lost*, though Milton does not attempt to excuse Eve:

> Adam and Eve illustrate two sorts of defection (I Tim 2:14). Eve made a mistake, 'being deceived' she was in the transgression: Adam made no mistake: his was an error of will, hers partly of judgment; nevertheless both proved fatal [. . .].
> By birthright gracious and accessible, she lends an ear to all petitions from all petitioners. She desires to instruct ignorance, to rectify misapprehension: 'unto the pure all things are pure,' and she never suspects even the serpent. Possibly

a trace of blameless infirmity transpires in the wording of her answer, '*lest ye die*,' for God had said to the man '[. . .] in the day that thou eatest thereof thou *shalt surely* die:' but such tenderness of spirit seems even lovely in the great first mother of mankind; or it may be that Adam had modified the form, if it devolved on him to declare the tremendous fact to his second self. Adam and Eve reached their goal, the Fall, by different routes. With Eve, the serpent discussed a question of conduct, and talked her over to his own side: with Adam, so far as appears, he might have argued the point forever and gained no vantage. (*LS*, pp. 17–18)

Either Eve misunderstood the command from God (which may even be Adam's fault), or else the language of the serpent deceived her, since she did not know that anyone might try to mislead her. Both interpretations rely on the slipperiness of language; and both also at least partially exonerate Eve. This is comparable to Milton's treatment of the fall of Eve in *Paradise Lost*, where Eve tells the serpent that 'God hath said, Ye shall not eate | Thereof, nor shall ye touch it, lest ye die' (Book IX, pp. 662–3). Milton's Eve's greatest sin, it seems, is to be 'credulous' rather than intrinsically wicked, though Rossetti's version goes further in vindication of Eve. Leaving the theology of this aside, Rossetti's disquisition highlights the interpretative nature of her beliefs and the significance of language for her religion as well as her poetry.

It thus seems possible that the dual and oppositional figures of the fallen/unfallen woman, in their personified guises in Revelation, in the Gothic novel, and in Rossetti's own poetry, are resolved through the figure of Eve. Rossetti's conscious association of Eve with the figure of the 'woman clothed with the sun' is not necessary to the text on which she is commenting, yet she chooses to draw our attention to Eve at this point, forcing the reader into a consideration of woman's supposedly dual nature, and also emphasizing the redeemability of any fall. No longer an outcast figure, Eve has overcome her liminality, through the grace of God, and stands in the New Jerusalem along with the rest of her sex. Having passed over the threshold of Eden after the Fall, she may be permitted to return after the Apocalypse. It is this sense of returning home which allows Rossetti to develop a sense of closure to the Gothic tropes of exile and boundaries. Milbank describes the movement of women as an important trope which tracks their progress, in Gothic and sensation fiction, physically rather than mentally, where the:

portrayal of the heroine charts her progress across a spatial field of forces as she crosses domestic boundaries, rather than the development of her mental processes over time. To cross boundaries, to plot, is the only way in which the woman can register on the narrative of events. The 'fallen woman' is a favourite character in sensation fiction for this reason, but the interest is not in her existence as a social problem, [. . .] but as a transgressor, in the literal image of the word. She 'errs' in moving between domestic house and market-place; her dissimulation as a plotter hides her private motive behind her public 'face'. In moving back into the private sphere for her own advancement, the errant woman creates a false mediation by revealing the private house as itself a market-place. (1992, p. 17)

To read Eve as a fallen women thus makes sense; for Rossetti to maintain complete confidence in her ultimate redemption and salvation is to be expected. Milbank's critique of the patriarchal society enacted in the novels of Radcliffe, for example, demonstrates that the crossing of boundaries requires the heroine to transgress, yet Rossetti reverses this in the final, triumphant scenes of Revelation.

In chapter 21 of Revelation, where 'a new heaven and a new earth' (21.1) are revealed to John, the city of the New Jerusalem, apostrophized as the Bride of Christ, is described in resplendent detail. In particular, its appearance from the outside is seen, set with gemstones and blazing with 'the glory of God' (21.11). Its walls and gates – presumably as the parts which John can see in his vision – are depicted, and Rossetti's commentary discusses these walls and gates:

Wherefore 'a wall' and wherefore 'gates'? 'Thou shalt call thy walls Salvation and thy gates Praise.' Isaiah writes *walls*, St. John *a wall*. New Jerusalem standing foursquare possesses under one aspect four walls; yet these being continuous and all four corner-stoned into unity seem to be one at least as indisputably as to be four. And (if so I may take the sense) Isaiah's *walls* reappearing as St. John's *wall*, sets forth the universal salvation as being from the alone Will, Might, Love of God: whilst the *gates* are twelve, because multitudinous mankind offering praise for so great a gift uplifts an innumerable voice. (*FD*, p. 497)

The wall is therefore constructed as inclusive, no longer the unpassable boundary but one which has many gates through which the Church can pass. False divisions are dissolved and thresholds unnecessary as all can enter. Moreover, 'those gates are of ingress not of egress, for none who enter thereby shall go out any more' (*FD*, p. 497). This city provides 'a genuine home' from which there is no need to leave; all wants will be supplied within, and no-one can be ejected (*FD*, p. 498). To trivialize the drama of Revelation, Rossetti's commentary provides, structurally speaking, a Gothic 'marriage plot', in which, despite travels, trials and a Fall, the Bride is reunited with her Beloved, and together they form a domestic centre from which there is no further transgressing of boundaries and no separation. In this final stage of heaven, no further threats can occur, no further boundaries penetrated and no fear or sadness or darkness can touch the hero and heroine. The mysteries of the plot by this stage have been discovered – Rossetti states that knowledge that was once forbidden will now be available; a family is reunited, and the future is secure, headed by the 'Great Householder Whose house is the universe'. This blissful ending is domestic, as the closure of Gothic novels tends to be. The happy ending is reinforced by the fulfilment of desires: 'All holy desires shall be fulfilled, – nor shall even mere blameless desires be nothing accounted of' (*FD*, p. 498).

The commentary takes pains to describe and discuss the gates of the holy city, which are beautiful objects in themselves, inlaid with pearls and other precious jewels. However, 'a gate is to be passed through, not resided in' (*FD*, p. 511). There is, therefore, no need to hesitate on the threshold, though 'The open gates bear permanent witness to human free will, still free even when made indefectible' (*FD*, p. 516). The exercise of free will, which caused the fall, is in Rossetti's version of the New Jerusalem enshrined in the very walls. Moreover, unlike the gates of Eden, these gates will never shut. Though much of this material is in the book of Revelation, much is also Rossetti's exegetical and descriptive discourse; there is no doubt that she adds considerably to the biblical account of the walls and gates of heaven in Revelation 21.10–21.

In Rossetti's poetry and prose, it is the world we know which figures as Gothic. Images of enclosure, such as in 'The Convent Threshold' and 'An Immurata Sister', feature as atmospheres which stifle growth and belief, while in nature, humanity is at its freest and closest to God. Rossetti configures the world in which we live as Gothic, because of the very nature of its fallenness. Many Gothic novels deal with what the characters perceive to be the end of their world – their own death or attack, death of a loved one, or the discontinuation of lineage; *The Face of the Deep* enacts for the reader the genuine Apocalypse, of which Gothic plots are a faint shadow. This seems quite probable if one accepts Kristeva's argument that 'all literature is probably a version of the apocalypse' (p. 207). Rossetti is renowned for her poems of patience and suffering, which enact this life as a waiting period for the next, in poems such as:

> Long and dark the nights, dim and short the days,
> Mounting weary heights on our weary ways,
>   Thee our God we praise.
> Scaling heavenly heights by unearthly ways,
> Thee our God we praise all our nights and days,
>   Thee our God we praise. (*FD*, p. 17)

The ultimate goal for Rossetti and her readers is finally to cross the threshold and enter the heavenly world which awaits; Death is not to be feared since 'Death is the gate to that City' (Quiller-Couch, 1934, p. 22). Critics have written of the significance of Gothic 'atmosphere', in which fear prevails, suffering is great and, moreover, the world seems dark, lit by only occasional glimpses of the sublime.[20] This atmosphere is frequently populated by symbols that are a reminder of the grave, such as insects, which are an often-used trope in Rossetti's work, and her work reflects 1 Corinthians 13.12: 'For now we see through a glass, darkly; but then face to face: now I know in part; but then shall I know even as also I am known.' Life on earth is thus a Gothic, grotesque, fallen reflection of life in heaven, and of the world as God intended, and this is reflected in Rossetti's fractured and fragmented work, particularly in the prose works which are collections of scripture, commentary, personal thoughts and poems. This fractured life is therefore a natural state of the human condition, from which we can escape only through Christ. Furthermore, Rossetti implies that the fractured way of seeing is the only way that is possible:

> Doubtless a thread of perfect sequence runs throughout Divine Revelation, binding it into one sacred and flawless whole. But not so do feeble eyes discern it. I can but study it piece by piece, word by word, unworthy even to behold the little I seem to observe. Much of this awful Apocalypse opens to my apprehension rather a series of aspects than any one defined and certified object. It summons me to watch and pray and give thanks; it urges me to climb heavenward. Its thread doubtless consists unbroken: but my clue is at the best woven of broken lights and shadows, here a little and there a little. (*FD*, p. 174)

David Punter in his essay on poetry and the uncanny, suggests that in 'The Ancient Mariner', the tension of the poem is in waiting to cross a threshold which we know cannot be crossed. This is because:

> according to myth, [. . .] within each threshold lives a small god; and such a god is capable of changing us, as we cross from the outside to the inside or vice versa, into something completely different, such that our very memory will be burned away, erased, will become the substance of erasure. (Punter, 2000, p. 196)

Though Punter's comments relate specifically to Coleridge's poem, they are strangely applicable for the Rossettian Gothic in *The Face of the Deep*. We 'know', with human understanding, that we cannot cross the threshold between earth and heaven, and yet it is finally proved, in Revelation, that through the grace of God we can. Moreover, that transformation to which Punter refers takes place in the Apocalypse. Theological beliefs about the exact nature of the resurrected in heaven vary, but Punter's description gives a reasonable (if unintentional) view of it. This final threshold can be crossed, permanently, and the shadows and fears of the Gothic world dismissed.

> Shadows to-day, while shadows show God's Will,
> > Light were not good except he sent us light.
> > Shadows to-day, because this day is night
> Whose marvels and whose mysteries fulfil
> Their course and deep in darkness serve him still.
> > Thou dim aurora, on the extremest height
> > Of airy summits wax not over bright;
> Refrain thy rose, refrain thy daffodil.
> Until God's Word go forth to kindle thee
> > And garland thee and bid thee stoop to us,
> > Blush in the heavenly choirs and glance not down:
> > To-day we race in darkness for a crown,
> In darkness for beatitude to be,
> In darkness for the city luminous. (*FD*, p. 166)

Conclusion

Christina Rossetti's poems have an intricate relationship with Gothic conventions and practice. From her earliest poems, which demonstrate a direct interaction with the novels of Maturin, to her mature prose works, which engage with some of the tropes of Gothic and draw on biblical sources, particularly the book of Revelation, her work offers a range of complex possibilities for a study of Gothic. Rather than suggesting that Rossetti's work is the result of the direct influence of Gothic, this book has aimed to provide a framework for exploring the numerous ways in which Rossetti produced a unique mode of nineteenth-century Gothic. Moreover, my argument has been predicated upon the concept that Gothic is a multistranded and sprawling collection of tropes, aesthetics, ideas and styles which cannot be easily contained by the word 'Gothic'. The 'Gothic' which I have traced in Rossetti's work originates only partly in her reading of Gothic literature; it is similarly indebted to Dante, to Pre-Raphaelitism, and most of all to her Christian faith and the Bible.

The introduction proposed that this book would approach Rossetti's work from an unusual angle. Since the reputation of Rossetti's poetry has in many ways suffered from being read as purely devotional, which narrows its appeal, or has been neglected in favour of a multitude of readings of 'Goblin Market', the approach of this book has been to examine her work by considering her use of Gothic. This does not imply that she is not a deeply religious poet; it is impossible to understand her writing fully without considering Rossetti's Tractarianism, as several recent studies have shown. Yet, as McGann has suggested, much of her work is still marginalized or neglected, possibly due to its reputation as primarily religious.[1] Such a focus on her faith may imply that Rossetti was not engaged with contemporary culture, or with literature other than the Bible. This book, therefore, has argued that this is not the case. Other critics already discussed have examined the relationship between Rossetti's work and Dante, or Pre-Raphaelitism, for example. Gothic, frequently read into Victorian novels such as those of the Brontës and Wilkie Collins, provides a means to remove

Rossetti from her familiar context of Victorian women poets and examine her poetry and prose against a wider backdrop of emerging nineteenth-century Gothic. A study of Gothic in Rossetti's texts also permits a reading of some of the elements which make up a fractured Gothic which appear in Rossetti's work, which are not usually discussed in studies of her work.

The exploration of these elements has included an examination of the possibilities which spectrality, a theoretically inflected approach for examining work in the field of nineteenth-century literature, can offer. Theories of spectrality are further-reaching than phantoms. This theoretical framework offers the space to consider work on the writer as spectral, linked to the interaction between writer and reader which is significant for both Gothic and Tractarianism. Most significant, though, is the portrayal of death and the afterlife which Rossetti's ghost poems offer. The use of spectres is often controversial in Gothic, whether they prove to be genuine phantoms or can be explained rationally, and it is true that there are many spectres in Rossetti's work, although they do not always conform to the ghosts of Gothic novels. Rossetti's spectres are always genuine, and offer a voice from beyond the grave and inside the mind, which is complicated by Rossetti's theological position. In this chapter a persistent situation emerges, that of the threshold to be crossed. A feature of Gothic novels, with the implication of imprisonment on one side and freedom on the other, the threshold between death and life proves to be crucial for Rossettian Gothic.

Though Rossetti read a range of Gothic novelists, there is no doubt that her deepest literary engagement related to the works of Maturin. Her early monologues have been little studied and are now rarely republished other than in complete collections of her poems, but a close examination suggests that they are indicative of a wide field of engagement with Gothic. The poems take moments of drama and conflict in the novels and offer a perspective, usually that of a heroine, which provides an interiority rarely seen in Maturin's novels, though more common in the work of Radcliffe. These poems have Gothic roots of which traces remain, fractured in their removal from their context of Maturin's narrative, but retaining what D'Amico refers to as 'motifs' of Gothic which persist throughout Rossetti's writing life. Some of the tropes which are explored in this chapter are not commonly considered to be an element of Gothic, such as a preoccupation with knowledge, related to the Fall in Eden; the use of language to deceive; and the self-sacrificing heroine. Rossetti is rewriting Gothic in these poems, transforming manipulated heroines into emblems of integrity, answerable to God rather than to mankind. Once again, Rossettian Gothic returns to matters of Christianity.

The grotesque as an aspect of Gothic offers a perspective on Rossetti's work which is akin to Ruskin's approach to the grotesque, as a moral dynamic in art and literature. Rossetti's poems demonstrate the effects of immorality and vice in the grotesques of 'The Dead City', a poem strongly reminiscent of Ruskin's Venice, for example. Though Rossetti is known as a poet of restraint, her grotesques demonstrate her unique use of disfigurement and distortion as a technique of contrast. My inference is that the postlapsarian world is occupied by human grotesques, in Rossetti's eyes. Many of her poems use this distorted excess to demonstrate a contrast between the ideal perfection of heaven and the gross irreverence and blasphemy of earth. Taking Christ as an example of perfected humanity, all other figures appear grotesque in contrast. From the hideous goblins and their evil fruit in 'Goblin Market', to the master of the dancing bear in 'Brother Bruin', and encompassing the wickedness of human nature in her devotional poems, Rossetti's grotesques pervade her work. Moreover, they complicate the relationship between the internal mind and external body, emphasizing the untrustworthiness of appearances and the disjunction that can occur between outward beauty and inward ugliness, though in some poems the physical appearance begins to reveal the horror of the immoral soul. Fear, in Gothic, is often essentially a fear for one's soul, and it is this fear which the Rossettian grotesque manifests.

This deployment of fear, as well as the grotesque, is evident in 'Goblin Market', Rossetti's most famous poem. Frequently anthologized and taught in schools and universities, the poem's popularity owes much to its openness to interpretation, from queer readings to Christian ones. 'Goblin Market', while not typical of Rossetti's oeuvre, offers itself as a starting-point for reading Rossetti's depictions of women, particularly the fallen women whose morality, if not virtue, she defends in other poems. Laura and Lizzie demonstrate not only the value of sisterhood, but also the redemptive possibilities of the fallen state. Here Rossetti transforms the tropes of Gothic, where woman's virginity is prized above all else and must be preserved for her character to remain intact; throughout her poems Rossetti's approach is forgiving, focusing as her brother did on the social hypocrisy surrounding female sexuality. The fallen woman in fiction is frequently doubled with the 'pure' woman, a device which is also apparent in 'Goblin Market', demonstrating another Gothic transformation: that of the doubling of traditionally 'good' and 'bad' characters into a more complex web of transgression, forgiveness and redemption.

This chapter also offered the opportunity to explore the multiple, and fascinating, ways in which 'Goblin Market' interacts with and draws upon earlier texts and traditions. Its relation to fairy tale, often considered a precursor to the Gothic genre itself, opens up some new ways of looking at the poem, though complicated by the poem's apparent eroticism, a trait which the 1972 *Playboy* article draws upon. This erotic content is also true of the vampire narratives, such as John Polidori's *The Vampyre*, on which Rossetti is thought to have drawn. Yet despite these secular and even occult influences, the poem remains one of Christian belief and morality, far removed from her other poems in style and content but rooted in an intertextual, multifaceted tradition of Christian Gothic.

'Goblin Market' provides an example of Rossetti's complex and ostensibly secular moral instruction; the final chapter of this book explores her mature devotional and exegetical texts which offer a specifically Christian edification. My discussion of these texts, particularly *The Face of the Deep*, provides some potential answers to the questions raised by Rossetti's Gothic, of origin and purpose. Its roots lie deeper than the Gothic novels which she read as a child, reaching back to her absorption in biblical texts, especially the book of Revelation. All her prose works appear preoccupied with the boundaries between life and death, between earth and heaven, and between the fallen and grotesque earth and the perfection of heaven. This becomes increasingly apparent in a close reading of *The Face of the Deep*, which contrasts the terrors that the Apocalypse will visit upon humanity with the unsurpassed splendour of heaven. In her discussion of the women depicted in the book of Revelation, Rossetti offers a perspective on the doubled figure of femininity which haunts Victorian culture, and provides a potential solution not only to the horrors of the Gothic world but also to the 'problem' of women, brought about by Eve's disobedience. Eventually, death offers humanity the opportunity to escape the Gothic world and move into a place free from terror. The final chapter of this book, exploring this relationship between Gothic and the Bible manifested in Rossetti's prose works, provides a conclusion in itself to the roots of Rossettian Gothic.

Gothic, I conclude, fractured and incoherent from its earliest manifestations in Walpole, is closely related to Christian belief, drawing upon its traditions and biblical texts. One of the many threads constituting the fabric of Gothic is Christianity; early Gothic novels are undoubtedly produced within a framework of Christian belief, and Rossetti's poems extend this, setting her poetic narratives in a fallen world that she expresses as Gothic. The two terms, 'religious' and 'Gothic', seem to collide, but they demonstrably fit together in Rossetti's work, from the Maturin poems through to her prose works. Rossetti combines her faith with darker elements drawn from Gothic, producing poetry and prose which refigures the world around her as dark and full of terrors, and apparently irreconcilable to its maker, a problem which will be resolved at the Apocalypse. For Rossetti, then, Gothic is absorbed into her work, sometimes so deeply that it is barely apparent, but its attributes serve as a vehicle for her beliefs; she expresses the world and her anxieties in terms of Gothic tropes. To read Rossetti purely as a religious poet, then, is to miss the implications of her mode of expressing her faith; her work is caught up in a web of intertextuality, subtle influences and overtly expressed theology which constitute an original mode of Gothic.

Notes

Introduction

1 A recent book explores this aspect of poetry: *The Longman Book of Gothic Verse*, ed. Caroline Franklin (2010).

2 For example, see Thompson (1991), Roden (2002) and Morrison (1990).

3 Rossetti herself eschewed biography and any personal details as Valerie Sanders suggests: '[m]ost Victorian women saw autobiography as a forbidden area, and deliberately situated themselves outside its formal parameters' (1989, p. 5), noting that Rossetti 'concealed her more personal thoughts among the leaves of an Anglican reading diary [*Time Flies*]' (p. 1).

4 Other biographical readings include Packer (1963), who reads many of Rossetti's poems in the light of a hypothetical affair with the painter William Bell Scott, a theory which is now usually discredited.

5 Rossetti's childhood reading is discussed in some detail by Jan Marsh (1994), and further information on books owned by the Rossettis can be found in Fredeman (1973).

6 A similar argument has been put forward by John V. Murphy, who suggests that certain 'characteristics provide a means of demonstrating that Shelley takes from the Gothic tradition devices, moods, and ideas that permeate his total work. Although much of the obvious Gothic trapping is lost, it becomes apparent that the major poetry uses Gothic traits for very serious ends' (1975, p. 9).

7 For example, Rosenblum (1986) examines what feminist criticism can do for a subject, most particularly the then popular theme of 're-voicing' women poets silenced by their gender, and is based on a textual analysis of Rossetti's poems. Other examples include Abbott and Leder (1987), Greer (1992), Mayberry (1989), Psomiades (1999) and Edmond (1988).

8 See Harrison (1988), Hassett (2005) and Roe (2006). Other notable works which engage with Rossetti's faith include Westerholm (1999), Arseneau (1991, 2004) and Burlinson (1994).

9 Though Chapman and other writers have commented on Rossetti's absence from the text, this idea is more pertinent to her earlier works than to her later, devotional poems, which frequently demonstrate a surprisingly open and confessional tone.

10 'Speaking with the Dead: Recovering Lost Voices', in Chapman (2000, pp. 28–45).

11 This is particularly supported by recent studies including Wolfreys (2002) and Chapman (2000).

12 For pertinent examples of critical responses to *The Castle of Otranto*, see Clemens (1999, pp. 29–40) and Clery (1999, pp. 71–9).

13 For example, *The Age; A Poem: Moral, Political, and Metaphysical. With Illustrative Annotations. In Ten Books* (1810), pp. 209–10, cited in Napier (1987, p. 28).

14 Napier suggests that the aesthetics serve a distinct purpose, which point the reader to the true 'meaning' of Gothic, if such a thing can be found: 'An attempt to isolate the distinctive qualities of Gothic narrative brings the reader repeatedly back to this characteristic: Gothic is finally much less about evil, "the fascination of the abomination", than it is a standardized, absolutely formulaic system of creating a certain kind of atmosphere in which a reader's sensibility towards fear and horror is exercised in predictable ways' (p. 29, citing Hume, 1971, pp. 266–7). Rossetti's work is less formulaic in its problematizing of Gothic tropes, but retains the 'atmosphere' which is frequently dependent on aesthetics.

15 William St Clair (2004, pp. 280–4) discusses attempts to control women's reading, in particular novels and romances, which itself indicates the likelihood of women's propensity to read novels 'which raise expectations of extraordinary adventures and cause readers to admire extravagant passions, and lead to unacceptable conduct' (p. 280). This idea of the potentially damaging effects of women's reading is demonstrated in Charlotte Lennox's novel *The Female Quixote* (1752).

16 As Murphy (1975) rightly points out, the aesthetics or 'outward manifestations of Gothic' are 'critical because they draw our attention to the mood and situation that often determine the Gothic pattern we seek' (p. 17).

17 A notable literary example of a female character who chose to live the Gothic is of course Catherine Morland of *Northanger Abbey*, whose desire to enact the melodrama of her favourite novels is a source of comedy. However, in contrast to this, it has been pointed out by Fiona Price (2009) that women writers such as Maria Edgeworth and Joanna Baillie offer a pragmatic response to contemporary aesthetics, providing 'healthy lessons of association' which 'suggest [. . .] a relationship between matter and mind, between the empirical observation of the environment and the moral and intellectual development of the individual', a concept which returns the woman from object to subject (p. 111).

18 To read in terms of inner and outer worlds is particularly appropriate for Rossetti's work, since a dual reading such as this pertains to typology, which, as Landow explains, is a significant presence in nineteenth-century literature, and was particularly espoused by the Tractarians, who believed that 'the physical world bears a divine impress which the sensitive eye can read in terms of type and symbol' (Landow, 1980, p. 112).

19   It seems likely that this notion is gendered, being tailored to the female characters in the Gothic novel, since such excessive and draining emotion is more channelled and focused in the Romantic poets, for example; Derek Colville (1970) writes that for Romantic writers, 'the imagination is raised from a receptive state of "mind-wandering" to one of intense concentration from which the normally sensed world fades' (p. 59). This clarity of focused emotion is much more apposite for the Gothic represented in poetry.

20   This is discussed by a number of other critics, including Norton (2000, pp. ix–x).

21   For example, the list from 'The Age', cited in Napier (p. 28), offers 'A castle', 'A giant', 'A blood-stained dagger', 'A knight', 'A monk', 'A lamp', 'Skeletons' and 'A ghost'.

22   Tennyson (1981) writes that 'one could illustrate almost every Tractarian topic and interest [. . .] with poems from the pen of Christina Rossetti' (p. 201). Subsequently, books such as D'Amico (1999), Roe (2006) and Hassett (2005) have demonstrated the truth of Tennyson's statement.

23   An excellent and comprehensive introduction to Tractarianism and Ritualism is provided by John Shelton Reed in *Glorious Battle: The Cultural Politics of Victorian Anglo-Catholicism* (1996).

24   For further discussion of the Tractarians and their influence on and engagement with literature of the period, see Knight and Mason (2006, pp. 87–119).

25   A precursor to this architectural poetry would be George Herbert's *The Temple* (1633).

26   This is discussed in detail in a number of books, including Griffin (2004), which contains a chapter devoted to the Oxford Movement, particularly relating to the novels of Anthony Trollope. Paz (1992), includes a chapter on 'The Tractarian Factor', points out that 'Anglo-Catholicism's ceremonial and theological implications got mixed up in the debate over the Gothic Revival. For some conservative Evangelicals, the Gothic style was "Popery done in stone"' (p. 133). Shell (1999) discusses the history of Catholicism and English literature, and suggests that, long before the Gothic revival in England, the 'Italian city-state' was used as a site for 'horrors' (p. 54), and that the anti-Catholic trend of Gothic has its roots in a much earlier unease with Catholicism.

27   This is also discussed by Eino Railo (1927). Railo considers a direct line of influence from Shakespeare, taking in Milton and Spenser, Radcliffe and the Gothic, and the Romantic poets.

28   Rictor Norton's anthology of early Gothic literature includes a section on poetry, much of which is by Radcliffe, and also includes Charlotte Smith, Coleridge, Nathan Drake, Hannah Cowley and Matthew Lewis. Norton discusses the influence of Gothic novelists on the Romantic poets, citing Keats's 'Eve of St. Agnes' and Byron's 'Manfred' as examples, yet there is no consideration of the Gothic nature of the poetry, merely a cursory note on the poets' interest in (and disdain for) novelists such as Radcliffe and Lewis.

29 This idea is entertained briefly by Punter and Byron (2004): '[I]t is also important to notice that as early as the 1740s we can trace the development of a form of poetry which was radically different from anything Pope advocated, and which came to be called "graveyard poetry". Graveyard poetry is significant here because it prefigures the Gothic novel in several ways and its emergence was sudden and dramatic' (p. 10). Similarly, Andrew Smith (2004) mentions this concept, suggesting that the graveyard poets 'made a significant contribution to developing a Gothic ambience (by dwelling on feelings of loss), and provided an investigation into life and death that constituted a peculiarly Gothic metaphysic' (p. 52).

30 Napier suggests that Wordsworth and Coleridge offer 'sublime moments of discontinuity' (p. 6), which the Gothic rarely achieves, despite its apparent predisposition towards fragmentation and the sublime; rather, poetry as a mode of Gothic is more receptive to such moments which provide uplift in the midst of the most reflective and melancholy moments. Radcliffe, however, tends to switch register, using motifs of gulfs, graveyards, mountains and brinks to demonstrate a momentous moral, for example.

31 Peter M. Sacks, 'Gray's Elegy', in Bloom (1986, pp. 119–23), queries whether this is truly an elegy since it seems to be mourning humanity rather than a specific person (if one disregards Gray's recent loss of his friend Richard West), but concludes that '[t]his individual death, albeit imaginary, is that of the poet himself', who provides 'a definition of the terms by which he should be mourned' (p. 119). Such a preoccupation with the death of 'the poet' is a common feature of graveyard poetry, and also of many of Rossetti's poems.

32 As Harrison has suggested, Dante Gabriel Rossetti's poems and paintings tend to fetishize the beautiful, dead woman, constructing her as a passive object of love, untouchable in death. Rossetti also utilizes the image of the dead woman, notably in poems such as 'After Death' and 'At Home', but for her, the dead woman speaks; she is rarely passive and almost never silent. Jamison argues that Rossetti uses a poetics of stealth to provide a subtle break with the aestheticized dead woman of nineteenth-century poetry. Contrary to the expressive poetics with which the female poet was traditionally linked, Rossetti's poems are restrained and interior, providing a contrast to the objective and exterior corpses of women frequently appearing in her brother's and other nineteenth-century poems. Furthermore, Jamison argues that for Rossetti as for Plath and Sexton, death is an act of self-creation which increases women's autonomy within the liminal space of the poem. The female form is released from its material body, and, like poetry itself, provides an 'alternative materiality' (p. 275).

33 The contrast between these two poems is quite clearly that of 'terror Gothic' (usually associated with Radcliffe) and 'horror Gothic' (usually associated with Lewis), a fracture in Gothic created by Radcliffe herself in her 1826 essay 'The Supernatural in Poetry'.

34 Hassett (2005) discusses 'Birchington Churchyard' and suggests that the elegy is 'poignantly lovely and austerely uncomforted. This churchyard poem intimates the consolation that is wanted but which [. . .] she is far too honest to profess' (p. 201). Hassett also suggests that this churchyard reflection demonstrates a more mature and less idealized depiction than her earlier poems such as 'Remember me when I am gone away'.

Chapter 1

1 Wolfreys (2002), especially the Introduction (pp. 1–24).

2 This idea is considered in a different light by W. David Shaw (1999), who examines the intentional ventriloquizing of the spectral poet speaking through the mouth of a fictional speaker in a poetic monologue. The poets he considers in detail are Browning, Tennyson, Arnold, Coleridge, Morris and Keats, though Rossetti's later monologic poems are mentioned briefly. This ventriloquism has a ghostly effect of raising the dead in many instances (pp. 9–11).

3 Furthermore, Tim Armstrong (2000), outlines the relationship between writing and death, linked by memory, and goes so far as to suggest that '[t]he career of the writer is founded on death' (p. 16), and that, therefore, a haunting attributed to an object or a place in fact occurs in the eye of the poet (p. 30) (e.g. in Hardy's poem 'Old Furniture').

4 For Bloom, however, the 'strong poets' are invariably male.

5 A. Schopenhauer, 'Essay on Spirit Seeing and Everything Connected Therewith' in *Parerga and Paralipomena*, ed. E. F. J. Payne (Oxford: Clarendon Press, 2000), pp. 225–309 (p. 238).

6 The double is a Pre-Raphaelite preoccupation, appearing in numerous Pre-Raphaelite poems and paintings, often using reflections and shadows as well as doppelgängers, such as *How They Met Themselves* (1861), by Dante Gabriel Rossetti; *The Awakening Conscience* (1853) and *The Shadow of Death* (1869–73), by William Holman Hunt; and *The Baleful Head*, by Edward Burne-Jones (1886–7).

7 Emma Parker (1998) proposes that Rossetti's poems of death can be explained by her 'wish that her work be remembered' as well as her own belief in life after death (p. 322).

8 Chapman suggests that for Rossetti, '[s]eeing what is not usually in focus is a theme to which Rossetti continually returns, as part of her Tractarian typological heritage; as she urges [. . .] in *Time Flies*, "less depends on the 'seeing' than on the seer"' (2000, p. 8).

9 Derrida (1994, p. xix). It is interesting to note that Tim Armstrong suggests that Hardy frequently 'describes the dead as wronged, misrepresented or unreported by

the texts of history' (2000, p. 90), though he concludes that: 'What saves the dead from history, then, is carried within the phrase 'mute thought' and its cognates: in the recollection of ghosts; in the evocation of the muttering and vanishing of the souls of the slain; in close attention to the curious calls of the dead' (p. 102).

10   This is in itself a problematic concept, however. Schaffer points out that '[t]he recovery of worthwhile female authors seemed more important than the question of their possible allegiance to a literary and cultural genre' (2000, p. 172), which is an issue that more recent feminist criticism has been addressing.

11   Garber (1987), Vine (1992), Rose (1991).

12   Marsh discusses this poem in her biography of Rossetti, and suggests that it is indicative of a genuine secret, which may be that she was abused by her father, Gabriele Rossetti. However, others, such as Burlinson, take issue with this suggestion, and argue that to probe the possible 'secret' is unproductive.

13   For further discussion of this, see Parker (1998, pp. 317–18).

14   In *Christina Rossetti in Context*, Harrison points out the necessity of an attempt to reconstruct context for Rossetti's poetry, commenting: 'Moreover, as only the most recent commentators have begun to indicate, her aesthetic values often derive from extremely diverse and sometimes ostensibly incompatible literary sources' (p. 1). The book covers a wide range of contextual issues, including Tractarianism, Dante and Pre-Raphaelitism, but little about Gothic.

15   Bloom posits that poems are too often read from a cultural viewpoint that values social aspects over the aesthetic: 'This reduces the aesthetic to ideology, or at best to metaphysics. A poem cannot be read *as a poem*, because it is primarily a social document or, rarely yet possibly, an attempt to overcome a philosophy' (1995, p. 18).

16   Crump cites 'The Daemon Lover', Sir Walter Scott (1771–1832), in *Minstrelsy of the Scottish Border* (1802–3).

17   This is not an unusual theme for a ballad; as Hugh Shields argues: '[w]riters in English attempted, as Bürger had done, to dress the traditional theme of the revenant lover in modern garb, using literary resources unknown to the old ballads' (1972, p. 98).

18   The 'supernaturalization' of which she speaks is that of 2 Corinthians 4.18: 'While we look not at the things which are seen, but at the things which are not seen: for the things which are seen are temporal; but the things which are not seen are eternal.'

19   Rossetti would have been familiar with the words of Deuteronomy 18.10–12: 'There shall not be found among you any one that maketh his son or his daughter to pass through the fire, or that useth divination, or an observer of times, or an enchanter, or a witch. Or a charmer, or a consulter with familiar spirits, or a wizard, or a necromancer. For all that do these things are an abomination unto the LORD: and because of these abominations the LORD thy God doth drive them out from before thee.'

20 'I hold without wavering that there is a Purgatory, and that souls there detained are aided by the suffrages of the faithful' ('Section 1: Statement of the Roman Doctrine Concerning Purgatory', para. 6).

21 Genesis 2.17: 'But of the tree of the knowledge of good and evil, thou shalt not eat of it: for in the day that thou eatest thereof thou shalt surely die.'

22 John Woolford notes that 'the sea is an ambiguous image in Rossetti's work. As a representative of life, it is turbulent and destructive, and she positions herself far from it, yet with a sense of it as the goal to which streams, and herself imaged as a stream, inevitably run. As that, it can stand for death' (2003, p. 33).

Chapter 2

1 Growing critical attention has been focused on the juvenilia of Jane Austen, George Eliot, John Ruskin, and others. For example, the Juvenilia Press was set up at the University of New South Wales for the purpose of bringing the juvenile works of such authors to a wider academic audience.

2 Other texts read, or at least owned, by Rossetti are indicated by Fredeman (1973), who states that books in Christina Rossetti's library included John Gay's *Fables* (1727), Jeremy Taylor, *Holy Living and Dying* (1837), the anonymous *Tales of Terror* (1808), Maturin, *Women* (1818), Oliver Goldsmith, *The Vicar of Wakefield* (1766), Newman's *Dream of Gerontius* (1865), Charles Cayley's *The Psalms in Metre* (1860) and Swinburne's *A Century of Roundels* (1883).

3 Rossetti's Maturin poems are considered seriously by two notable critics, who explore a single aspect of their impact: Rosenblum (1986) considers aspects of rivalry which develop from the *Women* poems, and D'Amico (1999) further considers the theology of these poems.

4 Rossetti wrote in a letter to Caroline Gemmer: 'So you think I once trembled on the "convent threshold" – Not seriously ever, tho' I went through a sort of romantic impression on the subject like many young people. No, I feel no drawing in that direction: really, of the two, I might perhaps have less unadaptedness in some ways to the hermit life' (dated 'June 27'), quoted in Harrison (1988, p. 189).

5 In a letter to W. M. Rossetti dated 28 April 1849, Rossetti wrote: 'I must beg that you will not fix upon any [of her poems, to pass on to Thomas Woolner] which the most imaginative person could construe into love personals' (Harrison, 1997, I, p. 16).

6 D'Amico writes that '[i]f Rossetti had simply been looking for distressed females and unhappy love affairs of which to write, the works of Lewis, Radcliffe, Scott and, later, Dickens would have provided several' (1981, p. 120).

7 Maturin, 1977, I, p. v. Subsequent page references are to this edition.

8 This idea was discussed in detail by Carlyle, who suggests: 'Was the tongue suspended there, that it might tell truly what we had seen, and make man the soul's

brother of man; or only that it might utter vain sounds, jargon, soul-confusing, and so *divide* man, as by enchanted walls of Darkness, from union with man? Thou who wearest that cunning, Heaven-made organ, a Tongue, think well of this. Speak not, I passionately entreat thee, till thy thought have silently matured itself, till thou have other than mad and mad-making noises to emit: *hold thy tongue* (thou hast it a-holding) till *some* meaning lie behind to set it wagging. Consider the significance of SILENCE: it is boundless, never by meditating to be exhausted, unspeakably profitable to thee!' (Carlyle, 1858, p. 324).

9 The monologic form is itself significant. Shaw argues that the monologue both addressed issues of divided selfhood and offered the poet the opportunity to become a 'hidden God' in ventriloquizing through their poems. The poem conforms to the traditional construction of the tragic soliloquy in many ways (see Belsey, 1985, pp. 42–7 for more detail on the tragic soliloquy).

10 See Nilda Jimenez (1979) for further details.

11 Except in direct quotation from Rossetti's poems, however, 'Zaira' will be used throughout.

12 Jerome McGann discusses Rossetti's theology in detail, suggesting that it should be taken seriously and considered in the light of contemporary theological debates. In particular, he comments on her use of the doctrine of 'soul sleep', adding that it provides 'the means for paradisal images which answer to her emotional needs' (1983, p. 139). While the relevance of Rossetti's emotional needs is debatable, her apparently fluctuating approach towards the nature of heaven suggests that it could be tailored to her literary requirements.

13 Marsh, in 'The Spider's Shadow', uses this poem as an illustration of Rossetti's 'fascination with death' (Liebregts and Tigges, 1996, p. 24), and, more specifically, with 'the sensation of oneself being dead and in the grave, buried, under the earth, but as if still sentient' (p. 25). Though Marsh's concern with the Rossettian aesthetics of Gothic succeeds in reclaiming her 'into the mainstream of Romantic writing, within a European tradition that places despair, spiritual anguish, alienation and self-disgust as central elements' this particular account of Rossetti's poetry fails to place Rossetti's faith in its necessary context (p. 30).

14 It is interesting to compare this poem with Letitia Landon's 1829 poem 'Revenge', which is in many ways a much more straightforward poem, desiring revenge upon an unfaithful lover, but in its four-line stanzas and use of bitter words as well as similar phraseology, it is clearly comparable. Rossetti read Landon's poetry in her youth and it is quite possible that she drew upon her predecessor's work as well as that of Maturin.

15 The full version, with W. M. Rossetti's excisions, is held by the British Library, Ashley MS 1364, in no. 1 of 6 notebooks.

16 Luke 20.33–36: 'Therefore in the resurrection whose wife of them is she? for seven had her to wife. And Jesus answering said unto them, The children of this world

marry, and are given in marriage: But they which shall be accounted worthy to obtain that world, and the resurrection from the dead, neither marry, nor are given in marriage: Neither can they die any more: for they are equal unto the angels; and are the children of God, being the children of the resurrection.'

17 It is interesting to note, however, that Anne Williams suggests that anxieties about femininity are to a certain extent reflected in the Gothic novel's concern with the Catholic 'mother' church (1995, p. 117).

18 Roe suggests that 'Rossetti's flowers and plants are all a testimony to God's love' (2006, p. 23).

19 Leviticus 16.22: 'And the goat shall bear upon him all their iniquities, unto a land not inhabited: and he shall let go the goat into the wilderness.'

Chapter 3

1 Ruskin's Gothic is of course the Gothic of medieval architecture, and I am not suggesting that literary Gothic is the same as architectural, but there are many similarities in Ruskin's approach to the Gothic and the approach of literary Gothic, as I shall discuss.

2 Certainly Ruskin, if not Rossetti, would have been aware of Burke's *A Philosophical Enquiry into the Origin of Our Ideas on the Sublime and the Beautiful* (1757). Burke links the sublime to terror, and describes it as causing a passion, from which 'arises the great power of the sublime' (1967, p. 57).

3 For example, Kayser (1957), and Clayborough (1965) provide detailed histories of the grotesque in English and European literature and history, including etymological considerations.

4 It seems likely that Ruskin's conception of 'nobility' corresponds to that of Keble, who writes in his *Lectures* of 'the more austere qualities of purity, integrity, strenuousness, goodness' (2003, I, p. 71).

5 However, Isobel Armstrong suggests that 'The Grotesque is not a sign of degeneration or decadence. Indeed, it is the vital possession of a healthy culture and takes different forms in different periods' (1993, p. 236). While Ruskin may have been writing about a fallen city, he nonetheless admires the grotesque as essential to the production of art.

6 The notion of the ludicrous as an aspect of the grotesque is noted by Lee Byron Jennings: 'The familiar structure of existence is undermined and chaos seems imminent. This aspect is intensified when concrete manifestations of decay appear and a feeling of hopelessness and corruption is developed. The ludicrous aspect, in turn, arises from the farcical quality inherent in such scenes of absurdity and approaching chaos' (1963, p. 18).

7 Moreover, it is not just in linking or dividing the physical and the transcendent that the grotesque is significant. Bakhtin proposes that '[w]e find at the basis of grotesque imagery a special concept of the body as a whole and of the limits of this whole. The confines between the body and the world and between separate bodies are drawn in the grotesque genre quite differently than in the classic and naturalist images' (1984, p. 31).

8 Rossetti's use of grotesque animal figures suggests the comment of Thomas Browne in *Religio Medici* (1642): 'There are no Grotesques in Nature; not anything framed to fill up empty Cantons, and unnecessary spaces. In the most imperfect Creatures and such as were not presented in the Ark, but, having their Seeds and Principles in the womb of Nature, are everywhere, where the power of the Sun is, in these is the Wisdom of His hand discovered' (1940, pp. 32–3).

9 For example, Chapman (2000). Yet the very existence of a potential secret is significant; Miller suggests that 'secrecy would seem to be a mode whose ultimate meaning lies in the subject's insistence that he is radically inaccessible to the culture that would otherwise entirely determine him' (1988, p. 185). This implies Rossetti's deliberate evasion of critical interpretation, yet in other poems, what might otherwise be a secret (e.g. the paternity of an illegitimate child) is immediately laid open to the reader. Isobel Armstrong describes the poem as 'flagrant coquetry' (Cosslett, 1996, p. 164).

10 This 'disappearance' of an author from a text suggests a different aspect of spectrality; that of the 'death of the author'. Roland Barthes, in *Image, Music, Text*, proposes that the figure of the author is a construction of the reader (and a modern one at that) which is always fallacious, being based on individual interpretations of a text and frequently misleading biographical details, which can cause the reader to fail to interact with a text: 'To give an Author to a text is to impose upon that text a stop clause, to furnish it with a final signification, to close the writing [. . .] once the Author is discovered, the text is "explained"' (p. 147). A spectre can never be explained, or explained away; if a 'final' meaning is assigned to a text, its spectres are dead though its author may have been revived.

11 This argument also permits the reading of classical authors, for example, whose beliefs were pagan but could still provide some moral guidance.

12 The widespread impact of physiognomy, particularly among the educated urban middle classes in the nineteenth century, is examined in detail in Pearl (2010).

13 In discussing *Sing-Song*, Hassett also refers to Rossetti's work as incorporating a form of 'serious play', which 'provides direct access to the pleasure of form, the source of the poet's "inward laughter," and demonstrates the range and mix of her tonalities' (2005, p. 119).

14 Discussing the grotesque or monstrous human form, Williams (1996) makes a similar point: 'The human body is the primeval matrix of all the chief figures and analogies by which human language seeks to understand reality; it is the model for

the world and the universe, just as it is the chief source of metaphors for the other and our relation to the other. The deforming of this governing form negates the equating of the limits of the real to the limits of discourse and reveals the realm of the monster as the step beyond the borders of affirmative discourse into the realm of the real' (p. 176).

15 It is interesting to contrast this with William Morris's long poem, *The Earthly Paradise*. Morris offers two perspectives of the earth: from God's point of view, telling the 'dwellers on the lovely earth' to 'take heed of how the daisies grow'; and from a human perspective, asking the 'brooder on the hills of heaven', reminding God of 'to what a heaven the earth might grow'. Morris's poem figures the earth, not as fallen, but as essentially good and beautiful, though doomed by mankind's own failures (1869, pp. 463–4).

16 It is worth noting, however, that Harrison writes that the final tercet of the poem 'enables the speaker (and prospectively the reader) to escape the traditional dialectics – of beauty and horror, desire and destruction, seduction and damnation' (1988, p. 90).

Chapter 4

1 For example, Campbell (1990), Helsinger (1991), Thompson (1991), Holt (1990), Morrill (1990) and Shurbutt (1992). Other significant interpretations of 'Goblin Market' include Carpenter (1991), D'Amico (1999, pp. 68–83), Hassett (2005, pp. 15–63) and Moers (1978, pp. 100–7).

2 Edmond also lists some significant interpretations of the poem on p. 170.

3 It is interesting to note here Mikhail Bakhtin's comment linking grotesque exaggeration and consumption: 'Such exaggeration is [. . .] most strongly expressed in picturing the body and food' (1984, p. 303).

4 It is possible to read the figures of the poem as another kind of caricatural grotesque, that of the consuming, shopping woman, as Lysack (2008) has done. She relates the desire for consumption in 'Goblin Market' to the consumer issues of 'imperialism and race' (p. 16) of the period.

5 Despite Duffy's reading, it is worth noting that the goblins specifically ask for hair from her head, in lines 123–5. Though one can see how Duffy's interpretation fits in with a sexual reading of the transaction between Laura and the goblins, this is a very loose interpretation of the text.

6 Waldman, however, discusses 'Shut Out' with reference to the figure of Eve, but without directly linking the narrator who is 'shut out' with Eve herself. Instead, it is figured as a Gothic poem which 'provides a warning that the subject must carefully discriminate between different opportunities for submission' (p. 38).

7   For example, Rosenblum (1986, p. 94). However, Anne Williams points out that, in the Gothic tradition, marriage cannot necessarily be read as a happy ending (1995, p. 138).

8   It seems likely that this line, 'Hardened by sun and air', is a pun on the poem's conclusion, in which the speaker is triumphant because she has borne a son and heir.

9   Dante Gabriel Rossetti shows a similar sympathy for the fallen women in many of his poems, most famously 'Jenny', but also 'Stratton Water' and 'Rose Mary'. Like his sister, he displays an awareness of the hypocrisy inherent in social attitudes towards women, which he exposes in his poetry.

10 Of course, later in the century Robert Louis Stevenson's *The Strange Case of Dr Jekyll and Mr Hyde* (1886) would incorporate these two characters into one figure.

11 For more discussion of the position of the fallen woman, see Anderson (1993).

12 For example, Battiscombe (1980) makes much of this aspect of Rossetti's personality, as the title of the biography implies.

13 It is noteworthy that Marina Warner discusses the concept of blondeness, or golden hair, as a fairy-tale construct of virginity (1994, pp. 371–86).

14 A significant difference, however, is that while Cinderella is a passive victim of her family's spite towards her, Laura participates willingly in her own moral fall, making her sister's redemption of her all the more significant.

15 Despite this, William Michael Rossetti suggests that she disliked Milton's poetry apart from his sonnets (WMR, p. lxx).

16 The influence of *The Faerie Queene* on Rossetti's work is discussed in Humphries (2008a).

Chapter 5

1   Ruskin, 'Of Queens' Gardens', in *Sesame and Lilies*, Cook and Wedderburn, XVIII, pp. 5–187 (p. 127).

2   Of these prose texts, several are also available online.

3   For example, Burgon stated: 'Inferior to us GOD made you: and our inferior to the end of time you will remain'; and 'If you set about becoming Man's rival, or rather if you try to be, what you can never become, Man's equal [. . .] you have in a manner unsexed yourselves, and must needs put up with the bitter consequence' (Meyrick Goulburn, 1892, II, pp. 236–7).

4   Examples of contemporary women writers' religious prose include Yonge's *Womankind* (1876), while more theological prose was produced by writers such as Josephine Butler's *The New Era* (1872) and *Hour Before the Dawn* (1878). Mark M. Freed also argues that with the publication of *Robert Elsmere* (1888), 'Mary Ward became a high-profile player in Anglican theological debate' ('The Moral

Irrelevance of Dogma: Mary Ward and Critical Theology in England', pp. 133–47, in Melnyk, 1998, p. 134).

5   The sentence quoted as epigraph to this chapter continues: 'There *is* one dangerous science for women – one which they must indeed beware how they profanely touch – that of theology. Strange, and miserably strange, that while they are modest enough to doubt their powers, and pause at the threshold of sciences where every step is demonstrable and sure, they will plunge headlong, and without one thought of incompetency, into that science in which the greatest men have trembled, and the wisest erred. Strange, that they will complacently and pridefully bind up whatever vice or folly there is in them, whatever arrogance, petulance, or blind incomprehensiveness, into one bitter bundle of consecrated myrrh. Strange, in creatures born to be Love visible, that where they can know least, they will condemn first, and think to recommend themselves to their Master, by scrambling up the steps of His judgment throne, to divide it with Him. Strangest of all, that they should think they were led by the Spirit of the Comforter into habits of mind which have become in them the unmixed elements of home discomfort; and that they dare to turn the Household Gods of Christianity into ugly idols of their own; – spiritual dolls, for them to dress according to their caprice; and from which their husbands must turn away in grieved contempt, lest they should be shrieked at for breaking them.' Ruskin, 'Of Queens' Gardens', pp. 127–8.

6   For example, in *The Mysteries of Udolpho*, the following passage describes the journey of Emily, Valancourt and St Aubert through the Pyrenees: 'The ruggedness of the unfrequented road often obliged the wanderers to alight from their little carriage, but they thought themselves amply repaid for this inconvenience by the grandeur of the scenes; and, while the muleteer led his animals slowly over the broken ground, the travellers had leisure to linger amid these solitudes, and to indulge the sublime reflections, which soften, while they elevate, the heart, and fill it with the certainty of a present God! Still the enjoyment of St. Aubert was touched with that pensive melancholy, which gives to every object a mellower tint, and breathes a sacred charm over all around' (Radcliffe, 1980, p. 28).

7   Davenport-Hines discusses a shift in attitude towards mountain scenery as the result of the writings of Thomas Burnett (1635–1715), whose work 'identified mountain scenery in all its horror as product and symbol of the Fall: such terrain was punitive of desire, a reminder of how God obliterates the perverse and the transgressive' (1998, p. 25).

8   For example, in *Melmoth the Wanderer*, a faint light from the moon illuminates and then vanishes from the scene of Isidora and Melmoth's wedding ceremony, casting the sinister rites into a gloom that is not just physical but spiritual: 'At that moment the moon, that had so faintly lit the chapel, sunk behind a cloud, and everything was enveloped in darkness so profound, that Isidora did not recognize the figure of Melmoth till her hand was clasped in his, and his voice whispered,

"He is here – ready to unite us". Maturin, *Melmoth the Wanderer*, p. 394. A different approach can be seen in *The Romance of the Forest*, where the light shining in darkness has a transcendent and spiritual effect: 'The first tender tints of morning now appeared on the verge of the horizon, stealing upon the darkness; – so pure, so fine, so ethereal! it seemed as if Heaven was opening to the view.' Ann Radcliffe, *The Romance of the Forest*, ed. Chloë Chard (Oxford: Oxford University Press, 1999), p. 30.

9   The Tenth Commandment reads: 'Thou shalt not covet thy neighbour's house, thou shalt not covet thy neighbour's wife, nor his manservant, nor his maidservant, nor his ox, nor his ass, nor any thing that is thy neighbour's' (Exodus 20.17).

10 Robert M. Kachur, 'Envisioning Equality, Asserting Authority: Women's Devotional Writings on the Apocalypse 1845–1900', in Melnyk, 1998, pp. 3–36 (p. 15).

11 Furthermore, Barbara Garlick (2002), states that Rossetti 'gestures towards a possible transcendent moment, a stepping through the mirror to confront the beatific vision, not through mystical union in the afterlife, but through language' (p. 158). Not only in heaven, but in her own written glimpse of heaven, can the threshold be crossed.

12 Sedgwick (1986) offers some pertinent comments on the necessity of the linking of surface and depth. Stating that the surface or aesthetics of Gothic are ignored at the risk of losing the meaning, she stresses the inextricable nature of surface and depth, discussing as an example markings on flesh and veils which serve as signifiers. She suggests that surface is in fact all that a writer *can* present; the meaning comes from the reader (pp. 140–67).

13 Revelation 2.20–23: 'Notwithstanding I have a few things against thee, because thou sufferest that woman Jezebel, which calleth herself a prophetess, to teach and to seduce my servants to commit fornication, and to eat things sacrificed unto idols. And I gave her space to repent of her fornication; and she repented not. Behold, I will cast her into a bed, and them that commit adultery with her into great tribulation, except they repent of their deeds. And I will kill her children with death; and all the churches shall know that I am he which searcheth the reins and hearts: and I will give unto every one of you according to your works.'

14 Revelation 17.3–6: 'So he carried me away in the spirit into the wilderness: and I saw a woman sit upon a scarlet coloured beast, full of names of blasphemy, having seven heads and ten horns. And the woman was arrayed in purple and scarlet colour, and decked with gold and precious stones and pearls, having a golden cup in her hand full of abominations and filthiness of her fornication: And upon her forehead was a name written, MYSTERY, BABYLON THE GREAT, THE MOTHER OF HARLOTS AND ABOMINATIONS OF THE EARTH. And I saw the woman drunken with the blood of the saints, and with the blood of the martyrs of Jesus: and when I saw her, I wondered with great admiration.'

15 Revelation 21.2: 'And I John saw the holy city, new Jerusalem, coming down from God out of heaven, prepared as a bride adorned for her husband.'

16 Revelation 12.1: 'And there appeared a great wonder in heaven; a woman clothed with the sun, and the moon under her feet, and upon her head a crown of twelve stars.'

17 Hassett suggests that 'A favourite figure [of Rossetti] is the half-moon' (2005, p. 213). The moon features in poems such as 'A Face of Plaintive Sweetness', clearly symbolic of as yet unredeemed womanhood.

18 Such complete final redemption is not to be assumed; usually it is a hope rather than a conviction: 'As elaborated in Augustinian theology, the condition of fallenness derives from the act of original sin. But although fallenness traces to an act of will, no amount of remorse or repentance enables us to transcend our fallen state through our own resolution. One can hope for a divine, uplifting act of grace, but such a dispensation will come only if one is among the predetermined number of the elect' (Anderson, 1993, p. 3).

19 Williams's response is of his time; other responses to the female figures of Revelation have been unequivocal and even extreme, such as D. H. Lawrence's response to Revelation 12.1: 'She has brought into the Bible what it lacked before: the great cosmic Mother robed and splendid, but persecuted. And she is, of course, essential to the scheme of power and splendour, which must have a queen' (1932, p. 155).

20 For example, Isidora's moments of transcendence in prison in *Melmoth the Wanderer*, or Julia's brief exhilaration after the ball in Radcliffe's *A Sicilian Romance*.

Conclusion

1 McGann argues in 'The Religious Poetry of Christina Rossetti' that this a problem for most Christian poetry, which suffers from its apparent 'thematic uniformity' in which theological differences and the poetics and approach of different poets 'tend to disappear into a basically congruent economy of Christian thought' (1983, p. 127).

Bibliography

Abbott, Andrea, and Sharon Leder, *The Language of Exclusion: The Poetry of Emily Dickinson and Christina Rossetti* (New York: Greenwood Press, 1987)

Anderson, Amanda, *Tainted Souls and Painted Faces: The Rhetoric of Fallenness in Victorian Culture* (Ithaca: Cornell University Press, 1993)

Armstrong, Isobel, *Victorian Poetry: Poetry, Poetics and Politics* (London: Routledge, 1993)

Armstrong, Tim, *Haunted Hardy: Poetry, History, Memory* (Basingstoke: Palgrave, 2000)

Arseneau, Mary, *Recovering Christina Rossetti: Female Community and Incarnational Poetics* (Basingstoke: Palgrave Macmillan, 2004)

—, *Symbol and Sacrament: The Incarnational Aesthetic of Christina Rossetti* (London, ON: University of Western Ontario Press, 1991)

Auerbach, Nina, *Romantic Imprisonment: Women and Other Glorified Outcasts* (New York: Columbia University Press, 1986)

—, *Woman and the Demon: The Life of a Victorian Myth* (Cambridge, MA: Harvard University Press, 1982)

Bagehot, Walter, *Literary Studies*, 2 vols (London: Dent, 1911)

Bakhtin, Mikhail, *Rabelais and His World*, trans. H. Iswolsky (Bloomington: Indiana University Press, 1984)

Barker, Juliet, *The Brontës* (London: Phoenix, 1995)

Barthes, Roland, *Image, Music, Text*, trans. and ed. Stephen Heath (New York: Noonday, 1977)

Battiscombe, Georgina, *Christina Rossetti: A Divided Life* (London: Constable, 1980)

Bauckham, Richard, *The Theology of the Book of Revelation* (Cambridge: Cambridge University Press, 1993)

Belsey, Catherine, *The Subject of Tragedy: Identity and Difference in Renaissance Drama* (London: Methuen, 1985)

Bettelheim, Bruno, *The Uses of Enchantment: The Meaning and Importance of Fairytales* (London: Penguin, 1991)

Bloom, Clive, *Gothic Histories: The Taste for Terror, 1764 to the Present* (London: Continuum, 2010)

Bloom, Harold, *The Anxiety of Influence: A Theory of Poetry* (New York: Oxford University Press, 1973)

—, (ed.), *Poets of Sensibility and the Sublime* (New York: Chelsea House, 1986)

—, *The Western Canon: The Books and School of the Ages* (London: Macmillan, 1995)

Botting, Fred, *Gothic* (London: Routledge, 1996)

Browne, Thomas, *Religio Medici*, facsimile of 1642 edition (London: Nelson, 1940)

Browning, Robert, 'To Thomas Forbes Kelsall', *Fortnightly Review* 18 (1872), 51–75

Burke, Edmund, *A Philosophical Enquiry into the Origin of Our Ideas of the Sublime and the Beautiful*, ed. J. T. Boulton (London: Routledge and Kegan Paul, 1958; repr. 1967)

Burlinson, Kathleen J., *Speaking Silence: Indeterminate Identities in the Writings of Christina Rossetti* (London: University of London Press, 1994)

Campbell, Elizabeth, 'Of Mothers and Merchants: Female Economics in Christina Rossetti's "Goblin Market"', *Victorian Studies* 33.3 (1990), 393–410

Carlyle, Thomas, *Critical and Miscellaneous Essays* (Boston: Phillips, Samson, 1858)

Carpenter, Mary Wilson, '"Eat Me, Drink Me, Love Me": The Consumable Female Body in Christina Rossetti's "Goblin Market"', *Victorian Poetry*, 29.4 (1991), 415–34

Castle, Terry, *The Female Thermometer: Eighteenth-Century Culture and the Invention of the Uncanny* (Oxford: Oxford University Press, 1995)

Chapman, Alison, *The Afterlife of Christina Rossetti* (New York: Macmillan, 2000)

Charlesworth, Michael, ed., *The Gothic Revival 1720–1870*, 3 vols (Mountfield, Sussex: Helm Information, 2002)

Clayborough, Arthur, *The Grotesque in English Literature* (Oxford: Clarendon Press, 1965)

Clemens, Valdine, *The Return of the Repressed: Gothic Horror from the Castle of Otranto to Alien* (Albany, NY: State University of New York Press, 1999)

Clery, Emma J., *The Rise of Supernatural Fiction, 1762–1800* (Cambridge: Cambridge University Press, 1999)

Colville, Derek, *Victorian Poetry and the Romantic Religion* (Albany, NY: State University of New York Press, 1970)

Cooke, Thomas, *A Practical and Familiar View of the Science of Physiognomy* (London: Camberwell, 1819)

Cosslett, Tess, ed., *Victorian Women Poets* (Harlow: Addison Wesley Longman, 1996)

D'Amico, Diane, *Christina Rossetti: Faith, Gender and Time* (Baton Rouge: Louisiana State University Press, 1999)

—, 'Christina Rossetti: The Maturin Poems', *Victorian Poetry* 19 (1981), 117–37

Dante, *The Commedia and Canzoniere of Dante Alighieri*, trans. and ed. E. H. Plumptre, 2 vols (London: Isbister, 1887)

Davenport-Hines, *Richard, Gothic: Four Hundred Years of Excess, Horror, Evil and Ruin* (London: Fourth Estate, 1998)

De Quincey, Thomas, *Confessions of an English Opium Eater and Other Writings*, ed. Barry Milligan (London: Penguin, 2003)

de Staël, Germaine, *Corinne, or Italy*, trans. and ed. S. Raphael (Oxford: Oxford University Press, 1998)

Defoe, Daniel, *An Essay on the History and Reality of Apparitions (1727)*, ed. G. A. Starr (London: Pickering & Chatto, 2005)

DeLaMotte, Eugenia C., *Perils of the Night: A Feminist Study of Nineteenth-Century Gothic* (Oxford: Oxford University Press, 1990)

Derrida, Jacques, *Margins of Philosophy*, trans. Alan Bass (Chicago: University of Chicago Press, 1982), pp. 308–30

—, *Specters of Marx*, trans. Peggy Kamuf and ed. Bernd Magnus and Stephen Cullenberg (New York: Routledge, 1994)

Dixon Hunt, John, *The Wider Sea: A Life of John Ruskin* (London: Orion, 1998)

Duffy, Maureen, *The Erotic World of Faery* (St. Albans: Granada, 1972)

Edmond, Rod, *Affairs of the Hearth: Victorian Poetry and Domestic Narrative* (Cambridge: Cambridge University Press, 1988)

Empson, William, *Seven Types of Ambiguity* (London: Penguin, 1930; repr. 1965)

Foucault, Michel, *Discipline and Punish,* trans. A. Sheridan (London: Penguin, 1991)

Franklin, Caroline, ed., *The Longman Book of Gothic Verse* (London: Longman, 2010)

Fredeman, William, *Books from the Libraries of Christina, Dante Gabriel, and William Michael Rossetti* (London: Bertram Rota, 1973)

Freud, Sigmund, *Collected Papers, Volume IV*, ed. Joan Riviere (London: Hogarth Press, 1949)

—, *Jokes and Their Relation to the Unconscious*, trans. and ed. James Strachey (London: Penguin, 1976)

—, *An Outline of Psychoanalysis*, trans. Helena Ragg-Kirkby, intro. Malcolm Bowie (London: Penguin, 2003; first published in 1940)

Frye, Northrop, *The Great Code: The Bible and Literature* (London: Routledge, 1982)

Garber, Marjorie B., *Shakespeare's Ghost Writers: Literature as Uncanny Causality* (London: Methuen, 1987)

Garlick, Barbara, ed., *Tradition and the Poetics of Self in Nineteenth-Century Women's Poetry* (Amsterdam: Rodopi, 2002)

Gosse, Edmund, *Critical Kit-Kats* (New York: Dodd, Mead, 1903), pp. 131–62

—, *Essays of Edmund Gosse* (London: Heineman, 1913)

Goulburn, Edward Meyrick, *John William Burgon, Late Dean of Chichester: A Biography, with Extracts from His Letters and Early Journals*, 2 vols (London: John Murray, 1892)

Gould, Joan, *Spinning Straw into Gold: What Fairytales Reveal about the Transformations in a Woman's Life* (New York: Randon House, 2005)

Gould, Sabine Baring, *The Lives of the Saints*, 16 vols (London: John Hodges, 1914; first published 1872–7)

Greer, Germaine, introd., *Goblin Market*, ed. Christina Rossetti (New York: Stonehill Publishing, 1975)

—, *Slipshod Sibyls: Recognition, Rejection and the Woman Poet* (London: Viking, 1992)

Griffin, Susan M., *Anti-Catholicism and Nineteenth-Century Fiction* (Cambridge: Cambridge University Press, 2004)

Hadfield, Andrew, *Edmund Spenser's Irish Experience: Wilde Fruit and Salvage Soyl* (Oxford: Clarendon Press, 1997)

Harpham, Geoffrey Galt, *On the Grotesque: Strategies of Contradiction in Art and Literature* (Princeton: Princeton University Press, 1982)

Harrison, Antony H., *Christina Rossetti in Context* (Brighton: Harvester, 1988)

—, ed., *The Letters of Christina Rossetti*, 2 vols (Charlottesville: University of Virginia Press, 1997 and 1999)

Hassett, Constance W., *Christina Rossetti: The Patience of Style* (Charlottesville: University of Virginia Press, 2005)

Hazlitt, William, *Lectures on the Dramatic Literature of the Age of Elizabeth: Delivered at the Surrey Institution* (London: John Warren, 1820)

Helsinger, Elizabeth K., 'Consumer Power and the Utopia of Desire: Christina Rossetti's "Goblin Market"', *English Literary History* 58.4 (1991), 903–33

Herdman, John, *The Double in Nineteenth-Century Fiction* (Basingstoke: Macmillan, 1990)

Hick, John, *Death and Eternal Life* (London: Collins, 1976)

Hogg, James, *The Private Memoirs and Confessions of a Justified Sinner*, ed. John Carey (Oxford: Oxford University Press, 1969; repr. 2009)

Holland, Norman N. and Leona F. Sherman, 'Gothic Possibilities', *New Literary History* 8 (1977), 279–94

Holt, Timothy, '"Men Sell Not Such in Any Town": Exchange in Goblin Market', *Victorian Poetry* 28.1 (1990), 51–67

Howells, Coral Ann, *Love, Mystery and Misery: Feeling in Gothic Fiction* (London: Athlone Press, 1978)

Hugo, Victor, 'The Preface to Cromwell', in *Prefaces and Prologues to Famous Books*, XXXIX (New York: Collier, 1909–14), online edition published 26 April 2001 <www.bartleby.com/39/41.html> [accessed 18 November 2008]

Hume, Robert D., 'Gothic Versus Romantic: A Rejoinder', *PMLA* 86 (1971), 282–90

Humphries, Simon, 'Christina Rossetti's "Goblin Market" and Spenser's Malbecco', *Notes and Queries* 55.1 (2008a), 51–4

—, 'Christina Rossetti's "My Dream" and Apocalypse', *Notes and Queries* 55.1 (2008b), 54–7

Hunt, Violet, *The Wife of Rossetti* (New York: E.P. Dutton & Co, 1932)

Jackson, Rosemary, *Fantasy: The Literature of Subversion* (London: Routledge, 1981)

Jamison, Anna, 'Passing Strange: Christina Rossetti's Unusual Dead', *Textual Practice*, 20.2 (2006), 257–80

Jennings, Lee Byron, *The Ludicrous Demon: Aspects of the Grotesque in German Post-Romantic Prose* (Berkeley: University of California Press, 1963)

Jimenez, Nilda, *The Bible and the Poetry of Christina Rossetti* (London: Greenwood Press, 1979)

Kaplan, Cora, *Sea Changes: Essays on Culture and Feminism* (London: Verso, 1986)

Kayser, Wolfgang, *The Grotesque in Art and Literature*, trans. Ulrich Weisstein (Bloomington: Indiana University Press, 1957)

Keble, John, *The Christian Year* (London: Church Literature Association, 1827; repr 1977)

—, *Lectures on Poetry 1832–1841*, trans. E. Francis and ed. Gavin Budge, 2 vols (Bristol: Thoemmes Press, 2003)

—, *Occasional Papers and Reviews* (London: James Parker, 1877)

—, 'Tract 89: On the Mysticism Attributed to the Fathers of the Church', *Tracts for the Times* <http://anglicanhistory.org/tracts/tract89/section6.html> [accessed 22 May 2009]

Kent, David A., ed., *The Achievement of Christina Rossetti* (Ithaca: Cornell University Press, 1987)

Knight, Mark, and Emma Mason, *Nineteenth-Century Religion and Literature: An Introduction* (Oxford: Oxford University Press, 2006)

Knoepflmacher, Ulrich C., *Ventures into Childland: Victorians, Fairytales and Femininity* (Chicago: University of Chicago Press, 1998)

Kooistra, Lorraine Janzen, *Christina Rossetti and Illustration: A Publishing History* (Athens, OH: Ohio University Press, 2002)

Kooistra, Lorraine Janzen, and Mary Arseneau, eds, *The Culture of Christina Rossetti: Female Poetics and Victorian Contexts* (Athens, OH: Ohio University Press, 1999)

Kristeva, Julia, *Powers of Horror: An Essay on Abjection*, trans. Leon S. Roudiez (New York: Columbia University Press, 1982)

Landow, George, *The Aesthetic and Critical Theories of John Ruskin*, chapter 5.3, 'Typological Symbolism in the Readings of Ruskin's Childhood' (2005), *The Victorian Web* <www.victorianweb.org/authors/ruskin/atheories/5.3.html> [accessed 29 December 2008]

—, 'The Dead Woman Talks Back: Christina Rossetti's Ironic Intonation of the Dead Fair Maiden' (2002), *The Victorian Web* <www.victorianweb.org/authors/ crossetti/ gpl1.html> [accessed 12 July 2007]

—, *Victorian Types, Victorian Shadows: Biblical Typology in Victorian Literature, Art and Thought* (London: Routledge and Kegan Paul, 1980)

Lawrence, David H., *Apocalypse* (London: Martin Secker, 1932)

Lewis, Mark and Andrew Payne, 'Ghost Dance: An Interview with Jacques Derrida', *Public 2: The Lunatic on One Idea* (1989), pp. 60–74

Lewis, Matthew, *The Monk*, ed. Howard Anderson (Oxford: Oxford University Press, 1980)

—, *Tales of Wonder* (London: Bulmer, 1801)

Liebregts, Peter, and Wim Tigges, eds, *Beauty and the Beast: Christina Rossetti, Walter Pater, R. L. Stevenson and Their Contemporaries* (Amsterdam: Rodopi, 1996)

Lysack, Krista, *Come Buy, Come Buy: Shopping and the Culture of Consumption in Victorian Women's Writing* (Athens, OH: Ohio University Press, 2008)

McDayter, Ghislaine, 'Consuming the Sublime: Gothic Pleasure and the Construction of Identity', *Women's Writing: The Elizabethan to Victorian Period* 2.1 (1995), 55–77

McEvoy, Emma, and Catherine Spooner, eds, *The Routledge Companion to the Gothic* (London: Routledge, 2007)

McGann, Jerome, 'The Religious Poetry of Christina Rossetti', *Critical Enquiry* 10 (1983), 127–44

Mann, Thomas, *Meditations of a Nonpolitical Man*, ed. and trans. W. D. Morris (New York: Frederick Ungar, 1983)

Marsh, Jan, *Christina Rossetti: A Literary Biography* (London: Jonathan Cape, 1994)

—, *The Legend of Elizabeth Siddal* (London: Quartet Books, 1989)

Marx, Karl, and Friedrich Engels, *The Manifesto of the Communist Party* (New York: Cosimo, 2009, facsimile of 1848 edition)

Maturin, C. R., *Melmoth the Wanderer*, ed. Victor Sage (London: Penguin, 2000)

—, *The Wild Irish Boy*, ed. E. F. Bleiler, 3 vols (New York: Arno Press, 1977)

—, *Women, or, Pour et Contre*, 3 vols (Edinburgh: Constable, 1818)

Mayberry, Katherine J., *Christina Rossetti and the Poetry of Discovery* (Baton Rouge: Louisiana State University Press, 1989)

Melnyk, Julie, ed., *Women's Theology in Nineteenth-Century Britain: Transfiguring the Faith of Their Fathers* (New York: Garland Publishing, 1998)

Milbank, Alison, *Dante and the Victorians* (Manchester: Manchester University Press, 1998)

—, *Daughters of the House: Modes of Gothic in Victorian Fiction* (Basingstoke: Macmillan, 1992)

Miller, David A., *The Novel and the Police* (Berkeley: University of California Press, 1988)

Millett, Kate, *Sexual Politics* (London: Virago, 1971; repr. 1977)

Moers, Ellen, *Literary Women* (London: Women's Press, 1976; repr. 1978)

Monroe, Judson Taylor, *Tragedy in the Novels of C. R. Maturin* (New York: Arno Press, 1980)

Morrill, David F., '"Twilight Is Not Good for Maidens": Uncle Polidori and the Psychodynamics of Vampirism in "Goblin Market"', *Victorian Poetry* 28.1 (1990), 1–16

Morris, William, *The Earthly Paradise*, 3 vols (Boston: Roberts, 1869)

Morrison, Ronald D., '"One Droned in Sweetness Like a Fattened Bee": Christina Rossetti's View of Marriage in Her Early Poetry', *Kentucky Philological Review* 5 (1990), 19–26

—, '"Their Fruit Like Honey in the Throat/But Poison in the Blood": Christina Rossetti and "The Vampyre"', *Weber Studies: Voices and Viewpoints of the Contemporary West* 14.2 (1997), 89–96

Murphy, John V., *The Dark Angel: Gothic Elements in the Work of Shelley* (London: Associated University Presses, 1975)

Napier, Elizabeth R., *The Failure of Gothic: Problems of Disjunction in an Eighteenth-Century Literary Form* (Oxford: Clarendon Press, 1987)

Neale, John Mason, *Annals of Virgin Saints* (London: Rivington, 1846)

Newman, John Henry, 'Tract 79: Against Romanism No. III: On Purgatory', *Tracts for the Times* <http://anglicanhistory.org/tracts/tract79.html> [accessed 16 March 2010]

Norton, Caroline, '"The Angel in the House" and "The Goblin Market"', *Macmillan's Magazine*, September 1863, 398–404

Norton, Rictor, *Gothic Readings: The First Wave, 1764–1840* (London: Leicester University Press, 2000)

Owen, Alex, *The Darkened Room: Women, Power and Spiritualism in Late Victorian England* (Chicago: University of Chicago Press, 1990; repr. 2004)

Packer, Lona Mosk, *Christina Rossetti* (Berkeley: University of California Press, 1963)

Palazzo, Lynda, *Christina Rossetti's Feminist Theology* (Basingstoke: Palgrave, 2002)

Parker, Emma, 'A Career of One's Own: Christina Rossetti, Literary Success and Love', *Women's Writing* 5.3 (1998), 305–28

Paulson, Ronald, *Representations of Revolution 1789–1820* (New Haven: Yale University Press, 1983)

Paz, Denis G., *Popular Anti-Catholicism in Mid-Victorian England* (Stanford, CA: Stanford University Press, 1992)

Pearl, Sharrona, *About Faces: Physiognomy in Nineteenth-Century Britain* (Cambridge, MA: Harvard University Press, 2010)

Pippin, Tina, *Apocalyptic Bodies: The Biblical End of the World in Text and Image* (New York: Routledge, 1999)

Polidori, John, *The Vampyre*, ed. Jonathan Wordsworth (Otley: Woodstock, 2001)

Price, Fiona, *Revolutions in Taste: Women's Writing and the Aesthetics of Romanticism 1773–1818* (Farnham: Ashgate, 2009)

Psomiades, Kathy A., and Talia Schaffer, eds, *Women and British Aestheticism* (Charlottesville: University of Virginia Press, 1999)

Punter, David, ed., *A Companion to the Gothic* (Oxford: Blackwell, 2000)

—, *The Literature of Terror: Volume 1: The Gothic Tradition* (London: Longman, 1996)

Quiller-Couch, Arthur, *The Poet as Citizen* (Cambridge: Cambridge University Press, 1934)

Radcliffe, Ann, *The Italian*, ed. E. J. Clery (Oxford: Oxford University Press, 1998)

—, *The Mysteries of Udolpho*, ed. Bonamy Dobrée (Oxford: Oxford University Press, 1974; repr. 1980)

—, *A Sicilian Romance*, ed. Alison Milbank (Oxford: Oxford University Press, 1993)

—, 'The Supernatural in Poetry', *New Monthly Magazine and Literary Journal*, 16.1 (1826), 145–52

Railo, Eino, *The Haunted Castle: A Study of the Elements of English Romanticism* (London: Routledge, 1927)

Reeves, Nancee, 'Vampires and Goblins: Coleridge's Influence on Christina Rossetti', *Journal of Pre-Raphaelite Studies* 21 (Spring 2012), 63–71

Ricoeur, Paul, and M. J. Valdes, eds, *A Ricoeur Reader: Reflection and Imagination* (Toronto: University of Toronto Press, 1991)

Robbins, Ruth, and Julian Wolfreys, eds, *Victorian Gothic: Literary and Cultural Manifestations in the Nineteenth-Century* (Basingstoke: Palgrave Macmillan, 2000)

Roden, Frederick S., *Same-Sex Desire in Victorian Religious Culture* (Basingstoke: Palgrave Macmillan, 2002)

Roe, Dinah, *Christina Rossetti's Faithful Imagination: The Devotional Poetry and Prose* (Basingstoke: Palgrave Macmillan, 2006)

Rose, Jacqueline, *The Haunting of Sylvia Plath* (London: Virago, 1991)

Rosenblum, Dolores, *Christina Rossetti: The Poetry of Endurance* (Carbondale: South Illinois University Press, 1986)

Rossetti, Christina, *Called to be Saints: The Minor Festivals Devotionally Studied*, ed. Maria Keaton (London: SPCK, 1881; repr. Bristol: Thoemmes Press, 2003)

—, *Christina Rossetti: The Complete Poems*, ed. Rebecca W. Crump (London: Penguin, 2005)

—, *The Face of the Deep: A Devotional Commentary on the Apocalypse* (London: SPCK, 1892; Bristol: Thoemmes Press, 2003)

—, '"Goblin Market": Ribald Classics', *Playboy* 20.9 (1973), 115–19

—, *Letter and Spirit: Notes on the Commandments* (London: SPCK, 1883; repr. Bristol: Thoemmes Press, 2003)

—, Notebooks 1–6, 1856–9 and 1861–6, London, British Library, MS Ashley 1364

—, *Poems and Prose*, ed. Jan Marsh (London: Everyman, 1994)

—, *Sing-Song* (London: Macmillan, 1872; repr. 1907)

—, *Time Flies: A Reading Diary* (London: SPCK, 1885)

Rossetti, Christina, and Dinah Mulock Craik, *Maude; On Sisterhoods; A Woman's Thoughts about Women*, ed. Elaine Showalter (New York: New York University Press, 1995)

Rossetti, Dante Gabriel, *Collected Poetry and Prose of D. G. Rossetti*, ed. Jerome McGann (New Haven: Yale University Press, 2003)

Rossetti, William Michael, *The Poetical Works of Christina Georgina Rossetti, with Memoir and Notes* (London: Macmillan, 1904)

Ruskin, John, *The Works of John Ruskin: Library Edition*, 39 vols, ed. E. T. Cook and Alexander Wedderburn (London: George Allen, 1903–12) and on CD-ROM (Cambridge University Press for the Ruskin Foundation, 1996)

Russell, Jeffrey Burton, *A History of Heaven: The Singing Silence* (Princeton: Princeton University Press, 1997)

Russo, Mary, *The Female Grotesque: Risk, Excess and Modernity* (London: Routledge, 1994)

Sanders, Valerie, *The Private Lives of Victorian Women* (Hemel Hempstead: Harvester Wheatsheaf, 1989)

Scheinberg, Cynthia, *Women's Poetry and Religion in Victorian England* (Cambridge: Cambridge University Press, 2002)

Schopenhauer, A., *Parerga and Paralipomena*, ed. E. F. J. Payne (Oxford: Clarendon Press, 2000)

Scott, Walter, *The Miscellaneous Prose Works of Sir Walter Scott*, 6 vols (Edinburgh: Black, 1878)

Sedgwick, Eve Kosofsky, *The Coherence of Gothic Conventions* (London: Methuen, 1986)

Shaw, W. David, *Origins of the Monologue: The Hidden God* (Toronto: University of Toronto Press, 1999)

Shell, Alison, *Catholicism, Controversy and the English Literary Imagination 1558–1660* (Cambridge: Cambridge University Press, 1999)

Shelton Reed, John, *Glorious Battle: The Cultural Politics of Victorian Anglo-Catholicism* (Nashville: Vanderbilt University Press, 1996)

Shields, Hugh, 'The Dead Lover's Return in English Ballad Tradition', *Jahrbuch für Volksliedforschung* 17 (1972), 98–114

Shurbutt, Sylvia Bailey, 'Revisionist Mythmaking in Christina Rossetti's "Goblin Market": Eve's Apple and Other Questions Revised and Reconsidered', *Victorian Newsletter* 82 (1992), 40–4

Shuttleworth, Sally, *Charlotte Brontë and Victorian Psychology* (Cambridge: Cambridge University Press, 1996)

Sickels, Eleanor, *The Gloomy Egoist* (New York: University of Columbia Press, 1932)

Simon, Ulrich, *Heaven in the Christian Tradition* (London: Rockliff, 1958)

Smith, Andrew, *Gothic Literature* (Edinburgh: Edinburgh University Press, 2004)

—, *Gothic Radicalism: Literature, Philosophy and Psychoanalysis in the Nineteenth Century* (London: Macmillan, 2000)

Smulders, Sharon, *Christina Rossetti Revisited* (New York: Twayne, 1996)

—, 'Woman's Enfranchisement in Christina Rossetti's Poetry', *Texas Studies in Literature and Language* 34.4 (1992), 568–88

St Clair, William, *The Reading Nation in the Romantic Period* (Cambridge: Cambridge University Press, 2004)

Starzyk, Lawrence J., 'Rossetti's "Jenny": Aestheticizing the Whore', *Papers on Language and Literature* 36.3 (Summer 2000), 227–45

Sullivan, Brad, '"Grown Sick with Hope Deferred": Christina Rossetti's Darker Musings', *Papers on Language and Literature* 32.3 (1996), 227–43

Summers, Montague, *The Gothic Quest: A History of the Gothic Novel* (London: Fortune Press, 1968)

Swann Jones, Steven, *The Fairy Tale: The Magic Mirror of the Imagination* (London: Routledge, 2002)

Tennyson, G. B., *Victorian Devotional Poetry: The Tractarian Mode* (Cambridge, MA: Harvard University Press, 1981)

Thompson, Deborah A., 'Anorexia as a Lived Trope: Christina Rossetti's "Goblin Market"', *Mosaic* 24.3–4 (1991), 89–106

Thomson, Philip, *The Grotesque* (London: Methuen, 1972)

Vevjoda, K., 'The Fruit of Charity: Comus and Christina Rossetti's "Goblin Market"', *Victorian Poetry* 38.4 (2000), 555–78

Vine, Steven, *Blake's Poetry: Spectral Visions* (Basingstoke: St Martin's, 1992)

Voller, Jack G., 'Christina Rossetti', in *The Literary Gothic* (2008) <www.litgothic.com/Authors/crossetti.html> [accessed 7 April 2010]

Waldman, Suzanne M., *The Demon and the Damozel: Dynamics of Desire in the Works of Christina Rossetti and Dante Gabriel Rossetti* (Athens, OH: Ohio University Press, 2008)

Walpole, Horace, *The Castle of Otranto: A Gothic Story*, ed. W. S. Lewis and Joseph W. Reed (Oxford: Oxford University Press, 1982; repr. 1990)

Warner, Marina, *From the Beast to the Blonde* (London: Vintage, 1994)

Westerholm, Joel, 'In Defense of Verses: The Aesthetic and Reputation of Christina Rossetti's Late Poetry', *Renascence* 51.3 (1999), 191–203

Williams, Anne, *Art of Darkness: A Poetics of Gothic* (Chicago: University of Chicago Press, 1995)

Williams, David, *Deformed Discourse: The Function of the Monster in Mediaeval Thought and Literature* (Exeter: University of Exeter Press, 1996)

Williams, Isaac, *The Apocalypse, with Notes and Reflections* (London: Rivington, 1852)

—, 'Tract 80: On Reserve in Communicating Religious Knowledge', *Tracts for the Times* <http://anglicanhistory.org/tracts/tract80.html> [accessed 6 April 2010]

Winnicott, Donald W., *Playing and Reality* (London: Routledge, 1971)

Wolfreys, Julian, *Victorian Hauntings: Spectrality, Gothic, the Uncanny and Literature* (Basingstoke: Palgrave, 2002)

Woolf, Virginia, *The Common Reader*, ed. A. McNeillie, 2 vols (London: Hogarth Press, 1986)

Woolford, John, 'Robert Browning, Christina Rossetti and the Wordsworthian Scene of Writing', *Wordsworth Circle* 34.1 (2003), 30–5

Yonge, Charlotte Mary, *Womankind* (London: Richard Clay, 1876; repr. 1889)

Zipes, Jack, *Breaking the Magic Spell: Radical Theories of Folk and Fairy Tales* (London: Heinemann, 1979)

Index